One Bible, Many Voices

Different Approaches to Biblical Studies

One Bible, Many Voices

Different Approaches to Biblical Studies

Susan E. Gillingham

First published in Great Britain in 1998
Society for Promoting Christian Knowledge, Holy Trinity Church,
Marylebone Road, London NW1 4DU

British Library Cataloguing-in-Publication Data
A catalogue record for this book is available
from the British Library

ISBN 0-281-04886-X

Typeset by David Gregson Associates, Beccles, Suffolk
Printed in Great Britain by
Redwood Books, Trowbridge, Wiltshire

To Abbie and Esther
with my love

Contents

Contents

Figure 7 from *Septuaginta*, Stuttgart, Deutsche Bibelgesellschaft, 1979.

Figures 10 and 11 from *New Bible Dictionary*, third edition, IVP, 1996, with kind permission from IVP.

Figure 12 from Η ΚΑΙΝΗ ΔΙΑθΗΚΗ, British and Foreign Bible Society, 1988.

Figure 13 from *Interlinear Greek Version*, 1974.

Figure 14 from R. M. Liuzza, *The Old English Version of the Gospels*, Early English Text Society OS 304, with kind permission from the Council of the Early English Text Society.

Figure 15 from J. Backhouse, *The Lindisfarne Gospels*, Phaidon Press with British Library, 1981.

Figure 22 from M. Perry and D. Iliff (eds), *Psalms for Today: Full Music Edition*, Hodder & Stoughton, 1990.

Wycliffe's and Tyndale's Versions of Hebrews 1.1–4 from D. S. Daniell and G. W. H. Lampe (eds), *Discovering the Bible*, University of London Press, 1970.

S. A. J. Bradley, *Anglo-Saxon Poetry*, Everyman, 1995, with kind permission from Everyman's Library Publishers.

Figure 23 from Jim Cotter, *Through Desert Places*, Cairns Publications, 47 Firth Park Avenue, Sheffield S5 6HF, 1989.

A. N. Smith (ed.), *Three Northumberland Poems*, Methuen, 1933.

Preface

This book has evolved over some ten years from two entirely different components. The first element which it incorporates was an extension studies course, entitled *Understanding and Using the Bible*, a distance-learning course for students of St John's College, Nottingham, who were undertaking vocational studies in theology. The second element comes from my later experience of teaching undergraduates reading theology at Oxford University. Here I have found the need for another approach – one aimed at students who have far less familiarity with the Bible as a text, but who expect an approach as academically rigorous and as free from any particular theological or confessional agenda as any other academic discipline in the University. It is to meet the needs of this latter audience (although the first is by no means excluded) that I have almost completely rewritten the earlier book.

My thanks are thus due to two different sets of colleagues. First I should thank Dr John Goldingay, who long ago suggested that I should rewrite the St John's course he had originally written, and the Revd David Muir, the director of St John's extension studies, and Ms Kate Hughes, my copy-editor in that original endeavour. I am most grateful to them for permitting me to rework the earlier material for this book. Second, my thanks for enabling the second stage to go forward are due to the Rt Revd Geoffrey Rowell, Bishop of Basingstoke, who encouraged SPCK to consider publishing yet another book on the Bible. Ms Judith Longman and Mr Philip Law, each once commissioning editors with SPCK, looked at the St John's course and were confident that I could develop a different book from it. For persuading me to contine the task, my thanks are due to Ms Lucy Gasson, also commissioning editor with SPCK; she gave me her time and enthusiasm and so enabled the project to progress. And for bringing the book to completion, I am very much indebted to Ms Trisha Dale, my final commissioning editor as well as copy-editor; her patience and attention to detail have been exemplary.

The purpose and audience for this particular book is upper-sixth-formers, first- and second-year undergraduates, and adult students coming later in life to read theology; it is assumed that each of these groups is approaching the Bible as an academic discipline. Yet the scope of the book is larger than this: it is really intended for anyone for whom biblical studies is a relatively new discipline, and who needs to understand the complexities of reading the Bible, without necessarily having any of the assumptions brought to the subject in believing ('confessional') circles. It is not that a confessional approach is seen to be unimportant; it is, quite simply, outside the immediate range of concern for someone wishing to undertake an A level, a diploma, certificate or degree in theology, engaging with the subject matter as they would in any other academic discipline.

The support of two Oxford colleagues in particular has been a real source of encouragement to me. Professor John Barton read and affirmed part of an earlier draft. While teaching some of the topics covered by this book alongside Professor Christopher Rowland, his advice in how to apply the theory in practice has been equally invaluable. My thanks are also due to four graduate students – Ms Claire Sands, Ms Sonya Ardan, Ms Francesca Stavrakopoulou and Ms Michelle Spearing – for all their administrative help and support, and to Dr Rex Mason, for his advice and support in the latter stages.

Three other people remain, whose support I value above all. First, my thanks are due to one who, as my fiercest critic and closest friend, has read the draft 'from outside' as it were, and sought to improve my style and clarity of argument with unfailing precision and consistent good humour; I owe him more than I can say. And second my thanks are due to my two daughters, Esther and Abigail, for all their patience in coping with an absent or present-but-distracted single parent; as a small token of gratitude, it is appropriate that I dedicate the book to them.

Although in many ways this book is written as a kind of reference book, I have tried very hard not to presume too much prior knowledge of my readers; nevertheless, I am aware I ask a good deal of them in terms of assimilating information and remembering it. It is hoped that, although mistakes remain – and these must be claimed as mine alone – the book will nevertheless be of some use for those embarking upon the complexities of biblical studies as an academic discipline.

Historical Background 1

The Old Testament
*c.*1000–167 BCE

First Temple
950–587 BCE

National and Political Concerns

    Assyria, Egypt, Babylon

Monarchy
Temple
Nation

prophets, priests, wise men,
psalmists, historians

Exile in Babylon
587–520 BCE

Universal and Cosmic Concerns

    Babylon, Persia

No Monarchy
No Temple
No Nation

prophets, priests, psalmists, scribes, historians

Second Temple
520–167 BCE

Ethnic and Cultic Concerns

    Persia, Greece

Theocracy
Second Temple
Under Foreign Rule

prophets' decline; priests, psalmists, historians,
scribes, wise men, apocalypticists

Historical Background 2

The New Testament
*c.*200 BCE – 135 CE

The End of the Second Temple Period 167 BCE – 70 CE

167 BCE
Desecration of Temple by Seleucid ruler, Antiochus IV 'Epiphanes'

63 BCE
Pompey's entry into Jerusalem: beginning of *Roman rule*

27 BCE – 14 CE
Augustus Caesar

4 BCE
Death of Herod the Great
Birth of Jesus Christ

14–37 CE
Tiberias Caesar

30 CE
Crucifixion of Jesus

37–41 CE
Caligula

40 CE
Paul's first missionary journey into Asia Minor

41–54 CE
Claudius

48 CE
Council of Jerusalem

	Paul's first letters	
54–68 CE		
Nero	Mark	64 CE
		Nero's persecution of Christians in
	Paul's later letters	Rome
69–79 CE		
Vespasian		70 CE
		Destruction of the Temple
	Most of the non-Pauline letters	

Second Jewish 'Exile'
70–135 CE

	Luke/Acts	
79–81 CE		
Titus		85 CE
	Matthew	Exclusion of Christians from
		Jewish synagogues
81–96 CE	Hebrews	
Domitian	John	Persecution of Christians by
	1, 2, 3 John	Emperor Domitian
	Revelation	
96–9 CE		
Nerva		
99–117 CE		
Trajan		
117–38 CE		
Hadrian		132–5 CE
		Jewish revolt ('Bar Kochba')
		quelled under Emperor Hadrian;
		Dispersion of Jews;
		Altar to Zeus on Temple site;
		Jerusalem renamed 'Colonia Aelia
		Capitolina'

List of Tables and Figures

Introduction

Whatever else is understood by postmodernism, it is all but universally agreed that it implies an open-ended, pluralistic understanding of the world. Whether speaking about it in linguistic, socio-political, literary or philosophical terms, the common consensus is a denial of the access to any objective truth: there are only subjective interpretations, each influenced by the cultural presuppositions of the interpreter. Following from this – and especially important for those engaged in theological study – there can be no absolute values; everything is relative, for every assertion is contingent upon a number of cultural variables. This is in part a reaction against modernist certainties, and a recognition that such certainties were an imposition of authority upon those whose interests were not best served by such a stance. This is not the place to provide an analysis or critique of postmodernism (which, by virtue of its own self-understanding, should also be seen as one voice among many): it is simply to observe that one aspect of it has radically affected the way we approach theology in general and biblical studies in particular. Walter Brueggemann, in *The Bible and Postmodern Imagination: Texts under Negotiation*, puts it as follows:

> In place of objective certitude and settled hegemony, we would now characterize our knowing in ways that make mastery and control much more problematic ... knowledge is inherently *pluralistic*, a cacophony of claims, each of which rings true to its own advocates. Indeed, pluralism is the only alternative to objectivism once the dominant center is no longer able to impose its view and to silence by force all alternative and dissenting opinion. (pp. 8–9)

Such a world-view has important consequences for theology as a serious academic subject. The increased emphasis on *religious studies* – a sociological and anthropological study of the history of all the world religions – is an attempt to keep up with the spirit of the age, and in many ways this has all been for the common good. But it leaves those who study *biblical studies* with a dilemma.

1

One choice is to approach the subject as a branch of religious studies, so that the study of the Bible is in effect a study of the history of the religion which gave rise to the books which are in the Bible. This has at least two consequent problems. At its best, it is not so much a study of the biblical texts as a study of the background to the biblical texts; and at its worst, by attempting to focus on the texts, it has to place too much emphasis on what is still a much disputed area – what we actually know about the chronological development of these texts within Near Eastern history.

Another choice, linked to the first in its historical concerns, but quite different from it in its opposition to the spirit of the age, is to continue to assert that these ancient biblical texts are still normative for us, and to affirm their traditional theological values. This also has attendant problems. In the first place, it assumes that one's own exposition of the theology which is supposedly self-evident within the text is indeed the correct one. Furthermore, it is somewhat overconfident in its assumption that texts which arose out of particular local situations have universal relevance and authority.

A third choice – this time more associated with the second by virtue of its theological concern, yet again entirely different from it in its avoidance of historical claims – is to view the biblical texts exclusively from a literary and linguistic perspective. Yet again this has its limitations. In applying modern literary and linguistic theories to ancient texts, this approach neglects any value gained from our insight into the text on account of its antiquity – when entirely different literary and linguistic conventions were used in comparison with our own. Furthermore, there is a very real danger of reducing a study of the Bible to a self-referential dialogue between the text and the reader, and so an individualistic interpretation replaces the communal one; yet traditionally speaking, the texts have been transmitted and understood from antiquity until the present time through different communities rather than through isolated individuals.

Although these three choices have been presented here somewhat briefly, they nevertheless represent the three main avenues for biblical studies today – the historical, the theological and the literary approaches. Obviously, it is possible to use part of one approach and some aspects of another for, as we have seen, each has inherent problems for the future of biblical studies if used in isolation. The phenomenon we call 'the Bible' is too diversified and complex a work to be subsumed under historical categories or under a systematic theology or under modern literary theory.

Nevertheless – and this depends very much on the type of academic or believing community in which biblical studies are undertaken – it is more likely than not that the potential student will discover a particular bias of reading, whereby one of the three methods is emphasized more than the other two. (This is not the place to discuss the nuances in each approach, and the interrelationship between one approach and another, for these will be assessed in a later chapter; the issue here is simply to recognize that biblical studies is rarely achieved without some sort of methodological bias.) Yet, as will become clear throughout the course of this study, any such bias contravenes not only what is good in the pluralistic spirit of our age, but also goes against the grain of the diverse nature of the Bible itself.

For the Bible is indeed a very disparate work. In calling the Bible a 'book', we misunderstand what it is really about. The English designation 'bible' comes from the Greek, *biblia*, which is in fact a plural noun, describing the number of books rather than the collections as a whole. (The best, albeit clumsy, English equivalent might be 'a body of literature'.) The Latin, also *biblia*, could denote either the feminine singular or the neuter plural. It may be that the preference for the former meaning has resulted in the Bible being seen in the same light as any other 'book'. But this is mistaken. Encompassing at least a thousand years in the making, the Bible offers as many different world-views as the cultures it represents. It is, we might conclude, one of the most pluralistic texts we possess.

Another misunderstanding arises from the way we refer to the different works in the Bible as 'books'. It is not just that it is anchronsitic to do so, in that there were no codices at the time of composition, but only scrolls and copies of scrolls. It is because not one so-called 'book' in the Bible can be viewed in the way we usually understand a 'book' today: none is the work of one hand, of one author, or even (in most cases) of one editor. Every single biblical 'book' is a highly composite work. For example, each of the first five books of the Hebrew Bible (the books which we call the Law: Genesis, Exodus, Leviticus, Numbers, Deuteronomy) was compiled over a period of some seven hundred years or more – from the earliest oral traditions to the finalized form of the text. Or again, the three major prophetic books (Isaiah, Jeremiah, Ezekiel) were compiled over periods of between at least two hundred and four hundred years, from the time of the earliest prophetic message to that of the final shaping of the text by disciples some generations later.

Hence, what is the case in macrocosm for the 'Bible' as a whole is also the case in microcosm for the works that make up the Bible. As a 'collection of collections', the Bible is a pluralistic text, made up of many parts with many divergent views about God and his relations with the world. Robert Carroll, writing in *Wolf in the Sheepfold: The Bible as a*

3

Problem for Christianity, puts the issue of the Bible's plurality in the following way:

> Even when [the Bible's] nature as a collection or congeries of books is acknowledged, or at least known, people still tend to think of it as a unity having one author and one message. These are illusions of time and familiarity. Not only is the Bible a book made up of many, diverse books, but it is also a number of different books, dependent upon the reader's perspective. In a very real sense there is no such thing as *the* Bible. There are only Bibles – Hebrew, Christian, Protestant ... Talk about 'the Bible' borders on the mythical ... It is an idea which takes different forms in different cultures and communities. (p. 7)

The contents of the Bible, as well as its process of compilation, make it well-suited for a multifaceted method of study, whereby the diversity evident in the making of the Bible is matched by a diversity of methods in the reading of it. Yet, as we have already noted, biblical studies is more often than not a discipline which works in independent ways with independent methods. A more sensible way forward would be one which was more integrative and interdependent, so that the deficiencies of one approach could be complemented by the strengths of another. This undoubtedly would mean tolerance, open-mindedness, and an agreed recognition of the positive value of pluralistic ways of reading; communities which achieve this are few and far between, but those who do so offer a far more positive contribution for the future of biblical studies.

Behind this book, then, is a plea for a pluralistic understanding of the nature of biblical studies. Part One, being concerned with the diversity of the Bible in its long history of transmission, is more informative. The first four chapters will demonstrate the disparate and diffuse nature of the biblical accounts – not only in terms of the process by which the biblical text acquired its final form, but also in terms of the process by which the collection was received after its final form – with different versions and different texts being used variously by different communities. Part Two is more evaluative, assessing the ways in which readers today might interact with this many-sided text. These four chapters seek to show how such a heterogeneous text is an asset rather than a problem for biblical studies. The first chapter in Part Two illustrates the enormous variety of approaches to reading the Bible theologically which have been formulated since the time of the New Testament. Most of these emanate from a religious tradition, but more lately they also come from a more secular setting. The second chapter here looks at the historical approaches to reading the Bible, and the third chapter, at the literary approaches; each of these has developed and changed considerably over the last two centuries or so, and thus each chapter ends with a discussion of the many variations in historical and literary approaches. The premiss behind all three chapters is that some integration of all three disciplines is necessary for balanced reading. The final two chapters seek to work out this theory of 'pluralistic reading' in practice, by way of one extended illustration. By using the Psalter (itself a complex body of literature) as an ideal model, and finally by reading one particular psalm (8) in this multi-faceted way, these chapters illustrate in practice how such a pluralistic approach can enrich our understanding of these texts.

This book seeks to show that pluralism, as one of the hallmarks of postmodernism, can serve more as friend than foe in relation to biblical studies. Far from threatening and fragmenting our under-standing of biblical faith, it offers a more reasonable, open-ended, integrative and ecumenical way forward. And for those embarking on biblical studies for the first time, it is vital that good habits of reading are cultivated sooner rather than later.

Part One

PLURALITY IN THE MAKING
OF THE BIBLE

1

A Biblical Library? The Smaller Parts of the Greater Whole

In any ordinary library, one would not expect the section on physics to offer the same sort of concerns as a book on the history of art; nor would one read an archival paper on criminal law and expect it to have the same aesthetic effect as would a piece of science fiction. So too with the Bible. Take, for example, the various didactic portions – these would include the legal and proverbial material in the Old Testament, as well as the parables and maxims of Jesus, and the exhortations of Paul – and compare these with the narrative histories, for example those in Joshua to 2 Kings in the Old Testament, and in the Acts of the Apostles in the New. It would not take long to perceive that didactic and narrative material each require a very different awareness of the historical and theological issues expressed through particular literary forms.

In understanding the Bible as a library of books, classified under several different sections, it is important to become aware of the most appropriate mode of reading for each separate work. Hence, identifying and classifying a particular piece of literature are essential before starting to read. The purpose of this chapter is to enable the potential biblical student to do this. Such a task works on three different levels, and because there is a great deal of diversity in the material represented at each level, the need for sensitive and integrated reading is essential. We shall move from the largest unit (marking the final stages in the biblical collection) to the smallest units, for it is important to understand how to read the whole before one reads the smaller parts.

The End of the Process: The Bible as a Body of Literature

The earliest languages in which the biblical writings were preserved were Hebrew, Aramaic and Greek. The Old Testament has been preserved in Hebrew and, in parts, in Aramaic; the New Testament was first written in Greek. Out of these two early linguistic traditions have emerged two quite different ways of subdividing each of these two major works, each subdivision showing the different cultural and theological concerns of particular compilers.

The Old Testament

Those who preserved and collected the Old Testament works in Hebrew created a threefold division for these books. The first is made up of five books called the *Tôrâ*, or the Law; however, this division is broader than the actual heading suggests, for the *Tôrâ* comprises not only legal codes but also a large proportion of material narrating the early origins of the Hebrew people.

The second division is called the *N^e bî' îm*, or the Prophets. This includes three major prophetic books, namely Isaiah, Jeremiah, and Ezekiel, and a collection of twelve smaller prophetic books, often referred to as the Scroll of the Twelve. Another part of the *N^e bî' îm* is a long narrative (Joshua, Judges, Samuel, Kings), concerning the time from the people's entry into the land until their exile from it. In Hebrew this portion is called the Former Prophets, and is thus a form of 'prophetic history', or history narrated from a prophetic viewpoint.

The third (and latest) collection is called the *Ch^e tûbîm*, or the Writings. This is a miscellany of material. Some of it is historical narrative, such as 1 and 2 Kings; this narrative includes parts of Ezra, Nehemiah, and 1 and 2 Chronicles. Some of it is didactic poetry; for example, the books of Proverbs and Job. One book, the Psalms, is of a liturgical nature. Five very short books, collected together on one scroll, are a combination of stories and poetry: Song of Songs, Lamentations and parts of Ecclesiastes are poetry; Ruth and Esther are stories. One other book is more concerned with apocalyptic issues (Daniel). The term used for the entire threefold division is, in Hebrew, *Tanach* – an acronym for the Hebrew words *Tôrâ* (Law), *N^e bî' îm* (Prophets) and *Ch^e tûbîm* (Writings). This particular classification indicates at least three clear diverse elements within the divisions of the Old Testament – often termed appropriately as the Hebrew Bible – and each division requires a different sensitivity on the part of the readers.

In the third century BCE, a Greek translation of the Hebrew was made in Alexandria, Egypt. Tradition has it that this was so that Ptolemy Philadelphus (285–46 BCE) could have a translated copy of the Hebrew Law (the *Tôrâ*) in his library at Alexandria. Its more practical purpose was that it catered for the many Jews who lived outside

Palestine, who had taken up a Hellenistic way of life and spoke and read Greek but not Hebrew. Other copies of the rest of the Hebrew Bible were gradually added to this copy of the Law – some were added in Alexandria, some further afield. The references to 'the law and the prophets and the others that followed them' in the Greek Prologue to Ecclesiasticus in about 132 BCE suggests that by this time much of the translation was complete. The whole translation became known as the Septuagint, or LXX; tradition has it that seventy-two scholars (six from each of the twelve tribes) were employed in the translation from the Hebrew, although the shorthand term for the whole is not LXXII but, more simply, LXX.

But, confusingly, the Greek translation adopted a fourfold division of this Hebrew Bible. The first, the Law, is the same as the Hebrew, incorporating the first five books of the Bible. The second division is termed the Histories, and, being more explicit and inclusive as to what might be termed history, comprises Chronicles, Ezra, Nehemiah and Esther (the latter four, in the Hebrew collection, were part of the Writings) as well as Joshua, Judges, Samuel and Kings (which, in the Hebrew collection, were part of the Prophets). The third division is called the Poetical Books, and includes Job, Psalms, Proverbs, Ecclesiastes and Song of Songs (all of which, in the Hebrew collection, were in the Writings), although the arrangement of the material is quite different from the Hebrew. The fourth division is the Prophetic Books. This comprises only the three major prophets and the Scroll of the Twelve, all of which were called the Latter Prophets in the Hebrew collection. However, even here, a different view of prophecy is evident, for the Greek omits the so-called 'prophetic history', and includes the book of Daniel, with its apocalpytic concerns about a new age being revealed at the end of time. (Daniel, in the Hebrew edition, was part of the Writings.)

Different theological and literary criteria have thus determined the ordering of these two collections. In addition, the Greek collection also has other books not included in the Hebrew Canon, which illustrate further the different concerns of these collectors. (We shall look more closely at this feature of the Septuagint in a later chapter.) In the *Hebrew* tradition, the Law is deemed paramount, because in theological terms it marks out the beginnings of God's dealings with the Hebrew people; the Prophets are seen as the interpretation of that Law, and thus follow it; and the Writings are an open-ended group, interpreting for their own time some of the issues set out in the Prophets. The *Greek* tradition is the same as the Hebrew in its acceptance of the Law as primary. But in the Septuagint, the Histories form a separate collection, on account of their backward look; the Prophets form a self-contained collection of prophetic personae, linked together because of their collective future vision; and the Poetical Books are an independent category in that they are timeless, although nevertheless concerned with the present moment.

Tables 1 and 2 outline the two different editions of the Old Testament, each with their divisions and subdivisions.

Table 1 The Threefold Division in the Hebrew Old Testament

The Tôrâ *or Law*

Genesis
Exodus
Leviticus
Numbers
Deuteronomy

The Nᵉbî' îm *or Prophets*

Joshua
Judges
1 and 2 Samuel
1 and 2 Kings
Isaiah
Jeremiah
Ezekiel
The Scroll of the Twelve

The Chᵉtûbîm *or Writings*

Psalms
Proverbs
Job
Song of Songs
Ruth
Lamentations
Ecclesiastes
Esther
Daniel
Ezra
Nehemiah
1 and 2 Chronicles

Table 2   The Fourfold Division in the Greek Old Testament

The Law

Genesis
Exodus
Leviticus
Numbers
Deuteronomy

The Histories

Joshua
Judges
Ruth
1 and 2 Samuel
1 and 2 Kings
1 and 2 Chronicles
Ezra
Nehemiah
Esther

The Poetical Books

Job
Psalms
Proverbs
Ecclesiastes
Song of Songs
Lamentations

The Prophetic Books

Isaiah
Jeremiah
Ezekiel
Hosea
Joel
Amos
Obadiah
Jonah
Micah
Nahum
Habakkuk
Zephaniah
Haggai
Zechariah
Malachi

The New Testament

The New Testament is essentially a Greek work. Here the division of material is less clear, but it is nevertheless possible to divide it into three or four groups of works.

In a threefold division, the first part would be the four Gospels and the Acts of the Apostles, for these books are the primary witness to the life of Jesus and to the birth of the Church. Insofar as they concern the didactic material and stories about the early origins of the Christian community, they correspond with the two themes evident in the Law of the Old Testament. The fourteen Epistles form a second collection, organized according to purported authorship; some editions begin with the letters attributed to Paul and end with the non-Pauline epistles (the 'Catholic' epistles), while other editions have the reverse order. Insofar as these might be seen as interpretations of the traditions found in the Gospels, they could be said to correspond with the Prophets, whose purpose in the Hebrew Bible was to interpret the Law. The final division is the apocalyptic book of Revelation (for, although the first two chapters include letters to seven churches, the overall concern of this book, like the book of Daniel, is undoubtedly apocalyptic). Being a more complex work, this could be compared with the place of Daniel in the Writings within the Hebrew Bible.

If, however, we use a fourfold division of the books which make up the New Testament, we end up with a classification which corresponds loosely to that of the Septuagint Old Testament. This is achieved by placing the Acts of the Apostles in a separate section. Using this model, the Gospels again parallel the Law; the history of the church in the Acts of the Apostles parallels the accounts of the origins and growth of the people of God as in the Septuagint division of the Histories; the Epistles, because of their appeal to present-day living, parallel the Poetical Books in the Septuagint; and Revelation, with its forward look, anticipating God's future intervention in the world, parallels the Greek Old Testament division termed the Prophetic books.

The differences between these divisions can be visualized as tables (see Tables 3 and 4). In presenting the New Testament in these two ways, we should make it clear that no edition of the Greek New Testament translation makes the threefold or fourfold division as distinct as this; it is a classification imposed on the text, deliberately making a parallel with either the Hebrew Bible or with the Septuagint. It could be argued that the fourfold division which is used for the LXX would be a more obvious pattern, for the New Testament writers had a closer relationship with the Greek (and indeed quoted from the LXX when they used the Old Testament) than they had with the Hebrew Bible.

Table 3   A Threefold Division of the New Testament (following the Hebrew Old Testament)

The Gospels

Matthew
Mark
Luke
John

and

the Acts of the Apostles

The Epistles

PAULINE

Romans
1 and 2 Corinthians
Galatians
Ephesians
Philippians
Colossians
1 and 2 Thessalonians
1 and 2 Timothy
Titus
Philemon

NON-PAULINE

Hebrews
James
1 and 2 Peter
1, 2 and 3 John
Jude

A Writing

Revelation

Table 4　A Fourfold Division of the New Testament (following the Greek Old Testament)

The Gospels

Matthew
Mark
Luke
John

A History

Acts of the Apostles

The Epistles

PAULINE

Romans
1 and 2 Corinthians
Galatians
Ephesians
Philippians
Colossians
1 and 2 Thessalonians
1 and 2 Timothy
Titus
Philemon

NON-PAULINE

Hebrews
James
1 and 2 Peter
1, 2 and 3 John
Jude

A Prophecy

Revelation

The Middle of the Process: The Bible as a Miscellany of Authors

It is impossible to know much about the identity of those responsible for the different divisions within the Bible. This is because no information is offered about their work other than in the references to the collections in other works. This may seem understandable; but less so is the fact that it is equally difficult to ascertain the identity of the actual biblical writers. This is in part due to the fact that, in the history of tradition, particular books were attributed to particular figureheads in the people's history, and attribution was thus read as authorship. Hence, using the Old Testament as an example, the term 'the Laws of Moses' was deemed to imply that Moses 'wrote' the entire Law; similarly, it was understood that David 'composed' the Psalms, and Solomon, the book of Proverbs. And all of the prophetic books were thought to have been written by the prophetic figures who inspired them; for example, Isaiah, Jeremiah, Ezekiel, Amos, Hosea. In the New Testament, again attribution traditionally presumed authorship. Hence the apostle Peter was understood to have written both 1 and 2 Peter, and the apostle John, the book of Revelation; Paul was originally credited with a far larger number of letters than is presumed today.

The issue of determining what we mean by an 'author' of the Bible is this: even though the figureheads in question (for example, Moses, David, Solomon, Isaiah, the apostles Peter, John and Paul) may well have been closely linked to the earliest traditions which inspired a particular book under their names, the compilation and editing were done by a number of others who had been inspired by their messages and who sought to preserve them in a way which was relevant for future generations. So when speaking of the 'identity of the writers of the Bible', we are not referring just to the names of those who acted, as it were, as patrons for particular books; we also need to include those from a wide spectrum of social and religious groups who were responsible for a work in its finished form. In this sense, it is very difficult indeed to make judgements, in any specific biographical or autobiographical sense, about the particular writers of particular books, for there were many of them. All we can ascertain, in a much more general sense, is the influence of various parties who were responsible for the formation of a book throughout its long history of transmission. Hence in the following discussion of the 'authors' of the Bible, we can only make observations in the most general terms.

17

The Old Testament

One of the most influential groups in the formation of the Old Testament is the *priestly writers*. They would have compiled the laws of Leviticus and Numbers; they would have presented the orderly account of the origins of mankind which forms the beginning and end of Genesis 1–11; and they would probably have been responsible for the compilation of the Chronicler's account of the people's history, from King David to the exile. The priestly writers encompass a long period in Israel's history. Their influence is likely to have begun in the first Temple period, between the period of the tenth and sixth centuries BCE, and continued throughout the second Temple period, from the sixth century BCE onwards (see p. xvi).

Another group comprises the *prophets*. This includes not only the named individual prophets, such as Isaiah, Jeremiah and Ezekiel, but also the disciples who collected and edited their works. It also includes the scroll of the twelve minor prophets; here, too, other prophetic disciples would have undertaken the process of collecting and editing individual works. The named prophets came from diverse cultural backgrounds, and it is likely that their disciples did too. For example, Amos and Hosea had more rural associations, and their concerns were with the northern kingdom in the eighth century BCE, while their close contemporary Micah, was a prophet from near Jerusalem, who addressed mainly the Judean king and the Jerusalem court. By contrast, some two hundred and twenty years later, the prophets Haggai and Zechariah were more closely linked to the Temple and its personnel, and their oracles were mainly concerned with the rebuilding of Jerusalem and the Temple. Another quite different prophetic group was responsible for compiling and editing the early history from settlement to exile with a particular prophetic bias (Joshua to 2 Kings, called 'the Former Prophets' in the Hebrew Bible). Their purpose was to provide a prophetic interpretation for the crisis of the deportation to Babylon.

Two other groups of writers cannot be classified in any one socio-religious grouping. The first of these we might term *poets* – some would be gifted officials who, on private and public occasions, composed many of the liturgical hymns and laments in the Psalter, others would be skilled bards, who composed less specifically liturgical works, but rather other works for public occasions such as reflective wisdom poetry, love songs and battle songs, celebrating victory or lamenting defeat in war. In earlier times, such poets would have been closely associated with the royal court; although the kings would rarely have composed themselves, under their patronage, court poets would have been responsible for parts of the books of Psalms and Proverbs.

A second group of unknown writers, spanning both the first and the second Temple periods, might be termed *storytellers*. These would be accomplished interpreters of earlier traditions, and their task was to explain the distinctive origins of their people by setting their stories within a larger historical context, editing material as diverse as Genesis, Exodus, Joshua, Samuel and Kings (in earlier times) and Ruth, Jonah and Esther (in later times, after the Exile).

Another influential group we might call *wise men*. As in other ancient Near Eastern cultures, such as Egypt and Babylon, where the traditions of wisdom similarly flourished, these would have been responsible for collecting and editing early folklore, and composing (or editing) easily memorable aphorisms. Some of them would have served in the court of the king, and may well have been responsible for the compilation of narrative and didactic material concerning the end of King David's reign which is found in Samuel and Kings. In post-exilic times, after the collapse of the court of the king, the wise men would still have maintained a moralizing stance in society; they would have been responsible for editing the didactic material which was preoccupied with the meaning of life, found in books such as Job and Ecclesiastes. During the second Temple period, they would have had associations with the *Temple scribes*, whose concern it was to organize and edit parts of the Law, the most obvious portions being the various lists and genealogies about the people's origins found at the beginning of Genesis, in Numbers, and in the books of Ezra and Nehemiah.

One much later group of writers, working towards the very end of the second Temple period (in the third and second centuries BCE) were the *apocalypticists* – those who, apparently frustrated with the oppressive state of affairs under foreign rule, sought to provide an alternative vision of restoration where God alone was king. It is likely that they were dissenting parties, and although their vision would have been influenced by the prophets, the wise, the priests and the scribes, they adapted the traditions of these parties for their own purposes. Evidence of their concerns is found mainly in material in the prophetic books; examples include Isaiah 24–7, Zechariah 9–14 and the book of Joel. The apocalypticists were also influential in the composition of the latter part of Daniel, the latest book in the biblical corpus to have been written.

Although the precise identity of these groups of writers is unclear, and although the precise extent of the influence each had will never be known, the fact that they existed and that their influence is clear (on theological and stylistic grounds) in so many Old Testament books leads on to one important observation: the Old Testament was compiled in a diffuse and pluralistic way, from the time of the existence of the earliest namesake of a book to the final stage of adapting the traditions for a much later community. Yet again, therefore, such a variety of contributors requires a similar variety of approaches when reading their different contributions.

The New Testament

The Old Testament is a good example of the complex relationship between the supposed author of a work and the later editors and compilers; and by now it should not be surprising to learn that this complexity is found in the New Testament literature as well, in spite of the more limited time-span (some one hundred years) for the composition of this entire work.

One further problem with the New Testament is that it is impossible to ascertain the influence of actual social groups, as was the case with the Old Testament; for example, the contributions of priests, prophets, scribes and apocalypticists simply cannot be observed in the same way in the different mass of material which comprises the New Testament. Indeed, the information we have regarding the social groups during this period throws little light on the writers and compilers of the books themselves. We now know quite a lot about the Pharisees, Sadducees, Essenes, Herodians, Zealots and scribes; all of these were parties known to have been influential in Jerusalem at the time of Christ. And, further afield, those who adhered to Gnosticism or to the mystery religions were also known to have a good deal of influence in first-century Judah and beyond. But – and this is quite different from the Old Testament – it is highly unlikely that any one of these groups was involved in the actual writing and transmission of any of the New Testament books.

One way forward is to determine first the extent of non-Jewish influence in the New Testament. (This is, of course, quite different from the consistently Jewish origins of the Old Testament.) There would appear to be at least one Gentile writer (the author of Luke/Acts), whose work comprises almost one third of the New Testament.

Second, it is then important to determine which of the New Testament Jewish books might bear the marks of *Palestinian* Judaism (in that they appear to originate from within Judah) and which might suggest more the influence of *Hellenistic* Judaism (in that their origins lie in more Hellenistic parts of Asia Minor). For example, the Gospels of Matthew and John each claim, by reference to their figurehead, to have closer associations with Palestinian Judaism in terms of their origins, even though their traditions may have developed in church communities in Asia Minor at a later stage. The same might be said of Mark with the link back to Peter in the history of tradition. So too several of the shorter letters may suggest a similar influence for the same reason; the actual letters of Peter, and those of James, Jude and John all make this link back to a key apostolic figure whose origins lie in Palestine. Furthermore, the book of Revelation, albeit a complex and composite work, nevertheless claimed to have its roots in the traditions associated with the apostle John and so back to Palestine in terms of origin too. In each case, all of these works would have been edited and adapted in church communities outside Palestine; at the very least their Palestinian origins bring these books closer, in terms of geography and culture, to the Jewish and Palestinian world of the Old Testament.

We are thus left with other books whose origins, at least, can be traced back to traditions outside Palestine altogether. In addition to Luke, most of the Epistles (comprising almost half of the New Testament) claim to have associations with various settings in the life of Paul, the later 'apostle', whose missionary influence extended far beyond the confines of Palestine. Paul's background appears to have been as cosmopolitan as any – he had a rabbinic education, yet was a Roman citizen, and his upbringing was in the Hellenistic Jewish community at Tarsus, in Asia Minor. The addressees of the various letters linked to his name are predominantly churches throughout Asia Minor – for example, Corinth, Galatia, Ephesus, Philippi and Colossae – and their cultural and theological concerns would be markedly different from those of Palestinian Christians. In origin, as well as in later development, these works bear the mark of more specifically Hellenistic influence.

Hence when approaching the question of the 'authors' of the New Testament, those books linked back in tradition to the various apostles may well suggest its origins lay amongst Jewish Christians in Palestine; but a good deal of other material comes from the more Hellenistic Jewish Christian world in Syria, Asia Minor and Greece. (We shall return to the issue of Palestinian and Hellenistic influences upon the early Christians in the following chapter; here we need only to note that it is possible to identify very different geographical and cultural settings behind the formation of the New Testament as a whole, even though it is difficult to tie these down any further to precise socio-religious groups.) Thus, even in the most general terms, we may perceive a wide variety of geographical and cultural influences throughout the New Testament at large, and this again indicates how works by different writers require different approaches and different expectations when reading them.

The Start of the Process: The Bible as a Plethora of Literary Forms

The Old Testament

It has always been a matter of some debate as to how much of the biblical material goes back to *earlier oral traditions* and how much is the result of a much later literary process. Within the Old Testament, oral traditions are most likely to be found in the poetic material. Examples include: working songs, war poetry and funeral dirges, found mainly in the Prophetic Books; poetry addressed to or about the king, found mainly in the book of Psalms; riddles and proverbial sayings, found especially in wisdom books such as Proverbs; and blessings and cursings, found especially in Genesis and Deuteronomy. This is not to deny that some earlier oral traditions may well lie behind some of the prose material. The most obvious examples include the myths and sagas found in the first chapters of Genesis, and the legends about popular heroes and heroines found in the prose parts of Job, and also in Ruth, Daniel and Esther.

The *written forms* of the Old Testament are equally various. There are several examples of archival records, in terms of reports and records taken from, for example, the royal court and the Temple. Here we might include: the lists and genealogies found in Numbers and in the earlier chapters of Chronicles; battle accounts, contracts and letters, found in the books of Joshua, Judges, Samuel and Kings; and law codes and cultic regulations, found in the latter part of Exodus and in Leviticus. In addition to these archival records, another equally large collection might be termed 'prose compositions'. This includes speeches, sermons, biographical accounts, reports of dreams and visions, prayers, oracles; all of these occur frequently in the prophetic books. Another category would be 'poetic compositions', such as poems about wisdom, hymns about God as Creator, individual and communal laments, all of which are especially dominant in prophets such as Isaiah, and in the first part of Proverbs, the Psalms, and in the book of Job. It would appear that the various writers – whether priests, prophets, poets, scribes, 'historians' or apocalypticists – borrowed freely from a range of literary forms at various stages of Israel's history.

The New Testament

The New Testament writers similarly borrowed and adapted a wide range of literary and oral forms, and, as with the Old Testament, these offer interesting correspondences with other works in the surrounding culture – not only from the Graeco-Roman world, but also those from contemporary Jewish sects, for example, those living at Qumran and Massada.

It is likely that a good deal or *oral tradition* lies behind the New Testament material. As well as a so-called 'sayings source' (called 'Q', from the German *Quelle*, meaning 'source') which is thought to be a collection of memorable sayings of Jesus, other examples include parables and maxims associated with the teaching of Jesus, but not included in Q. In addition to material from the Gospels, the Epistles also offer a few illustrations of oral traditions – for example, fragments of liturgy, hymns, prayers, greetings and formal exhortations.

Although the range of *literary forms* in the New Testament may not be as profuse as in the Old Testament, given the smaller volume of work, there is still evidence of some variety. Examples include the stylized discourses peculiar to the Gospels, especially in John; the material presented as memoirs, as biography, and as reports of dreams and visions in the Acts of the Apostles (which have correspondences with these forms in Old Testament Histories); and the eyewitness accounts, sermons, confessions of faith and moral instructions (all these have several Old Testament antecedents) found especially in the Epistles. Together, these all testify to a wide variety of traditionally crafted literary forms.

Hence even with the *formation* of the texts, the pluralistic nature of the Bible is a key issue, and this is the case as much with the New Testament as it is with the Old. This variety is illustrated in Tables 5 and 6. (For the sake of convenience, a fourfold model has been used for the New Testament as well as for the Old.)

Towards an Integrated Literary Approach
to the Bible

The model of a library is an appropriate one for this study. It should be clear by now that poetic stanzas require a different approach from legal codices; prophetic oracles cannot be read in the same way as genealogies; and ancient stories using legendary and mythical material cannot be interpreted in the same way as the New Testament Epistles. Whether

Table 5 Oral and Literary Forms of the Old Testament

The Law

Narratives, sagas, legends, myths, genealogies, tribal lists, law codes, cultic regulations, speeches, prayers, songs, blessings, curses

The Histories

Narratives, riddles, proverbs, battle reports, court archives, building projects, genealogies, letters, memoirs, accounts of visions, oracles, speeches, prayer, songs, hymns, laments

The Poetical Books

Didactic stories, maxims, proverbs, narratives, legends, songs, hymns, laments, court poetry, prayers

The Prophetic Books

Narratives, oracles, first- and third-person reports, accounts of visions, diatribes, letters, blessings, curses, myths, proverbs, legends, didactic stories

Table 6 Oral and Literary Forms of the New Testament

The Gospels

Narratives, pronouncement stories, parables, maxims, prayers, exhortations, sayings, discourses, reported oracles

A History

Narratives, memoirs, sermons, oracles, prayers, hymns, exhortations, discourses

The Epistles

Exhortations, moral instructions, catechisms, confessions of faith, hymns, prayers, formal greetings

A Prophecy

Exhortations, letters, moral instructions, reports and visions, prayers, hymns thinking primarily in historical, literary or theological categories, one has, as it were, to cut one's clothing to suit the cloth.

However, the pluralistic nature of these texts also reveals that each of the approaches has its limitations. First, the approach which has primarily an interest in the *historical nature of the text* is most prone to a lack of literary subtlety. Being more concerned with the contextualization of the texts, such an approach can often overlook the literary complexities within the biblical material. Most texts defy any precise 'historicization', because the history behind the emergence of the final form is so complex that it is impossible to determine with any great confidence the earlier and later stages of the final text. To appreciate a literary form, and to understand the writer's purpose in using one particular preferred style, does not necessarily get us any closer to the actual historical setting in which that form was first used. The literary forms cannot be understood from a historical perspective alone – and not least from a historical perspective which is often difficult to understand with any precision. Historical and literary concerns do not necessarily relate to each other neatly and clearly. For this reason, an attempt to create a 'history of religion' schema by reference to the texts themselves is ultimately a very tentative exercise.

The diffuse nature of the formation, composition and collection of these texts poses a different sort of problem for the *theological approach* – especially if there is a concern to propose some overall systematic theological unity from within the texts themselves. Here the danger is of indiscriminate selectivity, whereby verses are taken out of their original literary context, to be then used to support a different argument or to enhance a different spiritual lesson. Such a single-minded approach is not only highly tendentious but it is also insensitive to the literary complexities which lie behind the larger whole.

So it might appear that the best approach in which to have any real confidence is the *literary* one. Yet the sheer diversity of forms and styles, taken up by different writers at different times, creates great difficulties when attempting to read the text as an integral piece of literature. The literary approach is essentially holistic, seeing the text as an artefact, complete in itself. There is no doubt that this approach works best with those parts of the Bible which might cohere as a 'narrative' or 'story', although even here, the narrative may well comprise several smaller parts, which the holistic approach is apt to overlook. However, it has many limitations with regard to literary forms other than narratives – not least the poetic and didactic material – for it fails to do justice to the significance of the smaller parts which make up a typical biblical text, as also to the complex process of compilation. Oddly enough, this is the opposite problem to that found in the theological approach, where the smaller (theological) unit is over-emphasized, without due regard to the greater literary whole; here it is the greater (literary) whole which is overemphasized without due recognition to the complex number of the smaller parts.

And so we are back to the beginning of this chapter: there never can be one overall method of reading which can presume control over the text, claiming it has the most important interpretative key. All we can do is to decide upon the most appropriate approach for the text in question, and then allow other approaches to correct and complement the one which we have chosen. And in the final analysis, good reading is more often than not about sound common sense, intuition and imagination – and, as will soon be made clear, these are gained more in the practice of good reading than in the theory of it.

2

A Biblical Theology? Two Testaments, One Book?

Given that the Bible has been written and compiled in many different settings, it must contain many different theologies, each reflecting the concerns of the community from which each particular work derived. Yet in the Christian tradition, until the Enlightenment, the common belief was that the Bible could be viewed as one comprehensive theological whole; its centre was its collective witness to the person and work of Christ. This view still pervades biblical studies, as we shall see. But it has its problems: for example, Old Testament texts are not always open to being turned so that they point directly to Christ, and even in the New Testament, the 'collective witness' is so complex that it is impossible to establish with any certainty whether there is simply one centre at all.

Just as the previous chapter was concerned with the literary diversity of the Bible, this chapter has also as its focus the issue of diversity – this time in theological terms, but not only the theological diversity within each Testament but also the disparity between the two Testaments.

Theological Diversity in the Old Testament Literature

In the earlier part of the twentieth century, particularly in the early post-war years, a particular theological emphasis became evident in biblical studies. This was known as the 'biblical theology movement'. It became especially important in certain theological circles in Britain and in North America, and its chief concern was to rediscover one central, cohesive axis for a theology of the Bible. This was in part a reaction to a type of literary biblical criticism which dissected Scripture into smaller and smaller portions, without giving due attention to the whole. It was also a reaction to the sceptical view that we now know less about biblical history than we thought we did; hence instead of using history in any creative way – such as was the concern of the 'history of religions' school of thought – the key purpose of 'biblical theologies' was to develop more schematically the ideas and themes within the Old Testament. However worthy such a movement might be, its consistent problem has been the way it has had to generalize (often quite simplistically) the themes of the Old Testament in order to establish some unifying centre. A sample of the most relevant studies should illustrate this point.

One of the most straightforward proposals was made some forty years ago by E. Jacob. Writing in French in a book translated as *A Theology of the Old Testament* (1958), Jacob proposed that the Old Testament's theological unity was, quite simply 'God'. This was a unity of three parts: the characteristics of God, the action of God, and the opposition to God. But, many would argue, this is far too generalized to be effective. Other variations of this include a slightly more defined theological study by an American, G. E. Wright (1952). Old Testament theology, he argued, certainly cohered in its united witness to God, and this can be focused more on the way God has acted distinctively in history in order to bring about the salvation of his chosen people, Israel. Ironically, if Jacob's problem is that his notion of Israel's deity is too broad, then Wright's is that it is too narrow. There are too many parts of the Old Testament (notably in what may be termed 'wisdom literature' such as Proverbs, Job and Ecclesiastes) which have no explicit acknowledgement of this aspect of God's activity at all.

Some years later, W. Eichrodt, a German theologian, wrote his two-volume *A Theology of the Old Testament*, which, although more detailed than Wright's, nevertheless had the same problem. The essence of the Old Testament, he suggested, was in its theology of 'covenant'. For Eichrodt, the whole of the Old Testament reflected the people's perception of themselves as a 'covenant people', bound together through a common history by means of a long-established covenant relationship with their God. Yet the problem is again that a large proportion of the Old Testament – the wisdom literature included – seems to make no allusion to this concept of a covenant relationship.

Another German writer, G. von Rad, followed Eichrodt by writing one of the best known two-volume Old Testament theologies, translated into English in 1962 and 1965. Essentially it is a modification of Eichrodt's position. Like Wright, von Rad argues that the central Old Testament theme is '*Heilsgeschichte*', or 'salvation history', reflecting a particular view of God's special action in history, of which the idea of a covenant is a part. This, then, makes Old Testament theology uniform and distinctive, and marks it out from the polytheism of the surrounding cultures. However, not only does this beg the question as to whether the ideas of 'covenant' or 'salvation history' were understood in the same ways in different literature from different periods of Israel's history (for example, in the stories of Abraham, in the time of Moses, and in the accounts of David) but von Rad's emphasis on 'salvation history' raises two more fundamental issues.

First, it is unlikely that the notion of 'covenant' or 'salvation history' emerged in the very early stages of Israelite religion; the greater likelihood is that both are theological constructions, imposed upon the material describing earlier times but written at a much later stage, in order to gain a unified historical and theological perspective which had not previously been there. Hence these themes occur in some of the Old Testament literature, but by no means all of it; much depended upon the bias of the particular writers.

This leads on to the second issue – that it really cannot be demonstrated that all the three parts of the entire Hebrew Bible are concerned in the same way either with the idea of a covenant or with the idea of 'salvation history'. This of course takes us back to the criticism of Wright. Although convenant-thinking and '*Heilsgeschichte*' may well fit the prophets' view of history, as well as some of the material in the Pentateuch, neither can be seen to be a concern in most of the wisdom type of thinking evidenced in the final collection known as the Writings. There the predominant concern is more with universal problems of human experience than with any particular historical sense of the people's election by God. Von Rad deals with this problem better than did his predecessors, by emphasizing the different *traditions* which lie behind the overarching concern with salvation history, and so shows how it is possible to have different theologies making up the greater whole. But this very emphasis by von Rad shows in fact that it is difficult to construct a theology of the entire Old Testament.

Another keyword in searching for theological uniformity has been 'distinctiveness' – an approach which has some links with the above proposals in that it contrasts the supposed monotheism of the Old Testament with the polytheism of surrounding cultures. N. H. Snaith, for example, has suggested that the Old Testament, when compared with other collections of literature from the ancient Near East, is unique in its profession of faith in one God. This is a very early expression of 'monotheism' (developed, according to Snaith, in ways such as 'the holiness of God', 'the righteousness of God', 'the election-love of God' and 'the Spirit of God') and there is nothing quite like this, he claims, in the polytheistic cultures in neighbouring states. The problem with this argument is that it does not give due weight to the ways in which Israel's writers did in fact adapt their ideas of God from the polytheistic world around them. They did not live in a cultural vacuum, and their own religion was diverse and interacted in a complex way with the polytheistic, mythological views of their neighbours. Furthermore, like Wright's idea of covenant, this view assumes that monotheism came into Israel's faith at an early stage, rather than being a later development which was then written back into texts describing the people's early origins to create a sense that their religion was distinctive from a very early stage.

On this account, it is not surprising that several more recent studies have sought to show how attempts at unifying Old Testament theology face an impossible task. R. Albertz has written a two-volume work in German on the history of Israelite religion (1992), now translated into English. It continues the same critique offered above about the diverse and complex nature of Israelite religion. Albertz assesses the interrelationships of Israel's religious institutions, and comes to the following conclusion: there were *two* fundamental centres to Israelite religion: that which has been preserved through public, official state religion; and that which lies beneath the surface, whose concerns are more personal and heterodox, pertaining to familial beliefs and practices. Familial piety, although less perceptible from the Old Testament literature itself (because the writers wrote more naturally for the more public and official view) is, according to Albertz, as important an influence as the former. This view, which looks at the theologies of the Old Testament partly through the means of sociology of religion, would appear to be closer to the disparate evidence than the approach which selects one key theme or idea and tries to discover it through all the texts.

Other recent studies on the development of Israelite religion also support Albertz's view of the pluralism of Israel's religious institutions, and from this, the diverse nature of their theological beliefs. Apart from one or two exceptions (notably H. D. Preuss's *Old Testament Theology*, 1995 and 1996) most of the specifically theological studies published since the 1980s make it clear that it is extremely difficult to presume that every Old Testament book can fit neatly into a coherent theological whole. Three important examples from books published in the 1990s are W. Brueggeman (1992), R. Rendtorff (1993) and J. Goldingay (1995). All these writers take seriously the contextual approach which many other theologians are apt to disregard, affirming that there is a good deal of diversity, and also highlighting the difficulties in too readily assuming that there is a uniform theology. Goldingay's proposals are particularly interesting. Theological unity, he believes, is found (paradoxically) in the polarity of God's two fundamental activities – creation and salvation – and together these two themes create a coherence within their quite different theological emphases.

Thus far it can be seen that 'diversity' should be the operative word when speaking of Old Testament theology. There are too many deviations, even within the independent collections, let alone within the final body of literature as a whole, to assume any unifying theology is the key. For example, in the collection known as the Writings, the books of Ecclesiastes and Esther have very different views of God's hiddenness and providence; and even within the Prophets, books such as Jonah and Joel each in their different ways stand apart from the mainstream theology within the prophetic collection as a whole. Or again, looking at just one book within a division, one may even find that a number of 'theologies' are to be found within the so-called 'theology' of one book. The Psalter is perhaps the best example in this respect; given that it is a liturgical collection which spans some six hundred years of Israelite life, its ideas compromise a great variety of personal and communal expressions of faith and so defy any neat unifying theological appraisal.

Admittedly other writers have tried to modify the arguments which claimed too much uniformity, by arguing that Old Testament theology is a question of 'unity in diversity'. W. Zimmerli (yet another German writer) does this by identifying three major theological themes, rather than just one: God's gifts of land, priesthood and kingship. The difficulty here is that we are not told why there are only three. Other equally important themes could also be included – for example, those of prophecy, Temple and nationhood – and, if these are indeed equally important, this then simply increases the elements of diversity and so compounds the problem of asserting uniformity. This point is further illustrated in an earlier English work by H. H. Rowley. In *The Faith of Israel* (1956), Rowley selects themes such as 'Individual and Community', 'Death and Beyond' and 'the Good Life', and seeks to show how different writers contribute to these different themes in different ways.

Paradoxically, the success of Rowley's work is that it illustrates the sheer diversity of Old Testament theology, rather than the overall unity which it set out to demonstrate. There are few really successful Old Testament studies which hold the unity and diversity together in tension. One exception is a work by W. H. Schmidt, translated from the German as *The Faith of the Old Testament* (1983). This is really a study of the faith of various social groups as it became expressed in the various literary traditions. It is therefore a combination of the theological approach with the history of religions approach – more theological than Albertz, though close to it – and its sensitivity to the diversity of theologies within the literature as a whole works well.

Another way of asserting uniformity in Old Testament theology is by

'Christianizing' it – a practice which was common until the Enlightenment, as we saw earlier. This is achieved by assuming the Old Testament is basically full of disappointed hopes, which in turn point towards a need for fulfilment elsewhere – a fulfilment which is found only in the person and work of Jesus Christ. The translated title of W. Vischer's book makes the point: *The Witness of the Old Testament to Jesus Christ* (1949). So too do the works of the American, G. A. F. Knight, entitled *A Christian Theology of the Old Testament* (1964) and the British scholar, F. F. Bruce, aptly called *This is That* (1968).

The most recent systematic study of this type is that of B. S. Childs in *Biblical Theology of the Old and New Testaments* (1992). Starting with the assumption that the Bible is a unified whole because it is read as one collection, Childs proposes, with some degree of circularity, that the unity of Old Testament theology can be found only in the theology of the whole Bible. Hence the Bible's unity coheres in the implicit Christology throughout the whole. There are, of course, advantages in this view. First, it starts with what we actually have – the final text of the Bible (though there are more 'final texts' than Childs is inclined to admit, as we shall see in the following chapter, when we look at the formation of the biblical Canon). Child starts with the explicit focus on Christ expressed in the final part of the Bible, throughout the New Testament, and works backwards to the ways in which the same focus is evident, albeit somewhat hidden, throughout the Old Testament too. But the real problem, as we noted earlier with regard to any Christian interpretation of the Old Testament, is that the purported 'Christ-centredness' is often so hidden in the Old Testament that one wonders whether it is really there, except by way of deciding it *ought* to be there on account of what is known later. As with any Christian reading of the Old Testament, Childs starts with a theological position *outside* the text, rather than focusing primarily on the different theologies which are actually evident *within* it.

It is interesting that most of the publications which emphasize a unifying approach to Old Testament theology were written between the 1920s and 1970s and, apart from the few exceptions noted above, those which appeal more to a pluralistic understanding are more recent publications in the 1980s and 1990s. One of the most significant writers, who has influenced this change perhaps more than any other, is J. Barr. His main concern has been to correct any oversimplified approach to the Bible, and in six seminal publications, of which the most relevant here is probably his *The Scope and Authority of the Bible* (1980), he offers a sustained critique of those (Childs included) who try to impose on the biblical texts a theological framework it was never intended to have.

We may conclude that the most appropriate way forward is an approach to reading which takes the theological themes of each Old Testament book on their own merits, and, from this, the theological themes of each Old Testament division on their own merits. Even when there is a 'family likeness' with other theologies expressed elsewhere in the Old Testament, one has to be careful about assuming too much too soon; for even here, this likeness is often also found in literature outside the Old Testament collection, being a result of the shared cultural world-view of the writers with their neighbours. Whichever way one turns – to the smaller details of particular texts, to the larger view of the whole, within Israelite religion, or outside it – it is extremely difficult to speak with confidence of a uniformly consistent theology expressed throughout the whole of the Old Testament.

Theological Diversity in the New Testament Literature

Two particular factors militate against the possibility of one theological centre for the New Testament. The first concerns the specificity of each New Testament book. Whether Gospel or Epistle, each work bears the mark of an address to a particular church community, concerned with the issues relevant to the needs of a local situation. At the time of writing, there could hardly be an awareness of anything like a 'systematic theology'; each writer addressed a 'grass-roots' situation. In this sense, this is like the Old Testament theologies, where each writer is addressing particular needs in localized situations. However, because the New Testament literature is compressed into a much narrower time-span of some hundred years, the problem is apparent in a different way from the Old Testament, as will be seen shortly.

The second factor is that in this smaller body of literature there is nevertheless a far greater proportion of Hellenistic influence, through the writers and compilers who lived and worked in the church communities in Syria, Asia Minor and Greece. This is not to deny the possibility of some Hellenistic Jews also living in Palestine, but, as we noted in the first chapter, Palestinian Judaism had a distinctive theological emphasis, by way of its adherence to the land and the Temple, which in turn kept it much closer to its roots in the Hebrew Bible. And nor is it to deny that, in the later literature of the Old Testament (for example, in Ecclesiastes and in Daniel) Hellenistic influence is also apparent, but this having been said, it is still less substantial than in the New Testament. Hence the different proportions of Jewish and Hellenistic ways of thinking in different New Testament books is bound to create a diversity of theologies within the collection overall.

In spite of this, scholars have sought to discover one theological centre for the entire New Testament. In many ways, this has an affinity with the concerns in Old Testament studies; the biblical theology movement had supporters who defended a theological unity in *both* collections.

For example, the most general, though somewhat oversimplified way of asserting a New Testament theology is by referring to its united witness to Jesus Christ. Yet, as with the 'God-centred' approach proposed by E. Jacob for the Old Testament, this is not as straightforward as it may appear. In fact, it is even more of a problem than in the Old Testament. For instance, is the witness to the 'Jesus of history' – as expressed particularly in the Gospels – or is it to the 'Christ of faith' – as expressed more explicitly in the Acts of the Apostles, in the Epistles, and in Revelation? And is the witness to Christ to be understood in the context of a Gentile Christian community, as is probably the case with Luke/Acts, and with the letters to the Colossians and the Ephesians? Or is the testimony to Christ to be understood in different categories, as it addressed a Jewish Christian community, as with Matthew's Gospel, and the letters to the Romans and to the Galatians, and also with some of Revelation? The theological bias is bound to be different in each case. Although the 'witness to Christ' may be a connecting feature, by its very nature, this points to the theological diversity of the New Testament.

Another attempt at finding an overall theological focus is by use of some overarching term such as 'the saving acts of God in Christ'. This is similar to the 'salvation history' approach of G. E. Wright and G. von Rad in their arguments for a unified Old Testament theology. A typical New Testament approach of this kind is that of O. Cullmann, who develops a systematic schema of prophecy and fulfilment working throughout both the Old and New Testaments. Although there is some evidence to support this theory in part, the problem is that not all the New Testament material can be arranged neatly into such a schema, any more than this can be done in the Old Testament.

Another view more like Eichrodt's idea of the 'covenant' as the central theme in Old Testament theology, is to see one theological theme as the 'nerve centre' of New Testament thought. One of the first (and perhaps most radical) proponents of this view is A. Schweitzer (in English, 1910) who found that the apocalyptic preaching of Jesus was the central theological core. Schweitzer argued that Jesus preached about the end of the known world order, and he suggested that the New Testament witness is a united attempt to compensate for the fact that what Jesus anticipated happening never in fact came about. The New Testament is thus a unified attempt to correct the mistaken claims of Jesus, in the light of the delay of the second coming.

Continuing the thematic approach and locating it still within the apocalyptic preaching of Jesus, other scholars have attempted to place the theme of the kingdom of God as the heart of the New Testament message. This received much attention earlier in Germany (for example, in a study by J. Weiss). English scholars who have adopted this same theme include writers as early as C. H. Dodd (1936) and post-war writers such as J. Jeremias (1965). Still related to the kingdom of God theme, but somewhat different from it, is a theory proposed by E. Stauffer (in English, 1955), that the underlying motif throughout the texts is the conflict with the powers of evil. As we saw with the Old Testament, the problem with this and other New Testament theologies which take a thematic approach is that it works well with some of the material (in these examples, mainly with the Gospels and the Acts of the Apostles) but less so with others (for example, with some of the Epistles). The same criticism applies conversely if a theme such as 'justification' or 'grace' or 'righteousness' were superimposed as the nerve centre of New Testament thought; here this would work well with the Pauline material, but less so with the Gospels.

A different approach – again paralleling the previous Old Testament survey – is to take a theological theme from outside the New Testament, and to read this into the texts themselves. This has similarities with the appeal to the 'distinctiveness' of Old Testament theology as seen, for example, in Snaith's work. The most important New Testament theologian this century in this respect is R. Bultmann, who, adapting the ideas of several German theologians and philosophers from the middle of the last century onwards, proposed that the unifying concept throughout the New Testament writings could be described as 'faith seeking self-understanding'. Bultmann's two-volume *Theology of the New Testament,* published in English between 1952 and 1955, shows how he integrated many of the ideas of German philosophers with the ideas of New Testament writers. But the main problem in Bultmann's approach is that, by taking large unifying concepts such as faith and self-understanding, the result is so general that it could be applied to any theological literature, whether in the biblical collection, or beyond it.

A similar criticism could be made of yet another German, H. Conzelmann. The New Testament's centre, Conzelmann proposed, was its reflection upon the experience of Christian faith. The problem with all such thematic approaches is that they are apt to work only at one extreme: either the theme is too specific and hence excludes several of the New Testament works (as we have seen earlier); or it is too broad, taking its categories from outside the New Testament itself (along the lines of Bultmann and Conzelmann) and so it includes any kind of Christian writing which might have the same theological appeal.

Other writers use a 'unity in diversity' approach, such as that developed in Old Testament studies by W. Zimmerli, H. H. Rowley and W. H. Schmidt. Here one must again include B. S. Childs' *Biblical Theology of the Old and New Testaments* referred to previously, for it takes up the great theological themes of the entire Bible. Childs selects themes such as the identity of God, God the Creator, covenant, election and the people of God, Christ the Lord, reconciliation with God, law and gospel, humanity old and new, faith, and God's kingdom and rule, and applies each of these themes from the New Testament back into the Old – by using a specifically Christian lens.

We have already noted how such a Christian reading of the Old Testament is more often than not an imposition on to these texts, and does not deal adequately with the primary issue of the different Old Testament cultures suggesting different hopes and expectations about the future salvation of their people. This difficulty is further illustrated by two other earlier writers, A. M. Hunter and A. Richardson. For Hunter, the aspect of 'unity' is simply 'the Fact of Christ', or 'the divine plan of redemption', subdivided as the kingdom of God, the gospel, and the resurrection; the 'diversity' aspect is 'the Interpretation of the Fact', which looks at the theologies of Paul, Peter, John and Luke. Richardson's outline is similar: the 'unity' is the person of Christ; and the 'diversity' comprises several common themes – faith, knowledge, the power of God, kingdom of God, Holy Spirit, Messiah, resurrection, atonement, Israel of God, ministry, baptism and eucharist. As with similar Old Testament approaches, such a selection of interconnected themes fails to deal with different cultures which must have produced them. By using the biblical texts as a means of supporting predetermined themes, and by failing to give enough attention to the variety of socio-religious settings in which some of these themes may be expressed, it is again inclined to be a study of the history of ideas imposed upon the text, rather than a study of the theological, social and religious issues arising out of it.

Two other studies of the subject (and notably more recent ones) are seminal because they emphasize more constructively the diversity of New Testament theology. J. Dunn's earlier book on the nature of New Testament theology, *Unity and Diversity in the New Testament* (1977), looks at the different theologies by assessing the different forms and settings in which these theologies are expressed. Examples include preaching, creeds, Old Testament allusions, liturgies, accounts of spiritual experiences, prayers, and the teaching on ministry and sacraments. Dunn explores the sociological factors behind this diversity, and proposes that there are two fundamental influences on the formation of the theologies of the New Testament writers. The first, he argues, is Jewish Christianity, which initially stayed as close as possible to Judaism by 'Christianizing' the central beliefs about the Law; the second, he proposes, is Gentile Christianity, which tried to accommodate Greek and Gnostic thought by 'Christianizing' their moral and philosophical teaching.

Two further influences, Dunn also notes, are not so much socio-religious as theological and experiential. These are 'enthusiastic Christianity', which, being more experience-centred, emphasized life in the Spirit, and 'apocalpytic Christianity', which, being more depressed about the present times and hence more future-orientated, emphasized the life of the world to come. In spite of the fact that Dunn illustrates well the different theologies which make up the whole, the main difficulty in this schema is that it is part a history-of-religions approach, and part a history-of-ideas approach, and the two do not always fit well together in attempting to assemble a theology of the entire New Testament.

A more recent publication is J. Reumann's *Variety and Unity in New Testament Thought* (1991). Reumann assesses (usually critically) previous proposals for the uniformity of New Testament theology, looking at themes such as the kingdom of God, faith, God's plan of salvation, and the new age to come. Taking into account the different groups of theological contributors (the Gospel writers, Paul and the Pauline school, Peter, Hebrews, James, the Johannine school, and Jude and 2 Peter), Reumann proposes that if any centre holds, it is that of 'Jesus and the experience of faith'. In this he goes further than does Bultmann, because he places more emphasis on the many manifestations from such a centre, and he is less dependent upon ideas from outside the New Testament to substantiate it. A key point is that coherence is *not* the same as uniformity; an integrated reading of the New Testament requires due recognition of the disparate theological parts of the whole.

A common theme throughout this New Testament survey has been the way in which it echoes the similar survey of the Old Testament. On the more negative side, we have noted that we should expect diverse theologies within each division, and within each book in its division, and even within the composite parts of each book; we have seen that all these works bear the stamp of particular Christian communities, and each needs to be taken on its own merits. On the more positive side, perhaps using Reumann as one of the best guides, one can nevertheless ascertain several layers within the formation of these theologies, evident in many of the New Testament books. The starting point is the Palestinian Jewish influence, which had its base first in Jerusalem, around the key figures of Peter and James; the next stage is more explicit Hellenistic Jewish influence, through early Christian communities throughout Syria, Asia Minor and Greece, mainly centred around the key figure of Paul; and the latest stage might be seen as the influence upon Christianity of the great Gentile metropolis, Rome. Hence Christianity, by its very process of growth, had to be diverse. Between Jerusalem and Rome, it had to address the more conservative Jewish Christian communities – for example, those in Galatia and Thessalonica – as well as the more liberal yet divided Jewish and Hellenistic Christian communities – for example, in Philippi, Colossae, Antioch, Ephesus, Crete and Corinth.

Against this backcloth, it is difficult to presume anything other than diversity in the theological apologetic of the New Testament writers. Whatever uniformity we may wish to ascribe to the overall voice of the New Testament, it is usually so generalized ('the activity of God in history'; 'the one God who meets us in Jesus Christ') that it serves little purpose, other than to ascertain at the most basic level some coherence within the whole. The main contribution of such assertions is that (rather like credal affirmations in liturgy) they offer some boundaries for the diverse parts.

The Use of the Old Testament in the New

As we have seen, any attempt to assume one aspect of Old Testament theology and impose it upon the New might be viewed as a subjective and selective exercise. Yet in the history of Christian tradition, this is precisely what interpreters have done. For example, a relatively recent edict from Vatican Council II (1965), a promulgation on the Constitution of Divine Revelation, entitled *Dei Verbum* (Chapter IV, ø 16) states: 'God, inspirer and author of both Testaments, wisely arranged that the New Testament be hidden in the Old and the Old be made manifest in the New.' Although other church traditions might place the emphasis in a different place, the common consensus for those reading as believers is that the New Testament is the fulfilment of the Old (hence its term, 'New') and, moreover, that the Old Testament offers a proper interpretation of the New. But is this a legitimate theological exercise?

Two extremes need to be avoided. The first is to overplay the continuity, and to see that every page of the Old finds its counterpart in the

New; hence nothing exists in the Old for its own sake, but everything is to be turned 'Christwards'. We have noted several times that the pitfall in such an approach is that it undermines the integrity of the Old Testament as a body of literature in its own right. The second extreme is to overplay the discontinuity, so that an understanding of the Old Testament is deemed irrelevant for an appreciation of the New. This too has its problems. It is obviously true that the Old Testament can be read entirely for its own sake, as a book which witnesses to Jewish religion and culture, offering us important insights about the achievements of the Hebrew spirit, through its gallery of different personalities. On this account, the Old Testament may be better termed 'the Hebrew Bible', for this indicates it can be appreciated, in all its diversity, entirely on its own merits. Nevertheless, the converse is not the case; the New Testament cannot be read entirely on its own, for almost all the writers were steeped in the Jewish traditions of the Old Testament, and we can make little sense of their many allusions unless we look at the New within the context of the Old. The interpretation of the theologies of the New Testament does indeed require an informed understanding of the Old. To quote from a recent study of the New Testament by J. and K. Court (*The New Testament World*, CUP, 1990, p. 36): 'Christianity is unique among the religions of the world because it was born with a Bible [*sic*] in its cradle.'

Hence we should not overuse the Old Testament, trying to force every text into a Christian theological framework; but nor should we ignore it either. The key issue is not about the use of the Old Testament, but about the *way* in which it is used. This point is best illustrated from the New Testament itself.

In Chapter 1, we saw that, in both the Hebrew and the Greek divisions of the Old Testament, the Law (*Tôrâ*) was the organizational point of reference for the collection of writings. In the Hebrew Bible, the other two parts (the Prophets and Writings) fitted around this centre, and within the LXX, the other three parts (the Histories, Poetical Books and the Prophetic Books) did the same. By contrast, the primary focus in the New Testament's interpretation of the Old is not so much the Law, as the Prophets. The greatest selection of material is taken from the prophetic works (and also from the Psalms, but this is because they too were seen as prophetic in orientation).

This is not to deny that even in the Old Testament, despite the primary centre being the Law, there is ample evidence of the interest in the interpretation and fulfilment of prophecy. The books of Kings bring out this theme repeatedly. The phrase 'Thus X happened according to the word of the Lord which he had spoken through Y the prophet' is repeated several times throughout the books of Kings. (For example, in 1 Kings 12.15, from 1 Kings 11.29–39, and in 1 Kings 15.29, from 1 Kings 14.6–16; this pattern occurs at least four more times). Similarly, in the major prophetic books (Isaiah, Jeremiah and Ezekiel) a good deal of reinterpretation of earlier prophetic material takes place within the books themselves. For example, Isaiah 40–55 picks up several themes about God's promises to Zion (Jerusalem) which are found in Isaiah 1–39; the purpose in so doing is to emphasize that *now* is the age of the fulfilment of the prophecies spoken by Isaiah of Jerusalem (whose message is contained in Isaiah 1–39) albeit in a time some two hundred years earlier. The interest in prophecy, and in a later generation in the fulfilment of prophecy, is undoubtedly a major Old Testament concern.

It is not surprising that the New Testament takes this prophetic process of interpretation further still, because of the shared belief that, through the coming of Christ, the community was now living in the age of the fulfilment of Old Testament prophecies; a new era in their history had thus come about. On account of this, Matthew, John, Luke/Acts, Romans, 1 and 2 Corinthians, Galatians, Colossians, Hebrews and Revelation all use the prophecy/fulfilment schema in different ways.

Nowhere is this schema made more clear than in the Gospel of Matthew. More than ten times, drawing from the Prophets and the Psalms, Matthew uses the formula 'this took place to fulfil what the Lord had spoken by the prophet'. The phrase occurs four times in the birth narratives. For example, Matthew 1.22–3 ('Behold, a virgin shall conceive and bear a son') uses a prophecy from Isaiah 7.14; Matthew 2.15 ('Out of Egypt have I called my son') is a reference to Hosea 11.1; Matthew 2.17–18 ('a voice was heard in Ramah ... Rachel weeping for her children') uses Jeremiah 31.15; the fourth, in Matthew 2.23 ('He shall be called a Nazarene') has an unknown source. Six times Matthew inserts this formula at key points in the later narrative: at the time of the temptation (Matthew 4.14–16), after healing miracles (Matthew 8.17 and 12.17–21), after teaching in parables (13:35), at the time of the entry into Jerusalem (21.4–5) and after Judas' suicide (27.9–10).

However, the difficulty is that the actual use of Old Testament prophecy is not at all clear in each case. For example, in the Matthew 2.15 passage, the reference in Hosea originally meant the whole people of Israel; in Matthew, it applies to Jesus' own escape from Egypt, and so the prophecy is reused, with the implication that Jesus is the true embodiment of the people of Israel. Another difficulty is that Matthew 2.23 ('He shall be called a Nazarene') has no allusion in the Old Testament. It may be that the intention is to make a play on similar-sounding words. 'Nazareth', in Aramaic, sounds like 'branch', in Hebrew; in which case, the allusion may be to the 'branch' of Jesse (a reference to the Davidic king) in Isaiah 11.1, hence implying that Jesus is some sort of royal figure, born in Bethlehem, the home of King David. Matthew 21.4–5 is another interesting example. Referring to the prophecy in Zechariah 9.9, where an ass and colt are mentioned, Matthew's account of Jesus' entry into Jerusalem includes two donkeys, not one – in order to make clear that this is the precise fulfilment of the prophecy (although, in the original Zechariah prophecy, this probably only implies one animal).

In addition to this appeal to prophecy by using a particular formula, many other references to the Old Testament prophets are scattered throughout Matthew's Gospel. The prophet Micah is used in Matthew 2.5–6; Isaiah is used in Matthew 3.3, 13.14–15 and 15.7–9; and Daniel is used in Matthew 24.15. Furthermore, Matthew's account of the death of Jesus is interspersed with explicit and implicit references to the Psalms, using them as 'prophecies' to indicate that Jesus is a typical (suffering) Messiah figure. Psalm 22 is used regarding the casting of lots over Jesus' garments, the derision from the bystanders, and the cry of Godforsakenness, and Psalm 69 is used concerning the derision and mockery, and the offer of vinegar to drink.

What might be learnt from Matthew's particular use of prophecy in this way? First, that it is indeed selective and particular – a 'grass-roots' theology. Second, that Matthew was not the only work which used the Old Testament in this way. Indeed, this approach is by no means limited to the New Testament writers. Various Jewish communities as well as Christian congregations found this an important means of affirming that they, too, were living in the 'end times', waiting for the time of the fulfilment of earlier prophecy. For example, this same approach is also evident in the Dead Sea Scrolls, which have been found at Qumran.

Thus Matthew's use of prophecy offers one typical model of the way in which the New Testament writers developed their own theologies from different Old Testament examples. There are, of course, other ways in which other writers achieved the same end. Well-known figures of the past (Adam, Abraham, Moses, David) were used as 'types' (or 'antitypes', in the case of Adam) foreshadowing the person of Christ. Great events of the past (the Exodus, the giving of the Law, the gift of the land, the building of Jerusalem) became new ways of understanding the ministry of Christ. Great themes of particular Old Testament books were seen to point to Christ – for example, the Spirit of God in the valley of dry bones in Ezekiel 37, the Word of God as in the act of creation in Genesis 1, the Wisdom of God as described in

Proverbs 8, the Suffering Servant as in Isaiah 53. All these were explored and given new significance in the light of the teaching of Christ. In different ways, these were also models to illustrate further the fulfilment of prophecy and, when used by different New Testament writers in different settings, far from illustrating the overall unity throughout, they actually contribute further to the element of diversity in New Testament theology.

In addition to taking up various Old Testament passages in order to add new meaning to the person and work of Jesus Christ, several New Testament writers also used the Old Testament to give new significance to the nature and purpose of the newly established Christian community. For example, the Church is portrayed as the new Israel – here the accounts of God's election of the people of Israel are used (as in Romans 9.6ff. and in 1 Peter 2.9, 10). The Church is also seen as the new Temple (1 Corinthians 3.16; 6.19; 2 Corinthians 6.16; and Ephesians 2.20–2). In baptism the Church experiences redemption like that at the Red Sea (1 Corinthians 10.2). The Church is described as the inheritor of the promises once made to Abraham – for example in Romans 4.9ff.; 9.6–8 and Galatians 3.29 and 4.22ff. The Church has an inheritance better than that of Canaan – in Hebrews 3.18—4.13. The point should now be clear: the New Testament writers mined the various most relevant parts of the Old Testament to create their own theologies, in ways which suited the needs of their own communities, and they each did so (as was seen in the case of Matthew) in a very particular, selective way.

One obvious issue which arises out of this survey is that of '*proof-texting*' (that is, taking a text out of context and using it to prove a point in an entirely different context). It could be argued that, if the New Testament authors selected parts of the Old Testament in this way – and in so doing, hardly giving due weight to the different world-views in their original life setting, or to the earliest concerns of the Old Testament writers – does not this legitimize the process for those who do their biblical theology in the same way? There are many examples of commentators who have done just this throughout the history of the Christian tradition. Certainly the New Testament writers did not seem to worry about issues of dissonance between the world-view of the Old Testament and their own; nor were they especially concerned about distinguishing between different theologies in one Old Testament book and another. So does the end justify the means? The final section is an attempt to find a reasonable way forward.

Towards an Integrated Theological Approach to the Bible

We noted at the beginning of this chapter that whereas Chapter 1 illustrated the importance of sensitive reading with respect to the Bible as literature, Chapter 2 would illustrate the same with regard to the Bible as theology. In many ways, therefore, the guidelines offered both there and here correspond with one another. A pre-critical theological approach has just as many difficulties as a pre-critical literary one, and while affirming that both literary and theological approaches are essential, it is the appropriate use of each, in the face of such diversity, which is the important issue. Two observations are relevant in this respect.

First, *the theological approach needs to be complemented by the historical-critical method,* if it is to avoid being too superficial in its universalizing tendencies. For the historical method has one key asset: it emphasizes the particularity and cultural relativity of ancient texts, and from this, it is properly cautious about assuming too much connectedness between one ancient text and another. The problem of proof-texting is that a text, or a theological theme, is transplanted from one culture into another without recognizing the dissonance between the understanding of the text or theme in its earliest setting and in its later one. This can be overcome by giving due weight to the historical method, for it can act as a restraint on the generalizing and universalizing tendencies in a more enthusiastic theological reading of texts.

The theological approach is, very often, closely related to a 'confessional stance' – that is, a way of reading which is profoundly concerned with a 'faith response' between the reader as a believer and the text as the product of earlier believers. Such a stance is apt to be overly receptive, for it seeks to welcome the biblical texts into the life of the worshipping community, and thus it is prone to silence what is foreign and dissonant in order to receive only what are understood as shared beliefs and common experiences. (The liturgical formula, 'This is the word of the Lord', albeit perhaps unconsciously, encourages this process.) A historically orientated reading is even more an essential corrective here, for it emphasizes the particularity of a text and so modifies its universal appeal.

To take some examples: Old Testament texts which justify holy war, or which assume polygamy and slavery are a normative part of society, or which support a now archaic form of animal sacrifice cannot be incorporated into an overall theological schema in the same way as texts which speak of the ultimate harmony in the created order, or of the value of prayer or of the need for justice and the love of one's neighbour. The historical approach is an essential tool in creating a cultural sensitivity, in that it enables the reader to distinguish between what is contingent and hence culturally conditioned from what may be of permanent value. Furthermore, even after having established some core of what may be of permanent value, the historical approach also allows for due recognition of the many different theological voices (in other texts) which may express that value in diverse ways. For example, an awareness of historical contexts means taking into account the many different theologies of creation, of prayer and of ethics which are expressed throughout the Bible. In this sense, the historical approach serves not only as a restraining influence upon theological interpretation, but also as a constructive one.

Second, *the theological approach also needs to be complemented by the literary method,* for entirely different reasons. One positive feature of literary study of the Bible is that it has illustrated how one particular text, with all its different interpretations provided by readers throughout the centuries, is still in some ways a mystery. One of the features common to many of the theological approaches to the text is the inclination to simplify and universalize its meaning in order that those offering the interpretation may then *control* the meaning of a text. Hence the meaning proposed becomes the one true meaning; and this meaning is the means by which, as theological interpreters, they control the beliefs and behaviour of their community, whether for good or ill. But we have seen repeatedly how the complex nature of any biblical text (however small) defies such universalizing tendencies, and so undermines any authoritarian claims made for them. The literary method has often been confusing in the way it has put forward the idea of a multifaceted text in relation to the Bible, but it has undoubtedly enabled us to see that there are as many meanings in a text as there are readers and interpreters, as we all bring our singular experience to bear upon our reading. Literary sensitivity encourages theological pluralism, and given what we have noted throughout this chapter concerning the diversity of biblical theology, such pluralism seems to accord with the evidence.

Taking this one stage further still, it is not only that the text itself offers a multiple range of meanings; the events (or experiences) to which a text may bear witness also offer a multiple number of interpretations, of which the one text is but a small part. J. Reumann offers some important insights as to how this theological pluralism of event, text and interpretation works in practice. Affirming, as we have just done, that it is extremely difficult to ascertain only one 'moment of meaning' in any one text, and affirming too that a text can only capture one part of the meaning, Reumann asks how there can ever be just one interpretative moment of any one event. As an example, he uses the death of Jesus on the cross. Is the moment of meaning, he asks, to be found in the historical moment of Jesus expiring? Or does it occur in the earliest theological reflection on this, in some oral account of the death of Jesus? Or does it reside in the way one or other of the Gospel-writers retells the story? Or is it in Paul's more explicitly developed theological assertion of what was the result of Jesus' death, such as 'Christ died for our sins'? Or is ultimate meaning to be found in the period after the New Testament documents had been written, in some comprehensive and uniform theological combination of all of these beliefs? What then do we make of the meanings found in later Christian tradition, such as in the writings of Tertullian, or Augustine, or Anselm or Luther? And finally, might not the ultimate 'moment of meaning' – for us, at least – be found in the preaching about the death of Christ to hearers today? One event leads to many different interpretations; the many different interpretations are expressed in many different texts, across space and time.

Hence the literary approach teaches us that it is impossible to give any biblical text absolute meaning, because it is still only partially explored and hence is still in part a mystery. Furthermore, at the other end of the spectrum, the same approach demonstrates that we cannot take any one text in isolation, because this is but one small, fragmentary witness to something much larger than it can encapsulate. On both accounts, biblical texts are mysterious and not yet fully explored. If no text can be assumed to have absolute or final meaning, this has obvious ramifications in a defence of a *pluralistic* biblical theology.

This chapter has been about how we use constructively the diverse theologies evident throughout the Bible. Yet again we are brought back to the principle that no one approach can presume it is superior to the others, and that the integration of all the different ways of reading is the only reasonable way forward. The historical approach prevents us universalizing biblical theology from the particular local situations; the literary approach prevents us from particularizing the theologies too much within our own settings, without due concern for the wider issues; and the theological approach allows us to give due weight to the way in which texts have had meaning in the life of different communities – so that the opportunity is available for our being able to create new interpretations, properly controlled.

3

A Biblical Corpus? The Canon and the Boundaries of Faith

Whereas the first two chapters have been concerned with diversity within the biblical books, this chapter and the next one will look at the different ways in which the books were received in later tradition. Here we shall argue that, because it is impossible to draw up clear boundaries for the inclusion or exclusion of particular books, we do not possess just *one* authoritative collection (or Canon, meaning a rule of faith) called 'the Bible', or 'Scripture', but several different collections. This has important consequences for the ways in which we read those books which we have in our own particular Bible, for our reading is contingent upon the particular theological tradition – Jewish or Christian – with which we have become familiar.

The Emergence of a Canon in the Old Testament Collection

Two factors determined the eventual recognition by different communities of a fixed collection of Old Testament writings. One was the crisis facing the Jewish community from outside their faith, and the other, the sects and factions which developed within it.

The very earliest stages of the process of creating a Canon, or of 'canonization', began after the exile to Babylon in 587 BCE. At this time, ancient traditions were collected and preserved and, very gradually, the first delineation known as the 'Law' – the *Tôrâ* – began to emerge. This was not a sudden recognition; Judaism, itself evolving during this period, was too diffuse to make it so. So it was part of an evolving process. Within the other two divisions of the Hebrew Bible – the Prophets and the Writings – some works were 'coming in', and others were 'going out'. Throughout this whole period, and even until the first century CE, the formation of any one, whole, recognizable

46

Hebrew 'Bible' was in a state of flux. In order to understand this process better, we need to assess separately each of the three divisions in the Hebrew Bible.

The Law

It is probable that, *by the time of the monarchy from 1000 BCE onwards*, there were small collections of laws which were taught by priests and other officials at the local sanctuaries or at the city gates. One example is said to be part of the 'Book of the Covenant' contained in Exodus 21.1—23.19.

Moving forward some four hundred years, *by the time of the exile in 587 BCE*, there were probably several collections of laws which appear to have been used (for example, by the prophets) as a basis for reform. One example is the 'Deuteronomic Code' – part of a later collection of laws found within Deuteronomy 12—26, which according to 2 Kings 22—3, may well have inspired the reforms of the King Josiah in 621 BCE. Other legal collections, particularly priestly ones, emerged from different hands some time later.

After the return from exile in the sixth and fifth centuries BCE, an identifiable 'corpus of law' clearly existed, which included not only the Book of the Covenant and the Deuteronomic Law, but also some Priestly Code of Law – for example, the collections of the civil and cultic regulations in Leviticus and Numbers. This, combined with the narrative accounts of Genesis and Exodus, became known as 'the Law of Moses', and was seen to be binding upon the people: Nehemiah 8.1 and Ezra 7.14 describe a ceremony from about this time, where the people listened to the Law of Moses being read, and vowed to obey it.

Certainly *by the third century BCE*, the collection known as *Tôrâ* was complete. At this time, Genesis, Exodus, Leviticus, Numbers and Deuteronomy comprised a fixed, authoritative collection for the Septuagint translation in Alexandria.

The Prophets

During and shortly after the exile in the sixth and fifth centuries BCE, the 'prophetic history' (Joshua to 2 Kings) was probably compiled. By the time the books of Chronicles were compiled some two centuries later as an account of the same period of history, the traditions from this prophetic history appear to have been widely known in order for the Chronicler (the compiler of the books of Chronicles) to make additional comments and changes. Some time after the Exile, the works of the three major prophets (Isaiah, Jeremiah and Ezekiel) were being adapted in order to prepare the people for their gradual restoration to their land, and so they too were growing in their status throughout this period.

By the end of the Persian period in the late fourth century BCE, Isaiah and Jeremiah were probably accepted as canonical works, although Ezekiel's canonical status was still deliberated as late as the first century CE. The twelve minor prophets, preserved together on one single scroll, achieved a fixed status some time after the fourth century. Because the living voice of prophecy had ceased to be an influence in the Jewish community (that is after Malachi, by the fourth century at the latest), there was a growing need to preserve and reuse the inspired words of the prophets 'of old'. By 190 BCE, Ecclesiasticus 49.10 refers to the 'twelve prophets' as one collection.

By *the second century BCE*, the collection known as the *Nᵉbî'îm* (comprising the prophetic history, the three major prophets, and the Scroll of the Twelve) had sufficient status to be translated as one corpus from the Hebrew into the Greek, joining the other division known as the *Tôrâ*. However, the Greek did not include Daniel among the Prophets, suggesting there was still some measure of openness at this time regarding what was a fixed but not closed collection of books. What is clear is that, by the first century BCE, when 2 Maccabees 15.9 refers to 'the law and the prophets' this presumes that these two collections offered some normative source of authority and inspiration for the faith of that particular community.

The Writings

We noted in the first chapter that this is by far the most open-ended of the three divisions of the so-called Canon. When, *in 190 BCE*, the foreword to Ecclesiasticus refers to 'the law, the prophets, and the rest of the books' this implies that there was a recognizable third collection, but it also shows that at the time of this reference it was less defined. Almost three hundred years later, *near the end of the first century CE*, Luke 24.44 refers to 'the law, the prophets and the psalms'. This might imply that this final division now included only the Psalter, although it more probably presumes a larger collection which was headed by the Psalms. A similar reference by Philo, a first-century Jew, in his work *On the Contemplative Life* (3:25) speaks of 'the law, the prophetic words, and the hymns'; this similarly raises the question of the precise nature of this third division.

The findings at Qumran, dated *from the last two centuries BCE onwards*, offer no further clues. At Qumran, a work called *The Damascus Document* (in 7.14–18) and another entitled *The Manual of Discipline* (in 8.15–16) refer only to 'the law and the prophets' as a canonical collection; the Writings do not appear to be a recognizable complete division at all.

One interesting point is that, in other works from the Dead Sea Scrolls, the Psalms are constantly referred to, while other parts – such as Chronicles, Ezra and Nehemiah – hardly receive any mention at all. From this, we might conclude that the Psalter was the most important part of the division known as the Writings, but (unlike the Law and Prophets) other parts of this division kept expanding, rather than shrinking. The evidence from Luke and Philo, as well as from Qumran, all points in this direction. The variations and additions to this division in the Greek translations bear further witness to it. Hence we must assume that, unlike the *Tôrâ* and the *N'bî' îm*, no one normative collection known as the *Ch'tûbîm* was discernible until well after the time of Christ.

One further point of evidence is that, by the end of the first century CE, we know of two different lists of books which were seen to make up the 'Canon' of the *Tanach*, held by two different Jewish communities. The first and shorter list is based on the Hebrew text, and is known as the Palestinian Canon. This list corresponds in its final form with the threefold division of books for the Hebrew Bible presented by way of Table 1 in Chapter 1 (p. 12). This same list is referred to in the Talmud (a Jewish commentary on the books in the Hebrew Bible, especially the Law), which describes it as the outcome of discussions by a group of rabbis in about 90 to 100 CE at Jamnia, near Joppa, on the Mediterranean coast. The crisis brought about by the destruction of the Temple and the fall of Jerusalem in 70 CE, which resulted in the dispersion of the Jewish communities throughout Asia Minor, required a decision regarding the status of the Hebrew Scriptures in a time of change. Furthermore, the use of these scriptures by the Christian communities throughout Asia Minor demanded some clarity as to what were the canonical books of the *Jewish* faith. Because of these crises both within and without the Jewish community, particularly in Palestine, guidelines had to be drawn up to mark out the 'boundaries' of faith.

It is possible that Jamnia was a formal Jewish council which decided, once for all, these boundaries. The Talmud does not make it clear, but it is unlikely that things were as clear-cut as this. Jamnia may well not have been a council at all, but the result of its meeting was a firm decision for the inclusion of Ecclesiastes, Ruth, Daniel and Song of Songs (for the canonical status of all these books was by no means settled). The book of Sirach (or Ecclesiasticus) was also under discussion for inclusion. Eventually it was left out; and debates about whether or not to include the books of Esther and Ezekiel continued into the second century CE, when eventually they were fully accepted and allowed in. Table 7 outlines the list known as the Palestinian Canon, and it is evident that the status of the third division was by no means clear-cut. The **?** in Table 7 indicates where a book was still in some doubt, and the **??** indicates where there was even greater doubt.

Table 7   The Palestinian Canon

The Law	*The Prophets*	*The Writings*
	Former Prophets	
Genesis	Joshua	Psalms
Exodus	Judges	Proverbs
Leviticus	1 and 2 Samuel	Job
Numbers	1 and 2 Kings	
Deuteronomy		
	Latter Prophets	*Scroll of Five*
	Isaiah	? Ruth
	Jeremiah	? Song of Songs
	? Ezekiel	? Ecclesiastes
		Lamentations
		?? Esther
	Scroll of the Twelve	
	Hosea	
	Joel	
	Amos	
	Obadiah	
	Jonah	? Daniel
	Micah	Ezra
	Nahum	Nehemiah
	Habakkuk	1 and 2 Chronicles
	Zephaniah	
	Haggai	
	Zechariah	
	Malachi	

The standard Hebrew edition of the Bible, called the *BHS* (*Biblia Hebraica Stuttgartensia*, on account of its being published in Stuttgart), has followed the same order of the divisions in the Palestinian Canon (Law, Prophets, Writings) and of the books within those divisions. The order of the Writings, however, varies in several other printed editions, following the practice of other earlier manuscripts. For example, the books of Chronicles sometimes head up the list, and, in the 'Scroll of Five', Song comes before Ruth, and Lamentations before Ecclesiastes. But the threefold division, starting with the Law, then the Prophets, then the Writings, is constant. This indicates that by the first century CE there was a recognized movement from certitude (the Law, then the Prophets) to open-endedness (the Writings) with regard to the status of the various works.

Outside this particular collection was another miscellaneous group of books called the 'apocryphal books'; these were known as the 'seventy books' which, according to tradition, Ezra had to hide after he had published the so-called canonical books (cf. 2 Esdras 14.6, 45ff.). Most of these date from the second century BCE onwards, and, like most of the other books cited, originated in Palestine. Only two authors are identified by a name: Jesus ben Sirach (Ecclesiasticus 50.27) and Jason of Cyrene (2 Maccabees 2.23). The remainder of the 'seventy books' include 1 and 2 Esdras, Tobit, Judith, the longer Greek text of Esther, the Wisdom of Solomon, Ecclesiasticus, Baruch, the Letter of Jeremiah, the Prayer of Azariah and the Song of the Three Young Men, Susanna, Bel and the Dragon, the Prayer of Manasseh, books 1 to 4 of Maccabees, and Psalm 151. This additional group illustrates how the consolidating of a definitive list was a protracted process, insofar as the choices had to be made from a much larger collection.

Futhermore, many of the so-called 'seventy books' referred to above are actually included in a second Jewish list of books, known as the Alexandrian Canon. This list was made on the basis of the Septuagint, and, like the LXX, it originated outside Palestine, in Alexandria, in North Africa (now in modern Egypt). Because it was preserved and transmitted through many different Hellenistic Jewish communities, whose taste was inevitably more eclectic, it is not surprising that the list is much larger than the Palestinian Canon.

What makes the matter more confusing is that different manuscripts of the LXX offer different lists of books, and so the Alexandrian Canon may well have been just one longer collection among many. For example, the most complete manuscript of the LXX, *Codex Vaticanus*, from the fourth century CE, has no reference to Maccabees at all; *Codex Sinaiticus*, a slightly less complete manuscript also from the fourth century CE, lists both 1 Maccabees and 4 Maccabees; where *Codex*

Alexandrinus, a fifth-century CE manuscript, includes all four books of Maccabees. Some of the additional books are not even kept in a separate list. Baruch, for example, is mixed with the earlier prophetic books, because of its associations with the prophet Jeremiah, and Ecclesiasticus and the Wisdom of Solomon are incorporated into the poetical books.

One important point also needs to be recognized. The Christian Church, using the Greek version more than the Hebrew, because of the increasingly predominant Hellenistic influence upon Christianity, used the longer list in preference to the shorter, Palestinian-influenced one. Many of the additional books – not only those in the Alexandrian Canon but also those outside it – were important to the early Christian communities because they offered them additional theological material not found in the Palestinian Canon. These traditions – about angels, the resurrection of the dead, the coming of the Son of Man, and the personification of wisdom – provided a much richer resource for the Christian communities in their defence of faith concerning Jesus' birth, death, resurrection and teaching on the second coming. So even though many books were eventually excluded from the Christian corpus, they were a significant indirect influence on the Christians who wrote some parts of the New Testament. For example, Jude 14 quotes from Enoch as an authority; Matthew 2.23 uses a prophecy unknown in the Old Testament which probably came from a now unknown source; in the same way, 2 Corinthians 6.14, Ephesians 5.14 and James 4.4 quote from other texts not known within the Palestinian or Alexandrian Canons but nevertheless apparently accepted sources of authority within their own communities.

The list known as the Alexandrian Canon is offered as Table 8. (Again, the ? beside some books indicates that their eventual inclusion occurred only after some debate. The books marked with * beside them are those which were eventually excluded.) The order of these books – following the fourfold division, noted previously – corresponds overall with that offered in the standard edition of the Septuagint, edited by Rahlfs.

As indicated already, various later manuscripts demonstrate that several other books were also accepted into this longer list at one time or another. These books are additional to those 'seventy books' noted as part of an apocrypal appendage to the Palestinian Canon. They include the Letter of Aristeas (concerning the writing of the LXX), the Book of Jubilees, the Martyrdom and Ascension of Isaiah, the Ethiopic Book of Enoch, the Slavonic Book of Enoch, the Assumption of Moses, 2 Esdras, the Syrian Apocalypse of Baruch, the Greek Apocalypse of Baruch, 1 and 2 Baruch, the Testament of the Twelve Patriarchs, the

Table 8 The Alexandrian Canon

The Law	*The Histories*
Genesis	Joshua
Exodus	Judges
Leviticus	? Ruth
Numbers	1 and 2 Kingdoms (in
Deuteronomy	Hebrew, 1 and 2 Samuel)
	3 and 4 Kingdoms (in
	Hebrew, 1 and 2 Kings)
	Chronicles (= also
	'Paraleipomena', 'things left
	out')
	* Esdras A (= also '1 Ezra')
	Esdras B (in Hebrew,
	Ezra–Nehemiah)
	?? Esther
	* Judith
	* Tobit
	* 1 to 4 Maccabees

The Poetical Books	*The Prophetic Books*
Psalms	The Twelve Minor Prophets
* Odes of Solomon	Isaiah
* Psalm 151	Jeremiah (in Hebrew, a fuller
* Prayer of Manasseh	version)
* Additions to Daniel	* Baruch
* Additions to Esther	* Lamentations
	* Letter of Jeremiah
Proverbs	? Ezekiel
? Ecclesiastes	? Daniel
? Song of Songs	
Job	
* Wisdom of Solomon	
* Ben Sirach (= also 'Ecclesiasticus')	
* Psalms of Solomon	

Life of Adam and Eve, the Testament of Abraham, the Apocalypse of Abraham, and the Lives of the Prophets. Most of these suggested a provenance either in Palestine, or in Syria. Other books, from further afield, include the Sibylline Oracles Books 1 to 5, 2 Enoch (or the Secrets of Enoch) and 3 Baruch. Much of this material is apocalyptic in its theology, the language used is predominantly Greek, and the authors wrote pseudonymously, using as their authority renowned figures of the past. Yet again we may note the extensive range of literature out of which the selection of 'canonical' books was made.

Curiously, the Church in the East usually accepted the shorter collection in contrast to the reception of the fuller collection by the Church in the West. For example, fathers of the Western Church such as Clement of Rome, Polycarp, Hermas and Irenaeus of Lyons all quote freely from books outside the Palestinian corpus, accepting both their authority and their inspiration. Even as late as the fourth century CE, the North African Councils at Hippo and Carthage accepted a larger body of works which was more akin to the Alexandrian Canon. By contrast, in the Eastern Church, writers such as Melito of Sardis (second century CE), Origen (third century CE) and Athanasius (fourth century CE) used a shorter list of books. It was Jerome who tried to make this shorter Canon normative in the West, by choosing to translate into Latin directly from the shorter Hebrew text rather than from the Greek.

Hence between the third century BCE and the fourth century CE, the 'Hebrew Bible' and the 'Old Testament' meant different things to different Jewish and Christian communities. Obviously each community found its own criteria for inclusion and exclusion. Preference was given to the earlier material, particularly that written before the Persian period; the teaching in any new books had to agree with the teaching in *Tôrâ*: and each new book had to have a specifically Hebrew character – itself a broad term, although the medium of the Hebrew language was a key factor in establishing some authenticity.

In conclusion, there can be no doubt that it is a misnomer to speak of one 'Old Testament corpus'; certainly this was not so at such an early time as the formation of the New Testament. No one such collection existed; even the two lists representing the Palestinian and Alexandrian Canons were themselves 'fuzzy at the edges'.

The Emergence of a Canon in the New Testament Collection

The two factors which were influential in the gradual formation of a

Canon for the Hebrew Bible were significant in the formation of a Canon for the New Testament. These were the pressures upon the Christian communities from outside (this time from Hellenism and Judaism) and the questions about the limits of orthodoxy from within. The need for some distinctive 'rule of faith' was clear; the curious fact is that it took over three hundred years after the death of Christ before a major church council achieved it, and even then, this ruling was by no means fully accepted by all the Christian communities in the Graeco-Roman world.

One attempt to counter the pressure of *Hellenistic* influence was made by selecting those books that testified explicitly to Jesus as active in history: this went some way to dispelling the idea that the Christian faith was simply an adaptation of a Greek myth (for example, the myth of a heavenly redeemer) which was popular in the mystery religions. For this reason, the Gospels (although as we shall see, initially more than just the four) became central.

An attempt to counter *Jewish* opposition was made by selecting books which showed explicitly that Jesus fulfilled all the hopes and expectations of the Jewish faith expressed in the Hebrew Scriptures. In this way, the prophecy/fulfilment schema (referred to in Chapter 2) was important, not only in the Gospels, Matthew especially, but also in some of Paul's letters (for example, in Romans and Galatians), as well as in the Epistle to Hebrews; this was to demonstrate the fulfilment of the Old Testament in the New.

Two tests were used to counter the possible growth of heresy through the exclusion of spurious material. The first was an 'apostolic' test – a means of determining the close relationship between the writings and the apostles of Jesus. The second, 'ecclesial' test concerned the relationship of books not only with the person of Jesus, but also with early, well-established 'reputable' Christian communities throughout Palestine, Syria, Asia Minor and Greece. In *Palestine*, although Roman attacks on religious places 66–70 CE destroyed the prominence of the churches in Jerusalem and Caesarea, the fact that many traditions from all four Gospels and the Acts of the Apostles nevertheless originally derived from these communities increased the significance of these books. In *Syria*, the church at Antioch was particularly important – hence the importance of the works of Matthew, James and Jude which claimed to have strong affiliations with the Christian communities in this region. By far the greatest proportion of material comes from the churches in *Greece* and *Asia Minor*: later traditions linked the writings of John with Ephesus, and the communities visited by Paul (and, in some cases, by Luke), such as Corinth, Galatia, Ephesus, Philippi and Colossae, were all significant in collecting and selecting material which in later times became part of a final 'Canon'. Finally, the church in *Rome* also played a part in this process, and its associations with Mark, Luke, the letter of Paul to the Romans, and possibly Hebrews, were all deemed significant on this account.

Nevertheless, the growth of various collections of material into a corpus, whose authority was both recognized and shared by the Christian communities throughout the Graeco-Roman world, was long and slow. Indeed, as John Barton agues in *The Spirit and the Letter* (1997), there may have been little distinction among the early Christian communities between what counted as 'gospel' – the good news about Jesus learnt through preaching and teaching – and 'the Gospels'. It is obvious that as the Church spread further and further away from its origins in Jerusalem, an external need – that increasingly scattered communities should establish common bonds – led towards the desire for a more visible rule of faith; but the actual process is a difficult one to disentangle.

One way of countering splits and schisms within the churches was to emphasize most those books which were claimed by the writers (or later tradition) to have had close associations with the earthly and risen Jesus. The test was whether the author could be identified as an apostle, or as a brother of Jesus (or as in the case of Paul, as one 'untimely born', but a witness to the risen Christ on account of his vision on the Damascus Road). On this account, the Gospel of Mark was important because it presumed a link with the apostle Peter; the Gospel of Matthew, because of its link with Matthew himself, also an apostle; the Gospel of Luke, because of the association of Luke in the book of the Acts of the Apostles with the apostle Paul; and the Gospel of John, because of its association with 'the beloved disciple' – believed to be the apostle John himself.

In 1945, some twelve papyrus codices discovered at Nag Hammadi, near Luxor, on the Nile, revealed that other Gospels had also been in circulation during the first and second centuries CE. One such example is the Gospel of Thomas, dating from the late second century CE. Perhaps a few of the secret sayings of the risen Jesus from this Gospel, supposedly popularized by Thomas 'the Twin', one of the apostles, as well as by the brothers of Jesus, may be authentic. So too some of the sayings in the Gospel of Peter from Rhossus may be genuine, or at the very least, some are contemporaneous with the Q sayings source. However, the fact that it could not be verified that their authors were closely connected with the apostles themselves may well have been one reason for their eventual exclusion from the Canon. Gospels such as those of Thomas and Peter throw light on the history of the books of Hebrews and

Revelation: for, although both of these were eventually included into the Canon, they became the subject of much debate because it was similarly difficult to establish that their authorship could be traced back to the apostles Paul and John, and hence claim ultimate authority from Jesus himself.

The Pauline Letters

The earliest material is usually understood to be the epistles from Paul. This correspondence perhaps raises the most important question as to why any of these works were preserved for posterity (a question which could also be asked with regard to a number of Old Testament books, not least some of the prophets). Given that Paul's letters to the various Christian communities were addressing only one community at a time, why were they later given more universal significance? Who collected together such a diverse, parochial correspondence? There are two possible answers.

The first is simply that neighbouring churches shared their writings, and the authority of Paul's epistles gradually spread in this way. Colossians 4.16 gives one example of this practice ('and when this letter has been read among you, have it read also in the church of the Laodiceans; and see that you read also the letter from Laodicea') although we have no record of the 'letter to Laodicea', which is referred to there. Various other letters are referred to in the Corinthian and the Philippian correspondences, yet they have been omitted from the Pauline corpus, so this may indeed have been church practice, although it was not carried out totally effectively.

A second answer is that some of the disciples and converts of Paul decided to make definitive collections for posterity. Leaders who had worked with Paul – such as Timothy at Ephesus; the runaway slave Onesimus, later Bishop of Ephesus; and Aquila and Priscilla, who worked both in Corinth and in Ephesus – could have been influential in this process; however, it is more likely that the collections are largely due to those whose names are unknown. Some member of some community must have been responsible, for example, for a particular list of Paul's letters which was quoted by various church fathers in the middle of the second century. Rather like the personalities of the prophets of the Old Testament, the personality of Paul, popularized further through the book of the Acts of the Apostles, was evidently sufficiently compelling to encourage communities to preserve, copy and honour this correspondence to the key churches throughout Asia Minor and Greece.

The Four Gospels

A similar process of selection and preservation also applies to all four Gospels. Their authority seems to have been gradually established by the end of the second century. The connections with Jesus through an apostolic witness, as well as the associations with particularly important Christian communities, enabled the Gospels we now know as 'canonical' to survive over and against their competitors. Whether directly or indirectly, each appeared to have had clear associations with the Palestinian community in Jerusalem, yet each also had special associations with particular Christian communities beyond it, and this too may have aided their growth: Mark with Rome, Luke with Caesarea and Rome, Matthew with Antioch, and John with Ephesus.

It is interesting that attempts to create a complete corpus of more (or fewer) than the four Gospels continually failed. For example, Tatian, a Christian apologist in the Eastern Church at the end of the second century, attempted to write a history of the life of Christ based upon a continuous narrative of all four Gospels. Called the *Diatessaron*, it was used in the Syrian Church until the fifth century, when it was replaced by a translation called the *Peshitta*, which contained all four Gospels. Or again, Marcion, an unorthodox believer with links with the church in Rome, compiled at the end of the second century CE his own corpus of what he deemed to be 'acceptable' Christianity. This corpus not only excluded all the Old Testament (for Marcion saw it concerned a deity who was a 'demiurge', a God of law, not of love), but it also excluded most of the New Testament except for ten of Paul's letters (itself interesting because this shows that these at least were part of an established collection in Rome by then) and an edited version of Luke. But neither Tatian's nor Marcion's attempts at creating a shorter 'Canon' was universally acceptable. And conversely, other Gospels, such as those of Thomas, of Peter, and the Gospel according to the Hebrews, were used only in isolated independent communities; they did not gain the more universal acceptance enjoyed by the other four.

Ultimately the question as to *why* only four Gospels found general acceptance will never be answered, any more than will the question as to how the epistles of Paul were collected into one corpus. But it is clear that, by the end of the second century, the most influential Christian communities mutually acknowledged the Pauline letters and four Gospels (as well as a few other works) as their most critical link back to the time of Jesus Christ.

Thus far, the discussion has covered only the Gospels and Pauline Epistles – about two-thirds of the so-called New Testament Canon. This basic collection, still fuzzy at the edges, corresponds with the acceptance of the Law and Prophets within the Old Testament corpus; similarly, the lack of certainty about a third collection – a category which might be termed 'Other Works' – parallels the 'fuzzy edges' of the third division (that is, the Writings) in the Old Testament.

The 'Other Works'

Of these 'other works', the Acts of the Apostles was probably the least controversial. As we noted earlier, this is akin to the status of the Psalter in the Writings of the Old Testament. With its emphasis on the Jewish origins of the Christian faith, and with its link with Luke, it provided a good counter-attack to heretics such as Marcion. As the popularity of Paul grew, the accounts in the Acts of the Apostles probably further strengthened its appeal. Interestingly, although other 'Books of Acts' were also in circulation – the Acts of John, of Paul, of Thomas – they never gained wide acceptance, on account of their exaggerated style and the romantic and heterodox tendencies in their presentation of their stories.

In contrast to Acts, Revelation provoked the most discussion before being eventually included in a 'canonical' list. In some ways it was made acceptable by being prefaced by the seven letters to the seven churches, which made the work more rooted in a particular historical setting like the letters from Paul. These seven letters marked a contrast to the futuristic apocalyptic elements in the later chapters of Revelation, which on account of their weird imagery were more open to spurious interpretations. These chapters were hence too reminiscent of other apocalyptic works which were being excluded from the basic collection for the same reasons. Given that a good deal of unorthodox apocalyptic material had been in evidence from the second century BCE onwards, any work which might be termed 'apocalytic' (and even here, there was a good deal of confusion about the term) was treated with a certain amount of caution. Even up to the fourth century, Revelation was repeatedly excluded from the lists of canonical books to be used by the Eastern churches. Revelation was thus first really accepted in the West.

If Revelation was accepted in the West but rejected in the East, the opposite was the case with the letter to the Hebrews. Mainly due to its anonymity and to the difficulty of ascertaining whether it possessed any apostolic authority, it was excluded from the main lists of canonical books used by the Western churches almost to the end of the fourth century. Its acceptance by Jerome, in his translation known as the Vulgate, was the main reason for its being adopted by the churches of the West.

Of the seven 'non-Pauline Epistles', 1 Peter, 1 John and Jude received the most positive affirmation. 2 and 3 John and James were frequently disputed. Even more so was 2 Peter, whose history resembles that of the history of the acceptance of Esther into the Old Testament, and whose apocalyptic ideas aroused the same concerns as the book of Revelation. None of the leading church fathers referred explicitly to 2 Peter before Origen (third century), and even he regarded it as 'doubtful'. In the fourth century, Eusebius, and also Jerome, expressed doubts about its authenticity and its theology. However, by the end of the fourth century, it had been accepted into the collection of books which were used by the Greek and Latin churches – but its final acceptance was by no means a clear-cut decision.

It is thus impossible to draw up any one definitive list of the New Testament Canon from before the fourth century. Nevertheless, certain provisional lists are known. The best-known early 'list' is the Muratorian Canon, dating from the second century, although the beginning and ending of it have been lost. It appears to include all the later 'canonical' New Testament books except for Hebrews, James and 1 and 2 Peter, although it also includes books later excluded from the Canon, such as the Apocalypse of Peter and the Wisdom of Solomon. Another slightly later list is the *Festal Epistle of Athanasius* (367); this was ratified in Rome in 382 by what is known as the Gelasian Decree. This list is identical to the one affirmed by the Catholic Church at the Council of Trent in 1546. A further list, this time from the Eastern Church, also dates from the middle of the fourth century; this was part of the decisions made at the Council of Laodicea in *c.* 325. The purpose of that Council was to clarify and establish ecclesial law, and the last of its sixty decrees concerns the Canon of Scripture. A shorter collection of books is listed, although this still omits Revelation.

It could be argued that a decision about any definitive Canon of the New Testament has never been resolved universally throughout Christendom; each church tradition accepted as normative a different variation of the New Testament collections. Nevertheless, for the purpose of clarity, a list of New Testament books which were acceptable by the fourth century is shown in Table 9. Again, the ? indicates where a work was under discussion and dispute for some time; and the * indicates works initially included in some lists, but eventually omitted – in some cases, a good deal later – from all of the lists ratified by church councils. It can be seen that the picture is similar to the formation of the Old Testament Canon; two-thirds of the New Testament collection was established and acceptable, but the other third was still open to a good deal of flux and change. This, of course, has interesting ramifications as to how we should read a 'disputed' text of Scripture – either one which was eventually included or one which was eventually excluded. In theological terms, as well as literary terms, our approach to reading it should be the same as it is with any other book accepted into the Canon, in so far as every work should be treated reasonably on its own merits. But this raises a number of other literary and theological issues, which will be discussed at the end of this chapter.

Table 9   The Emerging New Testament Canon by the Fourth Century CE

Paul's Letters	*The Gospels*	*Other books*
Romans	Matthew	?? Hebrews
1 and 2 Corinthians	Mark	? James
Galatians	Luke	1 Peter
Ephesians	John	?? 2 Peter
Philippians		1 John
Colossians		? 2 John
1 and 2 Thessalonians		? 3 John
1 and 2 Timothy		Jude
Titus		? Revelation
Philemon		
		* Wisdom of Solomon
		* Apocalypse of Peter
		* The Shepherd of Hermas
		* Acts of Paul
		* Epistle of Barnabas
		* 1 and 2 Clement
		* The Didache
		* Gospel of Thomas
		* Gospel of Hebrews
		* Gospel of Peter

The Question of One Biblical Corpus

So is there therefore any essential difference between the accepted books and the marginal works? Do books such as Esther, Song of Songs, Daniel, Ruth, Ecclesiastes and Ezekiel, which were finally accepted into the Old Testament, deserve more attention than do the books such as 1 and 2 Maccabees, Tobit, Judith, Baruch, Ecclesiasticus and Enoch, which eventually were excluded from it? And do books such as Hebrews, James, 2 Peter, 2 and 3 John and Revelation, which were finally accepted into the New Testament, deserve more attention than works such as the Shepherd of Hermas, 1 and 2 Clement, and the Didache, which were finally excluded from it? Is our choice of reading ultimately a matter of personal taste? Or is it a question of circumstance, dependent upon the Jewish or Christian tradition (and hence upon the Bible translation) with which one is most accustomed?

Space prevents a very detailed discussion about the status of the more disputed Old Testament books, and hence our observations must be selective. But certainly 1 Maccabees, with its account of the history of the Jews from the time of Alexander the Great to the Seleucids, was seen to be as important a theological reflection on later Jewish history as were the books of Kings and Chronicles on the history of the monarchy. Similarly, the book of Tobit – which purports to relate the fortunes of an Israelite deported from the northern kingdom in 721 BCE, but whose faith and heroism win the order of the day – has much in common with the book of Daniel, which also uses a figure taken into exile (in Daniel's case, the setting is the Babylonian exile in 587 BCE). Both were written to encourage the flagging faith of the Jews some four hundred years later, suffering under Greek rule at the time of the Seleucid emperors in the second century BCE. Another example is Judith, which records the faith of a rich and pious widow at the time of the Babylonian exile, and as a story has much in common with the nationalistic ideals and the religious passion of another heroine of faith, Esther, in the Persian court some forty years later. Or again, the book of Baruch has much in common with the book of Lamentations; both, in the history of tradition, have associations with the prophet Jeremiah. Finally, the Wisdom of Ben Sira (Ecclesiasticus), with its many exhortations and promises and poems concerning wisdom, offers many correspondences with the book of Proverbs. It could certainly be argued that to appreciate fully the one 'canonical' book (in these examples, Kings, Chronicles, Daniel, Esther, Lamentations and Proverbs) it is also necessary to understand the one which has not been included (Maccabees, Tobit, Judith, Baruch and Ecclesiasticus). If we accept this premise, the boundaries of the Old Testament 'Canon', in theological terms, are indeed rather blurred.

Similarly, among the more disputed New Testament books, the excluded works of Clement – written to the Corinthians at the end of the first century in the name of the church at Rome, with its concern for the proper ordering of Christian observances, each in their proper place and each by the proper persons – has many parallels with the earlier Corinthian correspondence initiated by Paul. And the Shepherd of Hermas – so named because an angel, in the form of a shepherd, mediated to Hermas (a near-contemporary of Clement of Rome) through a series of visions the necessity of the repentance of the Church and the possibility of forgiveness of sins – has some resemblances in form and theology with the book of Revelation. Or again, the Didache, a short first-century manual about Christian morality (in its description of 'two ways') and church practice (with its instructions about baptism, fasting, prayer, the prophecy, bishops and deacons) has many associations with the didactic material in the Gospels, especially in Matthew and Luke, as well as in the book of the Acts of the Apostles. As with the Old Testament Canon, it could be argued that in order to appreciate a 'canonical' New Testament book (here, Corinthians, Revelation and Acts) our knowledge is enlightened by an understanding of the corresponding 'non-canonical' one (Clement, the Shepherd of Hermas and the Didache). If this is so, then the boundaries of the so-called 'biblical corpus' are again not very clearly defined in a theological sense.

Small wonder, therefore, that the different church traditions throughout the centuries have attributed differing levels of importance to different collections. An assessment of the three different Canons of the Orthodox Catholic and Protestant Churches should make this point clear.

The Canon of the Orthodox Church

The Orthodox Church includes the Eastern Churches of Egypt, Syria, Greece, Russia and Central Europe. The Syrian Church initially used the Palestinian Canon as its 'Old Testament', but gradually widened this to include not only the longer collection but other lesser-known writings as well. For the New Testament, Tatian's *Diatessaron* was used at first, instead of the four Gospels; and in addition to the letters of Paul, 3 Corinthians was also adopted. By the early fifth century, the four Gospels had replaced the *Diatessaron*, and 3 Corinthians was omitted; but the other Catholic epistles and Revelation were still not accredited with canonical status. Hence in the Syrian Church, the Old Testament Canon has a wider term of reference than that of the New.

The Greek Church, at the Council of Florence in 1441 and at the Synod of Jerusalem in 1672, understandably adopted for their Old Testament the Alexandrian Canon, because of its associations with the Septuagint. By contrast, the Russian Church, especially during the nineteenth century, adopted the shorter collection as in the

Palestinian Canon (in part as a conservative reaction to the liberal and inclusive tendencies of the eighteenth century). However, regarding the New Testament, both the Russian and the Greek Churches came to accept a Canon which was akin to that used by the Protestant Churches. Only the Ethiopian Church has a New Testament Canon which diverges from this practice; it includes more books, rather than fewer. The list includes some eight additional books – including, for example, the letters of Clement. Hence, even within the Orthodox tradition as a whole, a good deal of disparity is evident. The acknowledgement of one fixed and agreed Canon is not entirely clear.

The Canon of the Catholic Church

The Canon of the Catholic Church is equally interesting. This authoritative list from the Western Churches is essentially derived from the decrees at the Council of Trent in 1546. The decree called *De Canonicis Scripturis* named as canonical forty-five books of the Old Testament (Lamentations was counted as part of the book of Jeremiah), and twenty-seven books of the New Testament. Interestingly therefore, it was not until some fifteen centuries after the writing of most of the books that the Church in the West formally and finally declared its own collection as 'the Canon of Scripture'.

Admittedly, this decree was based upon the decisions made at the earlier church Councils (Hippo in 393; and Carthage in 397 and 419) which approved the list of books following the list in the Alexandrian Canon. But it also has to be said that the decisions taken at the Council of Trent were by no means unanimous. Cardinal Cajetan, on the eve of the Council, expressed doubts about the status of some of the additional books which were in the Alexandrian Canon; furthermore, the editions of German and French Bibles published just before the Council omitted some of these more disputed books; and even after the Council of Trent, Jerome's Vulgate, which also omitted them, was still widely used among Catholics.

The decision by the Catholic Church to acknowledge this fuller collection was mainly a theological one, with similar concerns to those of the Orthodox Churches. For example, in a time of change it was necessary to conform as closely as possible to the practices of the early church fathers (in this case, the fathers of the Western Church) who had similarly asserted the importance of the Septuagint and hence the Alexandrian Canon. And so it was that, much more recently, and for the same theological reasons, Vatican Council I (1870) and Vatican Council II (in the 1960s) each ratified the decisions of the Council of

Trent with respect to the Canon: forty-five books of the Old Testament, and twenty-seven books of the New.

Before discussing the state of the Canon in the Protestant Church from the time of the Reformation onwards, it is important to understand just how differently the Protestants and Catholics have viewed their own collections since this time and, with this, just what political and cultural emphases these different collections symbolized for each party in the earliest period.

The Catholic Canon makes a distinction between the shorter list of books for the Old Testament and the longer list of books by referring to those in the longer list as 'deuterocanonical': this same list in the Protestant Bibles is called the 'Apocrypha'. Furthermore, and some-what confusingly, an additional list of books is also acknowledged by the Catholic Church, including many of those books noted on p. 61 which were not included even in the Alexandrian Canon: this the Catholic Church terms the 'Apocrypha', while the Protestant Churches call it the 'Pseudepigrapha', or 'False Writings'.

The Canon of the Protestant Churches

Different terminology is a clear indication of different traditions. It should not be surprising to discover that, from the time of the sixteenth century onwards, the Protestant Canon has also had a chequered history, particularly with respect to finalizing an Old Testament collection. As we have noted, the Catholic Churches accepted the centrality of the Septuagint and hence for their Old Testament they also accepted the authority of the Alexandrian Canon. By contrast, the Protestant Churches turned instead to the shorter selection (that is, the Palestinian Canon) used by Jerome for the Vulgate (in the fourth century). As early as 1382, John Wycliffe's trans-lation of the Bible into English was based upon the Vulgate, and hence upon that list of books. Luther's translation of 1534 actually added the Apocrypha (or, in Catholic terms, the deuterocanonical books) with the note 'books which are not yet equal to the Sacred Scriptures and yet [which] are useful and good for reading'. Zwingli's translation of the Zurich Bible in 1527–9 likewise included the Apocrypha, but placed the books at the end of the Old Testament collection and ques-tioned their 'canonical' status. So too did Olivetan's Bible of 1534–5, used by the Calvinists.

English translations followed a similar pattern. The Authorized Version (King James Bible) of 1611 included the (Protestant)

Apocrypha, but kept it in a separate section between the two Testaments. Earlier, in the Thirty-nine Articles of the Church of England (1571), Article VI stated that the Apocrypha could be read 'for example of life and instruction of manners', but it was not to be used to 'establish any doctrine'. This somewhat open-ended attitude changed, however, in the seventeenth century. The Protestant scholar John Lightfoot (1643) was not unusual in his polemic against the 'wretched apocrypha', and several other Protestant scholars demanded its exclusion from future editions of the Bible. The Presbyterian Westminster Confession (1647) stated that the Apocrypha not [being] of divine inspiration, [was] no part of the Canon of Scripture, and therefore ... of no authority in the Church of God, not to be otherwise approved, or made us of, than other human writings'. After some dispute, the British and Foreign Bible Society (1827) omitted it altogether from their publications, except for some pulpit Bibles. One key reason behind this rejection was the Protestant suspicion about the source of Catholic doctrines such as purgatory, angelology and intercession for the dead, which was believed to have come from the Apocrypha. (This is a rather curious reason for Protestant suspicion for, as we noted earlier, the New Testament writers themselves had read, used and been influenced by these works.)

Still within the Protestant tradition, the New Testament Canon did not altogether escape disputes. Many Protestants – notably Luther – saw that there was a gradation of importance within the New Testament collection, with secondary value given to Hebrews, James, Jude and Revelation. (This was, he felt, in part due to the fact that a good deal of so-called 'Catholic' theology – such as purgatory, mediation by angels and intercession for the dead – gained some legitimacy by a reading of these books.) Luther placed these books at the end of his translation. Tyndale's English edition did likewise, although other editions since have kept the traditional order.

It should be clear from this survey that there has never been one such thing as a universal 'biblical corpus' of either the Old Testament or the New, whether we are speaking of the formation of a corpus in its earliest stages or of any uniform acceptance in the later stages of church tradition. This has important ramifications for the ways we read these biblical texts; some integrated reading is essential, but this has to be influenced by a recognition of the uncertain nature of the Canon. This sort of 'canonical reading', however, is entirely different in its cautious stance from another more confident form of 'canonical reading' which has been advocated and popularized, for example by B. S. Childs; we shall turn to this comparison shortly.

Towards an Integrated Historical Approach to the Bible

It should now be clear that to understand the history of the acceptance of the biblical books into their final collection requires some understanding of the history of the cultural and theological development of the different religious communities who accepted them. The diverse histories of the Churches, expressed through their many different traditions, and the histories of the interpretation of the biblical texts are inextricably bound together. It is not the case that the various Canons of Scripture shaped the Church; the traditions of the Churches have also shaped the various Canons of Scripture. Thus, when it comes to reading the texts, no one single method of reading can be used to interpret them. They have been the product of a variety of concerns, and they still require a variety of interpretations. And so a pluralistic approach, of which the broader historical approach is perhaps the most important part, is the only reasonable way forward.

The significance of the historical approach in this respect cannot be underestimated. As we have noted, the history of the adoption of the Canon expands one's understanding of what is involved in the reading of the Bible as an ancient text. To approach the text from a historical viewpoint involves looking as much at the stages *after* the formation of the texts as at the stages *before* the final form. The text's composition and gradual compilation into its final form are of course important, but just as significant is its continued preservation and transmission – what is termed the 'reception-history' of a text, both within the Jewish and the Christian traditions. In this sense, the historical approach is far more wide-ranging than its term implies. It moves from the earliest possible origins of a text, through to all the influences which are known to have brought it into its final form, and on to the different ways it has been understood – and, not least, translated – in the different traditions which have used it since that time. On this account, historically orientated readings also need to take seriously the broader *theological* considerations which have shaped the recognition of the text throughout its entire history.

We therefore need to examine what this means for the *theological* approach to the biblical text. If by this is implied a theology which has been formed most by matters of faith, one crucial consequence here is that the reader must give due recognition to the *wider* church community as a vehicle for biblical faith. The diverse theological traditions of the 'universal Church' are more important than the one particular theological tradition of the individual reader, however unified and satisfyingly coherent this may be. This is clearly the case when reading the more disputed one-third of the Old Testament collection, as so too when reading the more disputed one-third of the New. For, as we noted earlier, one cannot adequately read Esther without some recognition of the book of Judith, or Kings without a similar recognition of Maccabees, or 1 Corinthians without 1 Clement, or Revelation without the Shepherd of Hermas. Thus this sort of theological approach has to be informed by the *diversified history* of the Canon. Far from the Canon giving us the means of finding one overall theological uniformity, the Canon shows us how inclusive and open-ended much of the process really is. To this end the historical approach, when it is used to illustrate the extent of the history of the diversity of the canonical process, can illuminate the theological approach and offer the particular reader much broader horizons.

Furthermore, this sort of integrated historical/theological reading can help and inform the literary approach, where the primary concern is for the reader rather than for the context of the text. If the danger of the historical (or, more specifically, the historicist) approach is that it seeks to base too much on disputations about the nature of ancient history, then the danger of the literary approach is that it fails to attend to any of these disputations at all. The challenge of a pluralistic reading is that it allows a broader theological and historical context in which the literary discussions can take place.

An interesting analogy is offered by C. S. Lewis in his discussion of the 'Flatlanders'. These are an imaginary people who, living only in two dimensions, perceive only the length and breadth of the world around them, rather than having any concept of depth and height. Believing that the world is infinitely flat, they are unable to see the effect of three dimensions – the valleys and hills, and horizon and perspective. In the light of our earlier discussion, the canonical approach shows the importance of the dimension of 'depth' as well as 'height' in an integrated reading of the biblical texts. This implies broader historical and theological ways of looking at the texts; but it also involves a more profound view of the literary approach as well.

'Canonical reading', as we have interpreted it above, in all its historical, theological and literary variety, is essentially a pluralistic approach. This could not be more different from the canon-critical method (or canonical reading) proposed particularly by B. S. Childs. Childs, to whom reference was made in Chapter 2, has one major concern, and that is theological uniformity. Such uniformity, Childs defends, is discernible through the final canonical form of Scripture. For Childs, the final form is presumed to be the Hebrew text, and thus the Canon (for the Old Testament, at least) is a Palestinian one, and the date for its final stages of acceptance by the Jewish and Christian communities is the first century CE. Several problems emerge from Childs' proposals.

First, there is a significant historical problem with Childs' approach. As we have seen, the first century CE hardly provides a clear demarcation line for proposing a fixed final form for the whole Canon. Even the shorter Palestinian Canon meant different things to different Jewish and Christian communities as late as the fourth century CE. The emphasis on the 'final form' immediately raises the question of *which* final form, and for which community this was ultimately acceptable. An anomaly in Childs' position is that he does not see the *ordering* of the books as overly important; he recognizes, correctly, that there was still some change and flux at the time of the first century CE, but he does not then acknowledge that the order and number of the books in fact creates a structure and emphasis which is theologically significant. By the end of the first century CE, it would have been difficult not to have had a very different attitude to the Old Testament Law and Prophets (which were more fixed and ordered) compared with the Writings (which were more open-ended at this stage). Similarly, with regard to the New Testament, it is difficult to imagine that a first-century Christian could have had the same attitude to the Gospels and Epistles (which, although not universally established at this stage, were of important status in some communities) alongside other works (which were not in any settled form at all). What Childs leaves us with is a curious 'canon-within-a-canon', whereby his theological concerns override the historical considerations which are equally important.

A second difficulty is Childs' acceptance of the final authority of the Hebrew text and of those who preserved it. By effectively ignoring the Greek text, and hence also the Alexandrian Canon, Childs isolates a large part not only of the Jewish tradition but also of the Christian one. The Septuagint, rather than the Hebrew text, was used by most Christian communities in the earliest stages of Christendom. This is again puzzling, as Childs places so much emphasis on the Christianized reading of the Old Testament, while ignoring the main Greek medium through which that Christianized reading took place. Furthermore, his emphasis on the Hebrew text as preserved throughout some ten centuries, in what is known as the 'Massoretic tradition', is also an anachronism. This tradition (so-called because of the name given to a group of Jewish scholars from the eighth century CE in Tiberias who worked on the received Hebrew text and thus gave it the name the 'Massoretic Text') is hardly itself a first-century phenomenon, even though it was highly influential in the Middle Ages and was normative for later translations. Rather, it has as much to do with the state of affairs in the eighth to tenth centuries CE as it has to do with the concerns of the first century CE. This is thus another example of the way in which theological assumptions can distort the historical evidence.

Third, Childs' proposals are largely due to a negative view of the historical-critical method, which he regards as 'hypothetical'. Another paradox emerges here, insofar as Childs' own choice of date, text and canonical list is based on equally subjective and tentative criteria. The argument against the selective nature of the historical approach could certainly also be directed to Childs' theological appraisal of the canonical one, where Childs' selectivity is even more pronounced. Because he stresses the final form, he places little emphasis on the historical processes which led up to this formation, and similarly gives little attention to the historical processes which ultimately shaped and developed the 'final form'. He stresses the importance of 'believing communities' in the way they influenced the final form of Scripture, without adequately defending why *those* believing communities should themselves set the standards. Why discard the equal significance of other earlier believing communities, whose language, culture and theological concepts shaped the text in its earlier stages, as well as the influence of other later believing communities, whose theological, literary and linguistic concerns shaped and refined it in the later stages? Childs' definition of selectivity is itself based upon various assumptions about a necessary theological centre to the Bible, and these have shaped his own choice of material.

Fourth, Childs' method, in giving primary place to the 'final form', is not always consistent in practice. According to Childs, in order to understand texts within the Canon as a whole, it is important to establish that their theology is the same as the theological ideas expressed in other (canonical) texts. This is very much in line with the uniformity-of-theology approach which was discussed in the previous chapter. However, the critical problem is that the process of selection is what the reader brings to the text, rather than what resides in the 'givenness' of the whole collection. By making theological associations with other texts which seem to be 'close relatives', the result is likely to be an imposition of a theological framework upon the text. It is highly unlikely that the 'believing communities' who read the text in the first century CE would have made the same theological associations as we would do today, after some two thousand years of tradition and further interpretation. Hence, while appealing to a continuity of tradition, and a unity of theology, Childs' method of reading is paradoxically in danger of creating discontinuity resulting from a superimposed theological unity.

Important critics of Childs' canonical method include J. Barr (1982), J. Barton (1988 and 1997), and M. G. Brett (1991), and many of the views expressed above have been more fully developed in their works. The common observation in these publications is that Childs places too much emphasis on a search for theological uniformity, as noted above.

The 'integrated approach' proposed here, with its recognition of the value of the Canon, thus has little to do with Childs' canonical approach. When it comes to understanding the biblical texts, theology, literature and history are all vital components. A more pluralistic open-ended way of reading the texts is not only desirable; it is unavoidable, if one is to face honestly the evidence of the long, complex process of canonization. Childs' problem is that he limits the Canon to a fixed period of time, and his view of the history of the text is therefore distorted. By contrast, an integrated reading gives due weight to the many different worlds which have each played their part within the biblical collections – the world behind the texts, the world within the texts, and the world beyond them.

4

A Biblical Text?
The Variety of Versions

If the process of canonization was long and complex, the process following it – of translating and copying the texts – was more protracted still. And given that the idea of *one biblical corpus* is extremely difficult to maintain, that of a transmission of *one normative biblical text* is even more so. Obviously, at some point there must have been 'original biblical texts' – unless one takes the view that these only existed as oral forms, and that the different copies are the result of the different interpretations of an oral tradition. Whichever view one takes, any original and definitive 'biblical text' is out of our reach. All we have are the copies, and copies of copies, and translations of the copies. The diverse nature of the biblical texts is illustrated not only by the various early manuscripts and versions of the Old Testament texts, in Hebrew, Greek, Latin, Aramaic and Syriac, but also by the variety of the New Testament texts as well, in Greek, Syriac, Latin and Coptic. The multiplicity of translations points to the same issue even with respect to our own 'English Bible'. Thus, the purpose of this chapter is to illustrate that, when it comes to understanding the biblical texts as a whole, a pluralistic, open-ended way of reading is again the only way forward.

The Old Testament Text and the Hebrew, Greek and Latin Versions

The Jewish historian, Josephus, writing for a Roman audience at the end of the first century CE in a work called *Contra Apionem*, defended the Jews' reverence for their Scriptures as follows: 'although such long ages have now passed, no one has ventured to add, or to remove, or to alter a syllable' (1.42ff.). However, in the light of the evidence (not least, since the first century) it is questionable whether Josephus' confidence was really justified.

The Hebrew Text

The Hebrew text which most translators regard as authoritative is the Massoretic Text, referred to in the previous chapter. The name 'Massoretes' (meaning 'transmitters of tradition') was used to describe the group of Jewish scholars who worked in Tiberias, on the shores of Galilee, from about the seventh century CE onwards – that is, some six hundred years after Josephus. The Massoretes, concerned about both the intelligibility and the sacredness of the Hebrew text, offered a significant contribution towards the consolidation of the earlier, more disparate, tradition of transmission. From the time of the composition of the text until probably the first century CE, Hebrew was normally written without vowels; and because it was usually read aloud, the meaning was obvious in the pronunciation. A more modern consonantal script, without any vowels, is illustrated in Figure 1.

כל החיה אשר   17

אתך מכל בשר בעוף ובבהמה ובכל הרמש הרמש

על הארץ הוצא אתך ושרצו בארץ ופרו ורבו על

18 הארץ: ויצא נח ובניו ואשתו ונשי בניו אתו:

19 כל החיה כל הרמש וכל העוף כל רומש על

הארץ למשפחתיהם יצאו מן התבה:

Figure 1   Genesis 8.17–19 in a Consonantal Script (no vowels)

When Hebrew became less and less used as a spoken language, the understanding by ear had to be preserved in a written form, and so gradually a complete system of writing, by way of using vowels, emerged. That this was evident by the first century CE is apparent from the discussions about the Canon at Jamnia (*c.* 70–100 CE) when decisions were made not only about the Hebrew Canon, as we saw previously, but also about the consolidation of the actual text. Rabbi Akiba (*c.* 132 CE) was another Jewish influence who was interested in preserving the text in this same way. So too the compilers and collectors of the Babylonian Talmud attempted to fix the vowels in the texts they were editing.

By the time of the Massoretes in the seventh century, various attempts had been made to fix the vowels and signs in the consonantal text. The Massoretes were not so much innovators as ratifiers of an earlier tradition. Their own contribution was more the development of a system of punctuation marks, accents, and the additions of corrections of their own, whether of grammar, archaisms, changes in vocabulary, spelling or orthography. But what should be clear is that the Massoretes stabilized what had already been taking place before them in the copying of the texts. This is seen in their copious notes (called the 'Massorah') which showed where, in the margin, they had changed the text or ratified an earlier change.

There are at least two views concerning these changes. The more traditional view has been that these are corrections and improvements. By placing the word which the Massoretes called the *Q^erê* (meaning 'that which is to be read') with a sign under it (mostly either פ or ן) in the margin, they wrote out, usually in full, the corrected meaning of the word. By leaving the word in the written text (called the *K^ethîbh*, meaning 'that which is written') unaltered except for a small circle over it which indicated the change in the margin, they highlighted their corrected version in the margin. Another more straightforward view – proposed by J. Barr and developed by J. Barton in his most recent book on the Canon – is that the Massoretes were simply drawing together two equally important traditions: that which was written, and hence most likely to be read aloud from the text (the *K^ethîbh*), and that which was remembered in oral tradition as a correction of the reading (the *Q^erê*); hence what they were doing was providing a rule of thumb for the *reader*.

The Hebrew text we use today derives from this Massoretic Text (its shortened form being the MT). This particular text is believed to be due to the influence of a fifth-generation Massorete, Aaron ben Asher, who worked in the first half of the tenth century CE. To illustrate the *K^ethîbh* and *Q^erê* in the Massoretic Text, Genesis 8.17–19 is given again in Figure 2. The *sigla* (notes) in the margin indicate a grammatical correction to the verb in verse 18 of the text.

Figure 2   Genesis 8.17–19 Corrections to the Massoretic Text

The obvious problem, indicated at the beginning of this chapter, is that we do not have Aaron ben Asher's actual text at our disposal. Instead of texts, we only have access to copies made on papyri, or more commonly, on manuscripts. A particular text would be copied on to papyrus or parchment several times; but we have limited information about the Hebrew text at this stage, because so few complete manuscripts have survived. The earliest manuscript, believed to date back almost to the work of Aaron ben Asher, was found in 1896 in a depository for unfit scrolls (called a *genizah*) in an ancient synagogue in Cairo. This is called, appropriately, the Cairo Genizah Text, but it was in several fragments. Another link back to Aaron ben Asher text is the Aleppo Codex, also incomplete; this tenth-century codex was discovered in 1478 in Aleppo in Syria, and, through a variety of circumstances, found its way to Israel, and in 1958 became a key part of the Hebrew University Bible project in Jerusalem.

Another most important find was the Lisbon Codex, an attractively illuminated manuscript discovered in Portugal in 1483, and now in the British Museum. This fifteenth-century manuscript became the basis for a Hebrew edition of the Old Testament, compiled earlier this century by Norman Snaith, under the auspices of the British and Foreign Bible Society. Yet another manuscript was found in Venice; published in the early sixteenth century, this served as the standard rabbinical text for over two centuries. This 'Rabbinic Bible' which was printed in parallel columns, comparing the Hebrew texts and Aramaic translations alongside one another, marked the end of the process which the Massoretes had taken up; this was now a *printed* edition of Hebrew Scripture, rather than another handwritten copy, and so this finalized form consolidated and completed the Massoretic tradition.

One of the most significant and more complete manuscripts of the Massoretic Text is the Leningrad Codex (called 'L'), believed to have been written as early as 1009 CE. Brought to Germany from Leningrad in 1839, not only has it been the basis of translations of the Hebrew text into other languages, but it also is the standard text for the edition of the Hebrew Bible printed in Germany by Kittel and Kahle. This text is known as *Biblia Hebraica*, or the *BHK*, and is an edition which preceded the standard text used most today, called the *Biblia Hebraica Stuttgartensia*, or the *BHS*. An illustration of the Leningrad Codex, written in three columns, is given in Figure 3. Figure 4 shows the same part of the *BHS*, following most of the text in the right-hand column.

Even such a brief overview highlights two great gaps in our knowledge – gaps unrecognized by Josephus, who perhaps lived too early to observe them. At the earliest stage, the first prolonged break is the period beginning with the recognition of various authoritative

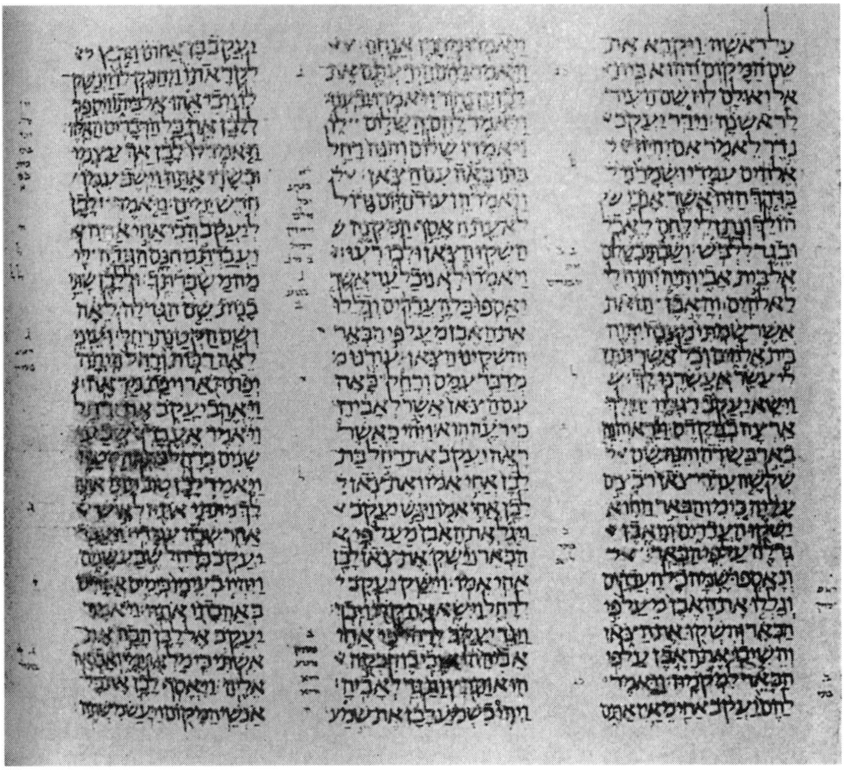

Figure 3   Genesis 28.19—29.22 from the Leningrad Codex

¹⁹ וַיִּקְרָ֛א אֶת־שֵֽׁם־הַמָּק֥וֹם הַה֖וּא בֵּֽית־אֵ֑ל

וְאוּלָ֛ם ל֥וּז שֵׁם־הָעִ֖יר לָרִאשֹׁנָֽה: ²⁰ וַיִּדַּ֥ר יַעֲקֹ֖ב נֶ֣דֶר לֵאמֹ֑ר אִם־

יִהְיֶ֨ה אֱלֹהִ֜ים עִמָּדִ֗י וּשְׁמָרַ֙נִי֙ בַּדֶּ֤רֶךְ הַזֶּה֙ אֲשֶׁ֣ר אָנֹכִ֣י הוֹלֵ֔ךְ וְנָֽתַן־לִ֥י

לֶ֛חֶם לֶאֱכֹ֖ל וּבֶ֥גֶד לִלְבֹּֽשׁ: ²¹ וְשַׁבְתִּ֥י בְשָׁל֖וֹם אֶל־בֵּ֣ית אָבִ֑י וְהָיָ֧ה יְהוָ֛ה

לִ֖י לֵאלֹהִֽים: ²² וְהָאֶ֣בֶן הַזֹּ֗את אֲשֶׁר־שַׂ֙מְתִּי֙ מַצֵּבָ֔ה יִהְיֶ֖ה בֵּ֣ית אֱלֹהִ֑ים

וְכֹל֙ אֲשֶׁ֣ר תִּתֶּן־לִ֔י עַשֵּׂ֖ר אֲעַשְּׂרֶ֥נּוּ לָֽךְ:

Figure 4   Genesis 28.19–22 from the *BHS*

collections ('canons') of the Old Testament, from around the first century BCE to the first century CE, when the Palestinian and Alexandrian Canons are known to have existed, and ending with the work of the Massoretes, between the seventh and tenth centuries CE: this is a gap of some six hundred years. At the later stage, the second prolonged break is the period between the completion of the texts by the Massoretes, around the ninth century CE, and the discovery of reliable, fairly complete manuscripts. These occur at any time between the eleventh century, in the case of the Leningrad Codex, and the fifteenth century, in the case of the Lisbon Codex. This is a period of some two to five hundred years.

These breaks in our knowledge of the process of transmission of the biblical text are certainly serious. Three other sources are partially helpful in offering insights into the formation of biblical texts during the time we know least about – between the second century BCE and the fourth century CE. These are (i) the findings at Qumran; (ii) the Samaritan Pentateuch; and (iii) a translation using the Hebrew by the Christian scholar, Origen.

THE QUMRAN SCROLLS

These scrolls have already been referred to briefly. Found from 1948 onwards in caves to the west of the Dead Sea, these manuscripts date from between 250 BCE and 68 CE. Hence, several are over eight hundred years earlier than the Massoretic Text. Some have been written on papyrus (for example, Deuteronomy and Kings) while others are on leather or vellum. Some of the scrolls have wide columns of over seventy letters; others have only fifteen letters per column. Two alphabets are evident. One is known as 'paleo-Hebrew' (ancient Hebrew) which almost certainly was derived from the Canaanites, a script probably used from before the Exile. The other is a form of Jewish 'Aramaic' script, using square letters, and is the script used in editions of the Hebrew Bible today. The oldest scrolls, found in Cave 4, are of Samuel (4 Q Sam b), Jeremiah (4 Q Jer a) and Exodus (4 Q Ex b).

One of the most important aspects about the Scrolls is that they have many affinities with the Septuagint, and seem to suggest a Hebrew prototype somewhat different from that used for the Massoretic Text which was written some six hundred years later (for the Septuagint and Massoretic Text certainly diverge in many places). Furthermore, the scribes at Qumran also help us to see that, important as the Massoretes may have been, they were not entirely innovative in their systematization of the Hebrew text. The Scrolls also have several examples of sectioning texts off into paragraphs, even into verses, which is a practice in the Massoretic Text. And, inevitably, there is also evidence of scribal errors – for example, failure to repeat letters or words, and confusion of letters of similar form. There is a wide variety of date, type and accuracy. This is because the Scrolls, belonging to a group believed to be called the Essenes, would have been brought by individual owners when they joined the community.

Qumran offers important information about this shadowy period in the transmission of the biblical texts, although, as may be seen above, it often raises as many problems as it solves. For example, the community possessed two Hebrew editions of the prophet Jeremiah – one shorter, and more like that preserved in the LXX, and one in length more like the version in the Massoretic Text. Clearly throughout this stage neither canon nor text were part of a fixed and stable tradition.

An interesting illustration of the state of the tradition at this time is found with the Scroll of Isaiah, now preserved in the Shrine of the Book of Jerusalem. Two such scrolls have been found, both in Cave 1 (1 Q Isa a and 1 Q Isa b). 1 Q Isa a was in fact one of the first Scrolls to be discovered and identified. It was written by a single hand, no later than the second century BCE; some additions were probably made about a century later. The spelling, vocabulary, syntax and morphology shows this to be a very early stage in the development of written Hebrew – which explains the hundreds of variants between this text and the Massoretic Text of Isaiah and so again suggests a difference between the prototype in the Scrolls and in the MT. It is argued that the Isaiah Scroll, written by the second century BCE, often with some affinities with the Septuagint translation (and so showing how far apart the Septuagint and the Massoretic Text actually are), could have been copied from one basic common text, *The Prophet Isaiah*, which other scribes both copied and translated. Nevertheless, the text of Isaiah, although *fixed*, was by no means *final*.

One illustration of this is the way in which the scribe has attempted to update the basic consonantal text, in order to make it more comprehensible for his audience, by adding substitute vowel sounds in order to make the consonantal text easier to understand. For example, the 'w' consonant is used to make an 'o' or 'u'; the 'y' to make an 'i' or 'e'; and the silent letter א (= ') makes an 'a'.

Another interesting example of the state of the textual tradition at this time is found in the Psalms Scrolls at Qumran, especially those discovered in Caves 4 and 11. One of these contains the last third of the Psalter, but in a very different order. It also contains 2 Samuel 23.1–7; Psalm 151 (also found in the Septuagint), celebrating David's victory over Goliath; three otherwise unknown psalms; a prose catalogue of David's poetic compositions; and then ends with Psalm 140.1–5;

134.1–3 and Psalm 151. This again shows that the Psalms were *not* an established basic tradition, either from a canonical or from a textual point of view; this is in contrast to the Scroll of Isaiah. Figures 5 and 6 are examples of versions of Psalm 151, about David's victory over Goliath from the Psalms Scroll. Figure 5 shows the way in which the vowelless script was written at Qumran. Figure 6 shows a much later printed edition of the vowelless script. An English translation of Psalm 151 is also given.

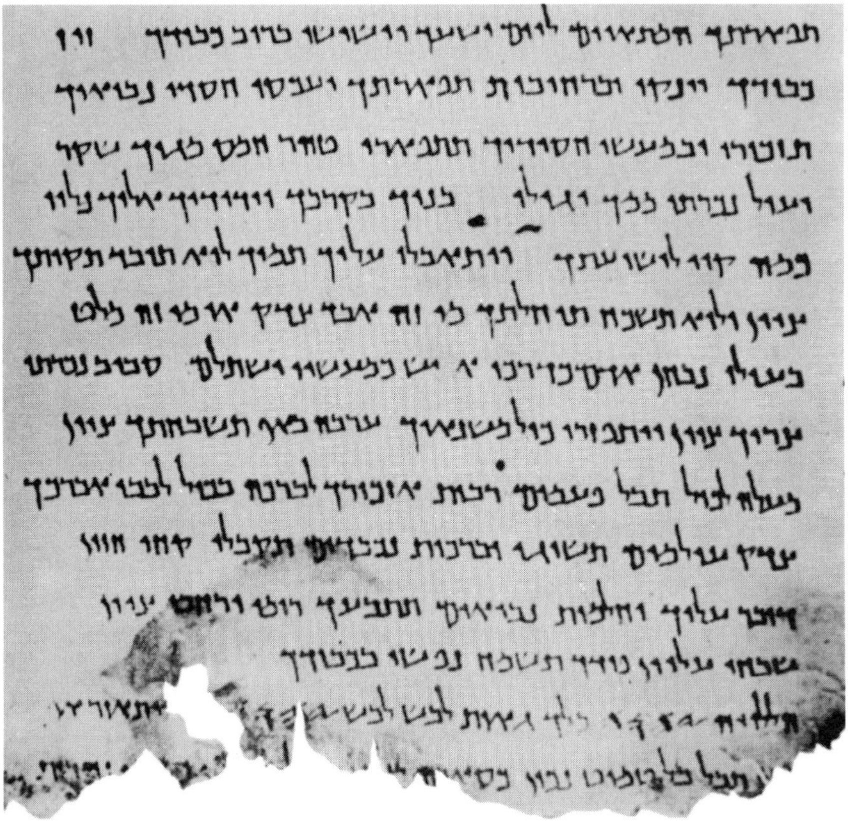

Figure 5   A Fragment of the Qumran Scroll of Psalm 151, taken from J. A. Sanders, *The Psalms Scrolls of Qumran Cave 11*, Clarendon Press, 1965, pp. 65–6.

In conclusion, while Qumran offers us resources to 'bridge the gap of time' between the composition of the texts and the discovery of actual manuscripts, it also illustrates further the multiplicity of tradition and textual transmission during this period.

תהלים קנ"א

1. קטן הייתי מן אחי
וצעיר מבני אבי
וישימני רועה לצונו
ומושל בגדיותיו

2. ידי עשו עוגב
ואצבעותי כנור
ואשימה ליהוה כבוד
אמרתי אני בנפשי

3. ההרים לוא יעידו לו
והגבעות לוא יגידו
עלו העצים את דברי
והצואן את מעשי

4. כי מי יגיד ומי ידבר
ומי יספר את מעשי אדון
הכול ראה אלוה
הכול הוא שמע והוא האזין

5. שלח נביאו למושחני
את שמואל לגדלני
יצאו אחי לקראתו
יפי התור ויפי המראה

6. הגבהים בקומתם
היפים בשערם
לוא בחר יהוה
אלוהים בם

7. וישלח ויקחני מאחר הצואן
וימשחני בשמן הקודש
וישימני נגיד לעמו
ומושל בבני בריתו

Figure 6   The Consonantal Text of Psalm 151

A Hallelujah of David the Son of Jesse.
1.   Smaller was I than my brothers
       and the youngest of the sons of my father,
     So he made me shepherd of his flock
       and ruler over his kids.

80

2. My hands have made an instrument
      and my fingers a lyre;
   And [so] have I rendered glory to the Lord,
      thought I, within my soul.
3. The mountains do not witness to him,
      nor do the hills proclaim;
   The trees have cherished my words
      and the flock my works.
4. For who can proclaim and who can bespeak
      and who can recount the deeds of the Lord?
   Everything has God seen,
      everything has he heard and he has heeded.
5. He sent his prophet to anoint me,
      Samuel to make me great;
   My brothers went out to meet him,
      handsome of figure and appearance.
6. Though they were tall of stature
      and handsome by their hair,
   The Lord God chose
      them not.
7. But he sent and took me from behind the flock
      and anointed me with holy oil,
   And he made me leader of his people
      and ruler over the sons of his covenant. (Psalm 151)

THE SAMARITAN PENTATEUCH

The Samaritan Pentateuch (SP) is a reworking ('recension') of the five books of the Law of Moses (Genesis to Deuteronomy). It comes from the Samaritan community on Mount Gerazim in the northern part of Palestine. Possibly as early as the fifth century BCE, this group split from mainstream Judaism, which was centred around the Jerusalem Temple in Judah in the south. However, the community's own traditions date this split much earlier. Seeing themselves as the true elect, of which 'the Jews' were the dissident group, they dated their separation from the eleventh century BCE when, at the time of the priest Eli, a cultic sanctuary was founded first as Shiloh and then at Jerusalem, thus leaving the Samaritan community to survive alone with their own sanctuary at Shechem, in the shadow of Mount Gerazim.

81

It is quite possible that some of the traditions of this community are ancient; all the existing copies of the Samaritan Pentateuch are in the Canaanite script, and so suggest an early date for the process of compilation. However, their work could not have received its final form until the late fourth century BCE, when Alexander the Great gave permission for the Samaritans to complete the building of their temple on Mount Gerazim. There are a number of interesting similarities between the Samaritan Pentateuch and the Septuagint against the Massoretic Text (some two thousand) as well as further correspondences with the Samaritan Pentateuch and Qumran scrolls, not least with the Exodus Scroll (4 Q Ex b). Overall, when compared with the Massoretic Text, this further indicates that the Qumran Hebrew text probably has a different provenance from the Massoretic Text (which many believe has come not from Palestine at all, but from the trans-Jordanian region).

But it is in the presentation of theology where the differences between the Massoretic Text of the Pentateuch and the Samaritan Pentateuch are most apparent. For example, the Samaritan text has quite a different view of the activity of God in the world: he is portrayed as utterly transcendent, mediating his presence only through angels (for example, Numbers 22.20 and 23.4, 5, 16). All anthropomorphisms, or ways of describing God in human terms, are avoided. The expression 'the breath of your nostrils' (Exodus 15.8) is changed to 'your breath'; the verb 'God repented' (Deuteronomy 32.6) is similarly changed to 'God forgave'.

Furthermore, the book of Deuteronomy, which stresses the importance of Mount Gerazim (in chapters 27 and 28) is the most important book of the five, and wherever possible, Mount Gerazim is added into passages where some northern sanctuary is implied (for example, Deuteronomy 5.21 and 27.4). Because Deuteronomy is so important, parts of this book have been inserted into the books of Exodus and Numbers (for example, Exodus 18.25 is followed by Deuteronomy 1.9–18; and Exodus 20.17 is followed by Deuteronomy 11.29–30 and 27.2, 5–7), in each case for a particular theological reason. These Exodus texts refer to Moses giving the law on Mount Sinai, and the editors have added to this the supposedly equal importance of Mount Gerazim – in each case to emphasize the importance of Mount Gerazim as the holy mountain above all others. Another important addition is made in the two accounts of the Ten Commandments (Exodus 20 and Deuteronomy 5): by combining the first two commandments, the Samaritan Pentateuch tradition then adds its own 'tenth': predictably, this is an injunction to the people to preserve Mount Gerazim as the centre of all worship.

Taken all together, the Samaritan Pentateuch highlights the freedom and variety which was still possible in the transmission of the Hebrew text between the fifth and third centuries BCE, and so tells us something about the status of the Law in the Canon as well as about the nature of the texts within that Law. The real problem with the SP is that the first complete manuscript copies date from the fourteenth century CE, and in this respect, the much earlier material at Qumran is more significant and useful, because the text we can actually observe and read pre-dates the Massoretes.

ORIGEN'S *HEXAPLA*

Origen's *Hexapla* is the name given to translations of the Hebrew text made between 231 CE (in Alexandria) and 245 CE (in Caesarea). Comprising some six thousand pages and some fifteen volumes, the work is called the *Hexapla* because it is a compilation of four Greek and two Hebrew texts set out in six columns. The first two columns are important for the insights they give regarding the later state of the Massoretic Text, if only by way of contrast with what we know from six hundred years later. The first column presents the Hebrew consonantal text as it was known by the third century CE; and the second column is a transliteration (a conversion into a different alphabet, not a translation) of the Hebrew text into corresponding Greek letters.

The other four columns are translations of the Hebrew into Greek by different Greek scholars – Aquila (128 CE), Theodotian (probably at Ephesus at the end of the second century), Symmachus (at the beginning of the third century) and, most importantly, the Septuagint. Three other Greek versions were used, but the six-column form was the norm. Origen's intention was to establish a more direct relationship between the Hebrew text he knew and the Septuagint. As an apologist and defender of the faith for the Christian Church, he wanted to demonstrate that, above all else, Christianity's roots were in Judaism and not in Greek religion. Hence Origen adapted the LXX so that it followed as closely as possible his Hebrew text; and when any part which was in the Hebrew text was lacking in the LXX, Origen expanded the LXX by way of reference to the other Greek versions (usually following Theodotian), giving clear signs in the LXX version to show where he had done so. The assumption was that, just as Judaism had given birth to Christianity which then became increasingly Hellenized, so too the Hebrew text was the original. Hence, the LXX had to be brought into line with the Hebrew. (This suggests a rather negative view about the independent value of the LXX; a view which is in need of correction since the discovery of the Qumran Scrolls, for it is now clear that the LXX is often close to the Hebrew in the Scrolls, and is thus earlier and more reliable than was previously assumed.)

Because the library in Caesarea was destroyed in the seventh century CE, no manuscripts exist of the *Hexapla*, except for two small fragments. The one on the Psalms, found in the Cairo Genizah Text, is still preserved in all six columns. However, it is clear that Origen's editing of the LXX and his popularizing of the Hebrew text was a great influence in making the biblical texts more available to the Christian communities from the third century onwards – albeit a constant reminder of their multiplex forms.

Although each of these examples sheds further light on the Hebrew text in its earliest stages, none of them makes the issue any clearer regarding one definitive Hebrew text. And when we turn to the editions of the text in languages other than Hebrew, the so-called 'Hebrew text' appears to be even more complex and diffuse than has been suggested here.

The Greek Text

The Greek text has come to us primarily through the Septuagint, and we have already seen with reference to Qumran, to the Samaritan Pentateuch and to the *Hexapla* that the Septuagint is in fact more closely aligned to the older (pre-Massoretic) rendering of the Hebrew text than may be thought. Hence the Septuagint not only offers important insights into the nature of the Canon in the third and second centuries BCE, but also into the nature of biblical translation at an early time. This is not to deny that, taking the LXX as a whole, there are several variations of style, and the nature of its rendering of the Hebrew into Greek varies from one book to another. Sometimes its translation of the Hebrew is quite literal (as in Kings, the Psalms and Ecclesiastes), and in other places it is more idiomatic (as in Esther, Job, Proverbs and Isaiah). This is probably because the translations were made over two centuries by several different hands, and in different places – not only in Alexandria, but also possibly in Palestine (perhaps the book of Psalms), Ephesus (Samuel–Kings) and in Antioch.

The most obvious divergencies from the Massoretic Text occur in the different arrangements of particular books. Examples include Exodus 35—40, a shorter edition of the book of Job, and 1 Samuel 17—18, where the text has been cut and revised. Jeremiah is one of the most significant examples, where the Greek version is much shorter and the book follows a variant order. Another example is the book of Proverbs which, like Jeremiah, changes the order of the contents. The LXX of Proverbs 24—31 runs as follows: Proverbs 30.1–14; 24.23–34; 30.15–33; 31.1–9; 25.1–29; 17; 31.10–31. The extract shown in Figure 7 shows how some of this is printed, taking the section running through Proverbs 24.30–4; 30.15–33 and 25.1–10, and indicating where the collection deviates from our Hebrew editions.

Another means of assessing the nature of the Greek Old Testament is indirectly through the New Testament writers, for they appear to use not only the LXX, but other Greek translations as well. Although these are now no longer in evidence, we do know of later translations which derived from them. The translations date between the second and third centuries CE, and are those used by Origen in the *Hexapla*: Aquila, Theodotian and Symmachus. At the end of the third century, in Antioch, a scholar named Lucian also made a translation of the Hebrew Bible into Greek; this was used by Jerome in his fourth-century Latin translation called the Vulgate, to which we shall refer again later.

A few fragments of the LXX, and of other Greek versions of the Old Testament dating from before 100 CE, have been found in caves like those at Qumran in the Judean desert. From this period, until medieval times, we possess some eighteen hundred manuscripts of the LXX – thus showing how much better informed we are about the Greek translation of the Hebrew Scriptures than about the Hebrew text itself. Although the condition of these manuscripts is variable, depending on whether they were produced on papyrus or on parchment, they offer useful information about the making of manuscripts throughout this period. Some are written in a continuous script known as 'cursive', a more informal type of writing; and others are written in large separate block letters called 'uncials'. In the ninth century CE another script was introduced at Constantinople; this was a more flowing writing in smaller letters, called the 'minuscule' script. It appears that at first the papyrus sheets were joined together to make scrolls, but as these were cumbersome to use, by the second century CE the papyrus were sewn together to make a book, or 'codex'. The codices were a significant influence in enabling a visual recognition of a collection of papyri brought together as a complete 'book'; this sort of cohesion was, of course, not possible with copies on scrolls.

The previous chapter made reference to the three most significant codices of the LXX. The first, *Codex Vaticanus* (known as 'B'), is an uncial codex from the fourth century CE. Written in three columns, it is the best quality of the codices, being a complete manuscript of the entire Old Testament, except that the very beginning is missing, so the text begins at Genesis 46.8. Some verses from 2 Samuel are also

21 φοβοῦ τὸν θεόν, υἱέ, καὶ βασιλέα
καὶ μηθετέρῳ αὐτῶν ἀπειθήσῃς ·
22 ἐξαίφνης γὰρ τείσονται τοὺς ἀσεβεῖς,
τὰς δὲ τιμωρίας ἀμφοτέρων τίς γνώσεται;
22a λόγον φυλασσόμενος υἱὸς ἀπωλείας ἐκτὸς ἔσται,
δεχόμενος δὲ ἐδέξατο αὐτόν.
22b μηδὲν ψεῦδος ἀπὸ γλώσσης βασιλεῖ λεγέσθω,
καὶ οὐδὲν ψεῦδος ἀπὸ γλώσσης αὐτοῦ οὐ μὴ ἐξέλθῃ.
22c μάχαιρα γλῶσσα βασιλέως καὶ οὐ σαρκίνη,
ὃς δ᾽ ἂν παραδοθῇ, συντριβήσεται ·
22d ἐὰν γὰρ ὀξυνθῇ ὁ θυμὸς αὐτοῦ,
σὺν νεύροις ἀνθρώπους ἀναλίσκει
22e καὶ ὀστᾶ ἀνθρώπων κατατρώγει
καὶ συγκαίει ὥσπερ φλὸξ
ὥστε ἄβρωτα εἶναι νεοσσοῖς ἀετῶν.

30 1 Τοὺς ἐμοὺς λόγους, υἱέ, φοβήθητι
καὶ δεξάμενος αὐτοὺς μετανόει ·
τάδε λέγει ὁ ἀνὴρ τοῖς πιστεύουσιν θεῷ, καὶ παύομαι ·
2 ἀφρονέστατος γάρ εἰμι πάντων ἀνθρώπων,
καὶ φρόνησις ἀνθρώπων οὐκ ἔστιν ἐν ἐμοί ·
3 θεὸς δεδίδαχέν με σοφίαν,
καὶ γνῶσιν ἁγίων ἔγνωκα.
4 τίς ἀνέβη εἰς τὸν οὐρανὸν καὶ κατέβη;
τίς συνήγαγεν ἀνέμους ἐν κόλπῳ;
τίς συνέστρεψεν ὕδωρ ἐν ἱματίῳ;
τίς ἐκράτησεν πάντων τῶν ἄκρων τῆς γῆς;
τί ὄνομα αὐτῷ, ἢ τί ὄνομα τοῖς τέκνοις αὐτοῦ, ἵνα γνῷς;
5 πάντες λόγοι θεοῦ πεπυρωμένοι,
ὑπερασπίζει δὲ αὐτὸς τῶν εὐλαβουμένων αὐτόν ·
6 μὴ προσθῇς τοῖς λόγοις αὐτοῦ,
ἵνα μὴ ἐλέγξῃ σε καὶ ψευδὴς γένῃ.
7 δύο αἰτοῦμαι παρὰ σοῦ,
μὴ ἀφέλῃς μου χάριν πρὸ τοῦ ἀποθανεῖν με ·

Figure 7   The Septuagint Version of Proverbs 24.21–2 (with additions); 30.1–14; 25.23–30

8 μάταιον λόγον καὶ ψευδῆ μακράν μου ποίησον,
   πλοῦτον δὲ καὶ πενίαν μή μοι δῷς,
   σύνταξον δέ μοι τὰ δέοντα καὶ τὰ αὐτάρκη,
9 ἵνα μὴ πλησθεὶς ψευδὴς γένωμαι καὶ εἴπω Τίς με ὁρᾷ;
   ἢ πενηθεὶς κλέψω καὶ ὀμόσω τὸ ὄνομα τοῦ θεοῦ.
10   μὴ παραδῷς οἰκέτην εἰς χεῖρας δεσπότου,
   μήποτε καταράσηταί σε καὶ ἀφανισθῇς.
11   ἔκγονον κακὸν πατέρα καταρᾶται,
   τὴν δὲ μητέρα οὐκ εὐλογεῖ ·
12 ἔκγονον κακὸν δίκαιον ἑαυτὸν κρίνει,
   τὴν δὲ ἔξοδον αὐτοῦ οὐκ ἀπένιψεν ·
13 ἔκγονον κακὸν ὑψηλοὺς ὀφθαλμοὺς ἔχει,
   τοῖς δὲ βλεφάροις αὐτοῦ ἐπαίρεται ·
14 ἔκγονον κακὸν μαχαίρας τοὺς ὀδόντας ἔχεῖ
   καὶ τὰς μύλας τομίδας, ὥστε ἀναλίσκειν
   καὶ κατεσθίειν τοὺς ταπεινοὺς ἀπὸ τῆς γῆς
   καὶ τοὺς πένητας αὐτῶν ἐξ ἀνθρώπων.

---

24 23   Ταῦτα δὲ λέγω ὑμῖν τοῖς σοφοῖς ἐπιγινώσκειν ·
   αἰδεῖσθαι πρόσωπον ἐν κρίσει οὐ καλόν ·
24 ὁ εἰπὼν τὸν ἀσεβῆ Δίκαιός ἐστιν,
   ἐπικατάρατος λαοῖς ἔσται καὶ μισητὸς εἰς ἔθνη ·
25 οἱ δὲ ἐλέγχοντες βελτίους φανοῦνται,
   ἐπ' αὐτοὺς δὲ ἥξει εὐλογία ἀγαθή ·
26 χείλη δὲ φιλήσουσιν ἀποκρινόμενα λόγους ἀγαθούς.
27   ἑτοίμαζε εἰς τὴν ἔξοδον τὰ ἔργα σου
   καὶ παρασκευάζου εἰς τὸν ἀγρὸν
   καὶ πορεύου κατόπισθέν μου
   καὶ ἀνοικοδομήσεις τὸν οἶκόν σου.
28   μὴ ἴσθι ψευδὴς μάρτυς ἐπὶ σὸν πολίτην
   μηδὲ πλατύνου σοῖς χείλεσιν ·
29 μὴ εἴπῃς Ὃν τρόπον ἐχρήσατό μοι χρήσομαι αὐτῷ,
   τείσομαι δὲ αὐτὸν ἅ με ἠδίκησεν.
30   ὥσπερ γεώργιον ἀνὴρ ἄφρων,

Figure 7 (continued)

missing, as well as some thirty psalms (105.27–137.6). The second, *Codex Sinaiticus* (known as 'S'), is also an uncial codex written on large pages with one column per page, and it also dates from the fourth century. It is not as complete as B. This may be because parts of it were recovered from a waste basket in the monastery on Mount Sinai as late as the nineteenth century. The third uncial codex is *Codex Alexandrinus* (known as 'A'), from the fifth century, presented in two columns. It is more complete than B, although the New Testament translation (which will be discussed later) is much less so.

An example of a text from *Codex Sinaiticus* (from Tobit 6.5) is given in Figure 8. A comparison with later examples will show that the Greek is very different in form and style from that of the New Testament.

Latin Versions

As far as the Latin version of the Old Testament is concerned, most translations are the work of Christians, using the Greek text rather than

Then the young man went down to wash himself. A fish leaped up from the river and would have swallowed the young man; and the angel said to him, 'Catch the fish.' So the young man seized the fish and threw it up on the land. Then the angel said to him, 'Cut open the fish and take the heart and liver and gall and put them away safely.' So the young man did as the angel told him; and they roasted and ate the fish.

And they both continued on their way until they came near to Ecbatana. Then the young man said to the angel, 'Brother Azarias, of what use is the liver and heart and gall of the fish?' He replied, 'As for the heart and the liver, if a demon or evil spirit gives trouble to any one, you make a smoke from these before the man or woman, and that person will never be troubled again. And as for the gall, anoint with it a man who has white films in his eyes, and he will be cured.'

When they approached Ecbatana, the angel said to the young man, 'Brother, today we shall stay with Raguel. He is your relative, and he has an only daughter named Sarah. I will suggest that she be given to you in marriage, because you are entitled to her and to her inheritance, for you are her only eligible kinsman. The girl is also beautiful and sensible. Now listen to my plan. I will speak to her

Figure 8 Tobit 6.5 from the *Codex Sinaiticus*

father, and as soon as we return from Rages we will celebrate the marriage. For I know that Raguel, according to the law of Moses, cannot give her to another man without incurring the penalty of death, because you rather than any other man are entitled to the inheritance' (Tobit 6.2–12)

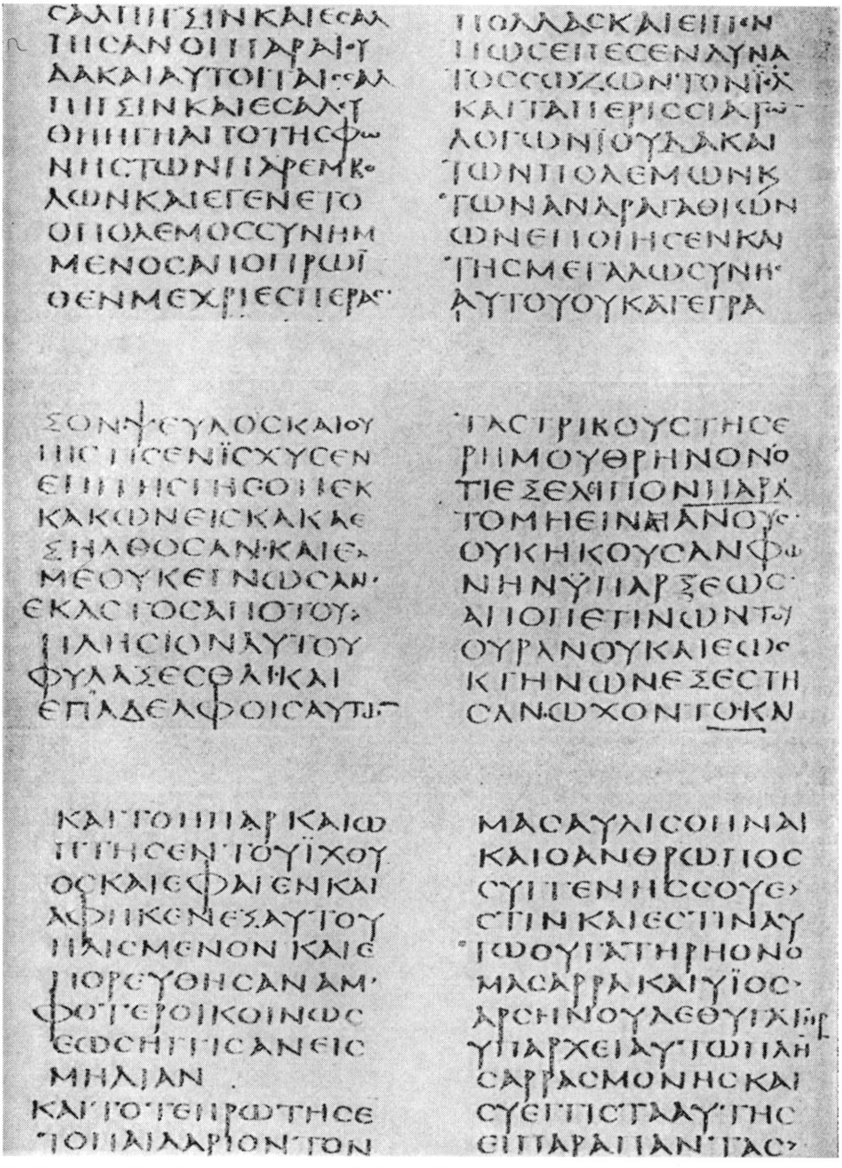

Figure 8 *(continued)*

the Hebrew. One interesting case concerns the Psalms, for one of the versions most used by Christians was the Gallican Psalter, translated from the Greek by Jerome in Bethlehem some time before 389 CE. Jerome also translated the Psalter into Latin directly from the Hebrew, and followed this with a translation of the entire Old Testament. This edition is known as the Vulgate ('V') on account of its being written in the common ('vulgar') Roman tongue. (Jerome also started a similar project on the Greek New Testament, although he only completed the Gospels.)

Because of its Christian stance, the Vulgate offers an implicit Christian interpretation of some old Testament passages. A good example is in Isaiah, where the prophecies which speak of a coming deliverer-figure are assumed to be referring to Christ. Similarly the oracles in the Psalms which refer to the king as a deliverer of the people suggest the same identification with Christ. Figure 9 is a less contentious extract from Judges 5.15–17, possibly dating from a Christian copy in the fifth century: the work of later correctors can also be seen.

Aramaic Versions

Just as the Septuagint catered for Greek-speaking Jews outside Palestine, and the Latin translations of the Old Testament catered for Christians in the Latin-speaking world, the Aramaic versions, as early as the second century BCE, catered for the several Jewish communities for whom Aramaic was the vernacular language. Aramaic appears to have been spoken by Jews under Persian rule from as early as the exilic period. Thus several smaller portions of the Old Testament were first written in Aramaic rather than Hebrew (Genesis 31.47; Jeremiah 10.11; Ezra 4.8—6.18; Ezra 7.12–26; Daniel 2.4—7.28). Fragments of Aramaic manuscripts have also been found at Qumran.

From the second century BCE onwards, a practice grew whereby Hebrew texts were translated from the Hebrew into Aramaic but preserved in an oral form. These were called the '*Targums*' (meaning 'translations') and although the rabbis initially looked on them with disapproval, they were so much used that eventually they were written down as elaborations of the Hebrew text. Unlike *midraš*, which was more discursive and acted more as an expanded commentary on Scripture, quoting other scriptural passages and a number of rabbinical sources, the *Targums* were deliberate attempts at copying the actual form and voice of the original, thus staying within the mode of a translation, albeit more as a paraphrase. The *Targums* developed as a

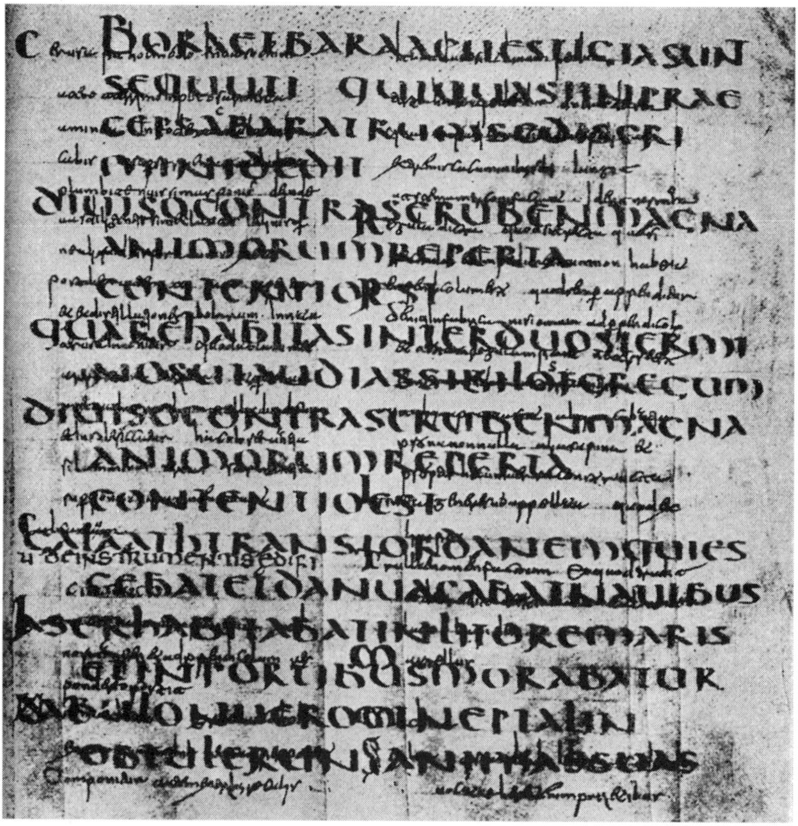

15. The princes of Issachar came with Deborah,
    and Issachar faithful to Barak;
    into the valley they rushed forth at his heels.
    Among the clans of Reuben
    there were great searchings of heart.
16. Why did you tarry among the sheepfolds,
    to hear the piping for the flocks?
    Among the clans of Reuben
    there were great searchings of heart.
17. Gilead stayed beyond the Jordan;
    and Dan, why did he still abide with the ships?
    Asher sat still at the coast of the sea,
    settling down by his landings

An English Translation from the Vulgate of Judges 5.15–17

Figure 9 Judges 15.15–17 from the Vulgate

result of the readers in the synagogues throughout the dispersed Jewish communities translating from the Hebrew into Aramaic, so that the worshippers understood the lessons of Scripture as they listened. These initially spontaneous translations gradually took on a more established oral form, and from this (much later, in the Christian era) into a written account of the lectionary readings.

The *Targum* of the Pentateuch is the earliest written form, the most important of which, probably originating in Palestine between the first and second centuries CE, is attributed to one Onqelos. These works were popular among the dispersed Jewish communities in what had once been the land of Babylon between the fourth and fifth centuries CE. The *Targums* of the Prophets are also important, of which the best known is attributed to Jonathan. This too may well have originated in Palestine, but was again better known in the old Babylonian region. Of the Writings (perhaps predictably), only fragmentary *Targums* exist. Although more paraphrase than actual translation, the *Targums* focus only on the Hebrew Scripture and in this way they differ not only from midrashic interpretations, but also from the *Mishnah* and the *Talmud*, which are not translations, but interpretations of the so-called 'oral law' of Moses. It is interesting that the first paraphrases of the Hebrew texts were made by the Jews – rather than by Christians – in spite of their supposed reverence, according to Josephus, for the sacred and unchangeable nature of their final text.

Syriac Versions

The translation of the Old Testament into Syriac was undertaken by Christians in the same way as was the Latin. This first took place as early as the first and second centuries CE in the district of Adiabene (now in modern Iraq) and in Edessa (now in modern Turkey). The most significant of these is a later edition called the *Peshitta* Bible (meaning 'simple version') referred to in the previous chapter. As a translation, some of it is more of a paraphrase than a literal rendering of the Hebrew. This edition was associated with Bishop Rabbula of Edessa, dating from the early fifth century. It is important because of the way it drew not only from the Hebrew text, but also from the Greek text, and (hence its more paraphrasing form in places) from the Aramaic *Targums*. A manuscript of the *Peshitta* Pentateuch, dating from 464 CE, is now in the British Museum. An extract from Genesis 29.32–3 is given in Figure 10.

What is clear is that although particular collections of writings gradually became axiomatic in different Jewish and Christian communities

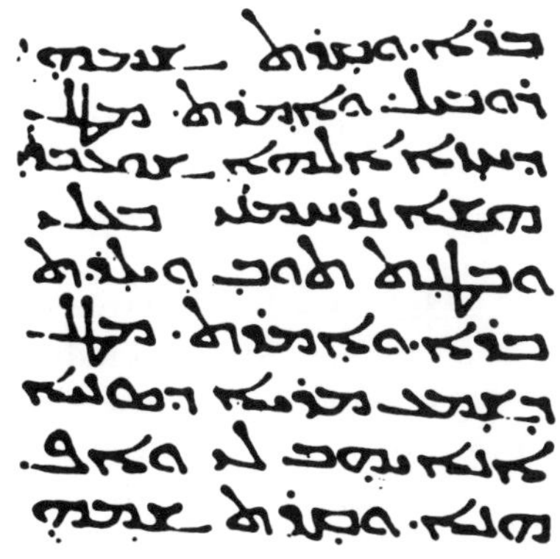

And Leah conceived and bore a son, and she called his name
Reuben, for she said, 'Because the Lord has looked upon my afflic-
tion; surely now my husband will love me.' She conceived again and
bore a son, and said, 'Because the Lord has heard that I am hated, he
has given me this son also'; and she called his name Simeon.

(Genesis 29.32–3)

Figure 10 Genesis 29.32–3 from the *Peshitta*

by the fourth century CE, the various recensions of each 'canonical
collection' from their own particular community were multiform, for
these had to meet both the cultural and the linguistic needs of such
different local communities, whether in Jerusalem, Qumran, Caesarea,
Alexandria or beyond. Any attempt to trace one definitive text of the
Hebrew Bible is thus an impossible task; none is known, and none
seems to exist. All we have is a multiple number of copies (manuscripts), and of translations (versions) of the copies. Table 10 is
intended to make this observation clear. The diverse texts and versions
referred to here have been arranged, as much as is possible, in some
chronological order, but the diversity and the late establishing of a
fixed text should be clear.

The New Testament Text and the Greek, Syriac, Latin and Coptic Versions

The various versions of the New Testament text can be described more
briefly than those of the Old Testament, partly because the process is
less diversified, and partly because the period of time for the whole
process is much shorter.

Table 10   The Old Testament Texts and Versions: Key Dates

The Hebrew Text

The Formation of the 'Hebrew Bible'	*c.* 10–2c. BCE	
Qumran Scrolls and Fragments	3c. BCE – 1c. CE	esp. Psalms and Isaiah
Nash Papyrus	1c. CE	fragments, e.g. of Ten Commandments
Origen's *Hexapla*	3c. CE	all OT (x2) in six columns
Manuscripts from Cairo Genizah Text	10c. CE	fragments of Massoretic Text (MT)
Aleppo Codex	10c. CE	fragments of MT
Leningrad Codex	11c. CE	nearly all MT
Lisbon Codex	15c. CE	nearly all MT
Manuscripts of Samaritan Pentateuch (dated back to 4c. BCE)	14c. CE	Genesis to Deuteronomy
Venice Codex	16c. CE	all MT (resource for 'Rabbinic Bible')

The Greek Text

Septuagint (LXX)	*c.* 3–1c. BCE	few fragmentary papyri
Aquila and Theodotian	2c. CE	surviving mss mainly via Origen's translation
Symmachus	3c. CE	mss mainly via Origen
Origen's *Hexapla*	3c. CE	Greek in four columns
Lucian's translation	3c. CE	all Old Testament
Codex Vaticanus (B)	4c. CE	Genesis 46.8–end of OT (minus 2 Samuel and 30 psalms): LXX codex
Codex Sinaiticus (S)	4c. CE	incomplete LXX codex
Codex Alexandrinus (A)	5c. CE	almost complete LXX codex

Other Texts

Aramaic *Targums* (2c. BCE)	1–2c. CE	copies of Pentateuch
	2c. CE	copies of Prophets
Jerome's Vulgate (Latin)	4c. CE	complete by 5c. CE
Peshitta Bible (Syriac)	5c. ce	complete form

Greek Codices and Papyri

Greek was the original language of the entire New Testament. Yet the problem of the 'time lag' between the time of writing and the time of known manuscripts is again evident. Quite a large proportion of the Gospels and Epistles was in copied form by the middle of the second century, as the most important churches at that time – for example, in Antioch, Alexandria, Ephesus, Rome, Lyon and Carthage – would have encouraged copies to be made for the other Christian communities in their care. Certainly by 331 we read in the historian Eusebius' account of Constantine and the Christian churches (in *Vita C* 4.36) that fifty copies of Scripture were commissioned for the new churches in Constantinople 'in fine parchment ... by professional scribes'. However, none of these copies is now extant. The oldest copies which are actually in existence are uncial codices dating from the end of the fourth and the fifth centuries. Hence although the gap in time between written account and known manuscript is much shorter than is the case with the Old Testament, it nevertheless exists.

However, in contrast to the Old Testament Hebrew texts, an abundant number of papyrus and vellum New Testament Greek manuscripts is now in evidence, dating between the fourth and tenth centuries. The three most important New Testament uncials are the same as those for the Old Testament in Greek. These were the work of Christian communities whose concern was to bring the Old and New Testaments together. These three, referred to earlier, are *Codex Vaticanus* (B), *Codex Sinaiticus* (S) and *Codex Alexandrinus* (A). B (the oldest) has its end missing (note that the beginning of Genesis was also missing for the Old Testament) and so ends at Hebrews 9.14. There is some evidence of a later editor tracing over every letter and omitting words which were considered incorrect. S contains the whole New Testament – the only uncial codex to do so (unlike its Old Testament, which we noted earlier is far less complete). In addition, it has two non-canonical books – the Epistle of Barnabas and the Shepherd of Hermas – two books which for some time were at the fringes of the New Testament collection. A lacks several works, including Matthew up to 25.6; John 6.50—8.52 and 2 Corinthians 4.13—12.6, and adds several others, including the Epistles of Clement and the Psalms of Solomon, showing the breadth of the collection still possible by the fourth century.

One other manuscript from the fifth century deserves mention: this is *Codex Bezae* (called 'D'), probably from North Africa. It contains only the Gospels, the Acts of the Apostles and part of 3 John, but because it is presented in both Greek and Latin on facing pages, it offers a useful

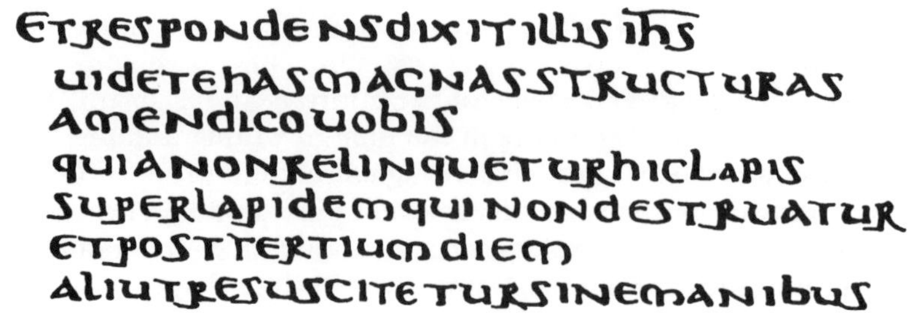

ETRESPONDENSdixiTillis ihs
uideTehAsmAGNASSTRUCTURAS
Amendicouobis
quiANONRELiNqueTURhicLApis
SUPERLApidemquiNONdESTRUATUR
ETpoSTTERTium diem
AliuTRESuSCITETURSINEmANibuS

And Jesus said to him, 'Do you see these great buildings? There will not be left here one stone upon another, that will not be thrown down.' (Mark 13.2)

Figure 11   Mark 13.2 from the *Codex Bezae* (D) with additional saying

comparison with the Latin translation at this stage, although it also suggests the work of several different scribes. Figure 11 gives an example from the Latin column of D. The extract is from Mark 13.2 with an additional quotation about Jesus raising up the destroyed temple on the third day.

Another two hundred Greek manuscripts have been preserved from the ninth century onwards, when the writing changed to the minuscule script. In spite of this, the critical edition of the Greek New Testament made last century by Westcott and Hort (1881–2) mainly used B and S, seeing these as the more 'neutral' traditions. Not until this century have different editions of the Greek New Testament also incorporated other manuscript discoveries alongside the work of Westcott and Hort (for example, the edition sponsored in 1955, used by the American, Scottish and German Bible societies).

The problem is thus not only that of the 'time lag' between the unknown 'original' and the manuscript, but also that of verifying which manuscripts are the most useful for reading. Figure 12 is an example of text from a critical edition of the Greek New Testament, from Luke 13.18–28. At the bottom of the page is the 'critical apparatus' – showing why certain choices have been made in the text, where there are obvious variations in the manuscripts. The letters A, B and D among the notes at the foot of the page indicate the use of the relevant codices. (ℵ is S.)

Just as the Qumran discoveries served in some way to bridge the gap between earlier Hebrew text and the later manuscripts, so fragments of papyri which have been found this century similarly bridge the gap between the original Greek text of the New Testament and the later manuscripts. Over ninety-six such fragments have been identified, dating between the second and eighth centuries. The fragments are so small that one could argue that, like Qumran to the Old Testament, they reveal more problems than they solve; but they do serve to confirm our view that this is indeed a multiplex tradition, and they do illustrate just how much the later manuscripts were dependent upon a disparate number of texts.

One such example is a third-century papyrus of John 1 and 20, in Greek, now in the British Museum. Called *P5*, in large measure this actually agrees with B and S. Another much longer papyrus codex, known as *P45*, and preserved in the Chester Beatty collection in Dublin, is important because it is over a century earlier than any known vellum manuscript, and comprises parts of Mark, Luke and the Acts of the Apostles. Another important papyrus, *P66*, is kept in the Bodmer collection in Geneva. This is again from John's Gospel, and dates from the third century as well. *P75*, in the same collection, is another much later (seventh-century) but much longer manuscript of Luke and John, particularly important because it is much more intact. But probably the earliest fragment of all is kept in the John Rylands Library, Manchester. Dating from about 135, and named *P52*, it contains just four verses of John 18.

Another more disputed manuscript which has recently received media attention is preserved in Magdalen College, Oxford. Known as *P46*, it contains parts of Matthew 26. (Parts of the same codex, called *P67*, fragments of Matthew 3 and 5, are preserved in Barcelona.) Although traditional scholarship has assigned the date to about 200, more recent paleographical work on the text has claimed that it may well date between 70 and 100 and hence may be the earliest manuscript of all. This assertion has been rejected on the grounds that the codicological and paleographical evidence is too slender and generalized to make over-precise comparisons with styles of writing in the Greek manuscripts at Qumran – and the consensus still favours the late-second-century date.

On the positive side, these fragmentary papyri confirm how early some of the Greek manuscripts really were; but more problematically, they again show how multivalent the textual tradition really was, for there are innumerable differences illustrating just how widely these works were used by a large number of different Christian communities. What we may conclude from all this evidence is that the form is often *fixed* – in that there are many similarities when comparing one manuscript with another – but it is by no means *final* – in the sense that it was still open to a good deal of alteration and explanation.

Ἔλεγεν οὖν, Τίνι ὁμοία 18
ἐστὶν ἡ βασιλεία τοῦ Θεοῦ, καὶ τίνι ὁμοιώσω
αὐτήν; ὁμοία ἐστὶν κόκκῳ σινάπεως, ὃν λαβὼν 19
ἄνθρωπος ἔβαλεν εἰς κῆπον ἑαυτοῦ, καὶ ηὔξησεν
καὶ ἐγένετο εἰς δένδρον, καὶ τὰ πετεινὰ τοῦ οὐρανοῦ
168.5 κατεσκήνωσεν ἐν τοῖς κλάδοις αὐτοῦ. Καὶ πάλιν 20
εἶπεν, Τίνι ὁμοιώσω τὴν βασιλείαν τοῦ Θεοῦ;
ὁμοία ἐστὶν ζύμῃ, ἣν λαβοῦσα γυνὴ ἔκρυψεν εἰς 21
ἀλεύρου σάτα τρία, ἕως οὗ ἐζυμώθη ὅλον.
169.2 Καὶ διεπορεύετο κατὰ πόλεις καὶ κώμας δι- 22
δάσκων καὶ πορείαν ποιούμενος εἰς Ἱεροσόλυμα.
170.5 Εἶπεν δέ τις αὐτῷ, Κύριε, εἰ ὀλίγοι οἱ σωζόμενοι; 23
ὁ δὲ εἶπεν πρὸς αὐτούς, | Ἀγωνίζεσθε εἰσελθεῖν 24
διὰ τῆς στενῆς θύρας, ὅτι πολλοί, λέγω ὑμῖν,
171.5 ζητήσουσιν εἰσελθεῖν καὶ οὐκ ἰσχύσουσιν. ἀφ᾽ 25
οὗ ἂν ἐγερθῇ ὁ οἰκοδεσπότης καὶ ἀποκλείσῃ τὴν
θύραν, καὶ ἄρξησθε ἔξω ἑστάναι καὶ κρούειν τὴν
θύραν λέγοντες, Κύριε, ἄνοιξον ἡμῖν, καὶ ἀποκρι-
θεὶς ἐρεῖ ὑμῖν, Οὐκ οἶδα ὑμᾶς πόθεν ἐστέ. τότε 26
ἄρξεσθε λέγειν, Ἐφάγομεν ἐνώπιόν σου καὶ ἐπίο-
μεν, καὶ ἐν ταῖς πλατείαις ἡμῶν ἐδίδαξας· καὶ 27
ἐρεῖ λέγων ὑμῖν, Οὐκ οἶδα πόθεν ἐστέ· ἀπόστητε
ἀπ᾽ ἐμοῦ πάντες ἐργάται ἀδικίας. ἐκεῖ ἔσται ὁ κλαυ- 28
172.5 θμὸς καὶ ὁ βρυγμὸς τῶν ὀδόντων, *ὅταν ὄψησθε
Ἀβρααμ καὶ Ισαακ καὶ Ιακωβ καὶ πάντας τοὺς

---

19 δενδρον **ℵBD** *al* it sy^sc co arm ; R] *add* μεγα 𝔭⁴⁵AWΘ
fr fr3 *pm* lat sy^p ς   24 (ισχυσουσιν.] , R^m)   25
εγερθη ο οικ.] ο οικ. εισελθη **D** *d* : εισελθη ο οικ. fr3 lat
27 λεγων υμιν **B** *892*] υμιν **ℵ** lat sy^p sa : Λεγω υμιν
ADWΘ fr fr3 *pl d* (sy^sc) ς ; R | Ουκ οιδα π. εστε] Ουδεποτε
ειδον υμας **D** *d e*

He said therefore, 'What is the kingdom of God like? And to what
shall I compare it? It is like a grain of mustard seed which a man took
and sowed in his garden; and it grew and became a tree, and the
birds of the air made nests in its branches.'

And again he said, 'To what shall I compare the kingdom of God?
It is like leaven which a woman took and hid in three measures of
flour, till it was all leavened.'

He went on his way through towns and villages, teaching, and jour-
neying toward Jerusalem. And some one said to him, 'Lord, will
those who are saved be few?' and he said to them, 'Strive to enter by
the narrow door; for many, I tell you, will seek to enter and will not
be able. When once the householder has risen up and shut the door,
you will begin to stand outside and to knock at the door, saying,

---

Figure 12   Luke 13.18–28 showing the 'critical apparatus' in the Greek

"Lord, open to us." He will answer you, "I do not know where you come from." Then you will begin to say, "We ate and drank in your presence, and you taught in our streets." But he will say, "I tell you, I do not know where you come from; depart from me, all you workers of iniquity!" There you will weep and gnash your teeth, when you see Abraham and Isaac and Jacob and all the prophets in the kingdom of God and you yourselves thrust out.' (Luke 13.18–28)

Figure 12 *(continued)*

Syriac Translations

Other translations which pre-date the Greek codices of B, S and A by between one and two hundred years are in Syriac and Latin (from the end of the second century) and in Coptic (from the third century). As well as two other early forms of the Gospels in Syriac, one other important translation in Syriac is Tatian's *Diatessaron* (meaning 'four in one'), translated from the Greek in about 170 CE. As was noted in the previous chapter, this edition combines all four Gospels into one, and also includes non-canonical materials such as 'Joseph the Carpenter' and 'the Gospel of the Hebrews'. Until the fifth century, this collection was the official Syriac text, when it was taken over by the *Peshitta*, which combined both Old and New Testaments. After this the *Diatessaron* was considered heretical, and most copies were destroyed; hence we now only know of translations in Latin and in Arabic.

Coptic Manuscripts

Manuscripts of the Coptic New Testament, from near Thebes in southern Egypt, dating from the third and fourth centuries, have mainly been found this century. Although these are not complete – comprising only the Gospels and the Acts of the Apostles – they show a reliance on both the Hebrew and the Greek versions.

Armenian Versions

Similarly, the Armenian version, dating from the fifth century, a translation (probably) from the Syriac and the Greek, is important insofar as there are more surviving manuscripts of this version (admittedly the manuscripts date from the ninth century onwards) than any other version other than Jerome's Vulgate.

Latin Versions

The New Testament was translated into 'Old Latin' in North Africa and Europe by the end of the second century. Tertullian of Carthage (160–220) quotes from such Latin versions, as does Cyprian of Carthage some time later (200–58). There are over fifty fragments of Old Latin versions in evidence, dating from between the fourth and thirteenth centuries, thus demonstrating that Jerome's Vulgate was by no means the first attempt at producing the Scripture in Latin. However, Jerome's is by far the most important Latin version. The New Testament translation comprises only the Four Gospels, being part of his Vulgate edition between 383 and 384, but apparently using the older Latin and Greek texts. The rest of the New Testament in Latin was completed by other scholars later in the late fourth and early fifth centuries. This whole Latin version has always been the primary source for translation into other languages by those in the Roman Catholic Church.

Our conclusions here mirror those offered for the Old Testament. The Greek text, like that of the Hebrew, is found in various recensions, and in different canonical collections, depending upon the linguistic and cultural needs of the Christian communities who used them. Like the Old Testament, there is again the problem of gaps in our knowledge up to the time when manuscripts have been discovered. The earliest copies are hidden from us, and even the later manuscript versions occur in disparate versions. One definitive biblical text, whether of the Old or of the New Testaments, is therefore a contradiction in terms. As with the chart summarizing the texts and versions of the Old Testament (Table 10) a corresponding chart for the New Testament could also be helpful. This chart (Table 11) not only presents the same multiplicity which was seen in the Old Testament, but also presents the material here, as before, in chronological order.

Translating the Bible into English

The process of translating the Bible into English is another example of the way that culture and language influence in various ways the theological intentions of the translators, so that, even when speaking of the English Bible, it is impossible to propose any one definitive text as having final authority.

The first significant example of an English rendering of the Bible dates from around 670 CE. Caedmon, an illiterate peasant boy who worked at the Abbey of Whitby, had an unusual gift of recounting,

Table 11 The New Testament Texts and Versions: Key Dates

The Greek Text

The Formation of the 'New Testament' books *c.* 1–2c. CE

Examples of Papyri

P45	2c.	parts of Mark, Luke, the Acts of the Apostles
P46	2c. (1c. ?)	very small part of Matthew 26
P52	2c.	parts of John 18
P67	2c.	parts of Matthew 3, 5
P5	3c.	parts of John 1, 20
P66	3c.	parts of John
P75	7c.	much of Luke and John

Examples of Codices

Codex Vaticanus (B)	4c.	Matthew–Hebrews 9.14.
Codex Sinaiticus (S)	4c.	All NT, Epistle of Barnabas and Shepherd of Hermas
Codex Alexandrinus (A)	5c.	Matthew 25.6–Revelation apart from John 6.50—8.52; 2 Corinthians 4.13—12.6
Codex Bezae (D)	5c.	parts of Gospels, Acts of the Apostles, 3 John

200+ minuscule mss from 9c. onwards of all parts of NT

Other Texts

Diatessaron (Syriac)	2c.	Four Gospels in one
Coptic Versions	3–4c.	Gospels and Acts of the Apostles
Armenian Versions	5c.	Parts of all NT
Latin Versions:		
Old Latin	2c.	Fragments of NT
Jerome's Vulgate	4c.	Parts of Four Gospels
Additions to Vulgate	4–5c.	Rest of NT

through dreams, stories of the Bible in the form of poetry. This gift resulted in his vocation as a monk, and throughout his life he composed poems from the stories in Genesis and Exodus and in other Old Testament historical books, as well as from the Gospels and other apostolic teachings. The only surviving fragment traditionally ascribed

Nu þe sculan herian   heofonrices peard,
metudes myhte   7 his modȝeþanc,
3 purc puldorfæder,   spa he pundra ȝehpilc,
ece drihten,   ord astealde ;
he ærest ȝesceop   ylda bearnum
6 heofon to hrofe,   haliȝ scyppend,
tha middunȝeard   moncynnæs uard ;
eci dryctin   æfter tiadæ
9 firum foldu,   frea allmectiȝ.

Figure 13   Caedmon's Hymn (from MS Hatton 43)

to Caedmon is a few lines of poetry composed using biblical idiom, although by no means is this a translation of one particular biblical text. Known as Caedmon's Hymn, the West Saxon Version (from MS Hatton 43, taken from A. N. Smith, ed., *Three Northumbrian Poems*, Methuen, London, 1933, pp. 39–41) is as shown in Figure 13.

The translation of the extract of Caedmon's Hymn (taken from S. A. J. Bradley, *Anglo-Saxon Poetry*, Everyman, London, 1995, p. 4) is as follows:

> Now we must laud the heaven-kingdom's Keeper, the Ordainer's might and his mind's intent, the work of the Father of glory: in that he, the Lord everlasting, appointed of each wondrous thing the beginning; he, holy Creator, at the first created heaven for a roof to the children of men; he, mankind's Keeper, Lord everlasting, almighty Ruler, afterwards fashioned for mortals the middle-earth, the world.

In contrast to Caedmon's intuitive and aesthetic rendering of the Bible, Bede, a monk in the monastery at Jarrow, and a contemporary of Caedmon, actually translated parts of the Bible from the Vulgate into Old English. This work was technical and literal rather than intuitive and poetic. The best known examples were the Lord's Prayer and John's Gospel, referred to by Bede himself in his 'Letter to Egbert of York' and in the 'Letter about Bede's Death by Cuthbert the Deacon', although no fragment of these translations actually exists today. A later example of an Old English version of the Bible (taken from R. M. Liuzza (ed.), *The Old English Version of the Gospels*, OUP, 1994, p. 12) is shown in Figure 14. It is a translation of the Lord's Prayer (Matthew 6.9–11).

The Lindisfarne Gospels offer another example of biblical translation into English, showing again the influence of monastic communities in the late seventh and eighth centuries. These Gospels, now in the

Fæder ure þu þe eart on
heofonum; Si þin nama gehalgod [10] to becume þin rice gewurþe ðin
willa on eorðan swa swa on heofonum. [11] urne gedæghwamlican hlaf
syle us todæg [12] and forgyf us ure gyltas swa swa we forgyfað urum
gyltendum [13] and ne gelæd þu us on costnunge ac alys us of yfele
soþlice

Figure 14   The Lord's Prayer in an Old English Version

British Museum, are intricately decorated copies of the Gospels in
Latin, written on vellum. A translation of the Latin, in Old English, was
added some two and a half centuries later between the lines. Figure 15
(from J. Backhouse, *The Lindisfarne Gospels*, Phaidon Press with British
Library, London, 1981, p. 18) is from the latter part of the Beatitudes
(Matthew 5.5–7).

In the ninth century, another translation of the Bible into Old
English was undertaken by Alfred the Great. After the defeat of the
Danes and the establishment of schools and monasteries throughout
the land, King Alfred set scholars to work on translating many different
Latin books, including parts of the Vulgate, of which (so tradition has
it) the Ten Commandments and Psalms were the work of Alfred
himself. Most of the copies of the Bible were made by monks
throughout the Middle Ages.

The first complete translation of the Bible into English was not made
until 1382. This was the work of John Wycliffe, Rector of Lutterworth
in Leicestershire. His concern for the reform of the Church and his
preaching tours throughout the land convinced him that the Bible
should be translated into the vernacular which the ordinary people
could then understand. Opposed by the ecclesiastical authorities, who
felt the reading and teaching of the Bible should be the responsibility
of trained clergy, Wycliffe died in 1384, amidst bitter controversy
concerning his completed translation. Although a number of copies
were made of the translation, many of them were destroyed by church
leaders after his death. Wycliffe's translation of the first verses from
Hebrews 1 reads:

> God, that spak sum tyme bi prophetis in many maneres to oure fadris, at the
> laste in these daies he hath spoke to us bi the sone; whom he hath ordeyned
> eir of alle thingis, and bi whom he made the worldis. Which whanne also he
> is the brightnesse of glorie, and figure of his substaunce and berith all
> thingis bi word of his vertu, he makith purgacioun of synnes, and syttith on
> the righthalf of the maieste in the heunes; and so myche is maad betere than
> aungels, bi hou myche he hath eneritid a more dyuerse name bifor hem.

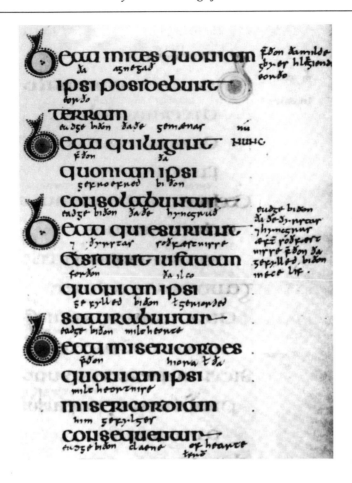

Blessed are the meek,
for they shall inherit
the earth;

Blessed are those who
hunger and thirst for
righteousness, for they
shall be filled;

Blessed are the merciful,
for they shall obtain mercy
       (Matthew 5.5–7)

Figure 15   Matthew 5.5–7 in the Lindisfarne Gospels

Wycliffe's translation was made and copied by hand. By contrast, the invention of the printing press in the middle of the fifteenth century resulted in hundreds of copies of other translations, in Britain and in Europe, being available. One significant contribution, which influenced English translations from the sixteenth century onwards, is the Greek edition of the New Testament published by the Swiss scholar, Erasmus (?1469–1536). Brought up to be so familiar with the Vulgate that he all but believed that the New Testament was originally a Latin work, Erasmus first published his own translation of the Greek New Testament into Latin during his time in Oxford in the early part of the sixteenth century. Some time between 1516 and 1522 he then published his own scholarly edition of the Greek New Testament by reference to the Latin, in part in order to illustrate the integrity of the Latin translation.

William Tyndale was a Bible translator who made use of the printed editions of Erasmus' work. As a Reformer, his theological writings were not accepted in England; his translation of all the New Testament and almost half the Old was undertaken mainly in Germany. In contrast to Wycliffe, who used the Vulgate, Tyndale used the available manuscripts of the Hebrew Old Testament as well as the Greek New Testament of Erasmus. But opposition to Tyndale's work was as severe as it was to that of Wycliffe, and in 1535 he was arrested and a year later was burnt at the stake. Tyndale's translation of Hebrews 1.1–4 reads:

> God in tyme past diversly and many wayes, spake vnto the fathers by prophetes: but in these last dayes he hath spoken vnto vs by his sonne, whom he hath made the heyre of all thynges: by whom also he made the worlde. Which sonne beynge the brightness of his glory, and very ymage off his substance, bearynge vppe all things with the worde of his power, hath in his awne person pourged oure synees, and is sytten on the right honde of the maiestie an hye, and is more excellent then the angels in as moche as he hath by inheritaunce obteyned an excellenter name than have they.

Tyndale's last prayer before his execution was 'Lord, open the King of England's eyes!' Two years later, Henry VIII ordered that a copy of the English Bible should be placed in every church in the land. Within thirty years of Tyndale's death, eight new, different, versions were published. By now doctrinal and indeed political forces were at work so that different translations marked the ebb and flow of more than scholarly disagreement about sources.

Coverdale's Bible (1535) was the work of Miles Coverdale, a close companion of Tyndale, who incorporated into his translation several of the Old Testament books translated by Tyndale in prison, but which he had been unable to print. Coverdale's translation of the Psalms is to be found in the 1662 Book of Common Prayer.

Matthew's Bible (1537) was written under the pseudonym of Thomas Matthew, otherwise John Rogers, who was a friend of Tyndale, and who was also burnt at the stake for his work, during the reign of Queen Mary.

Taverner's Bible (1539) was a revision of Matthew's Bible; Taverner was an Oxford scholar and an expert in Greek.

In the same year the *Great Bible* was printed; this was the edition which was placed in every church, at the command of King Henry VIII.

The *Geneva Bible* (1557) was a version made abroad during the reign of Queen Mary, in whose reign all English translations were again forbidden and who restored the Latin Vulgate for use in all churches.

The *Bishop's Bible* (1568) was made ten years after Queen Elizabeth's accession, so called because its translation was commissioned by Archbishop Matthew Parker, and was intended to be a superior edition which included the best of all previous English translations.

The *Douai Bible* (1582: New Testament; 1609–10: Old Testament) was an edition made by English Catholics who fled to France. Its distinctiveness was that it was based on the Vulgate, rather than on the Hebrew and the Greek as other editions had been; published at Rheims and Douai, it was revised in later years as one of the standard texts for English Catholics.

Finally, in 1611 the King James Bible was printed as the edition to supersede the Bishop's Bible. This became the standard text for Protestants in Reformation and post-Reformation times, for both public and private use. The translation of Hebrews 1.1ff. below shows how far the interpretation had developed since the work of Wycliffe and Tyndale.

> God, who at sundry times and in divers manners spake in time past unto the fathers by the prophets, Hath in these last days spoken unto us by *his* Son, whom he hath appointed heir of all things, by whom also he made the worlds; Who being the brightness of *his* glory, and the express image of his person, and upholding all things by the word of his power, when he had by himself purged our sins, sat down on the right hand of the Majesty on high; Being made so much better than the angels, as he hath by inheritance obtained a more excellent name than they.

The King James Bible became the standard text for some two hundred and fifty years. Other landmarks in the English translations include the publications of the *Revised Version* (1881, the RV); the *Revised Standard Version* (1946, 1952, 1973, the RSV, also known as the *Common Bible*); the *New Testament in Modern English* (a free translation by J. B. Phillips, 1958); the *New English Bible* (1961 and 1970, the NEB); the *Jerusalem*

Bible (1966, the JB); the *Living Bible* (a paraphrase by Kenneth Taylor, 1971, the LB); the *New International Version* (1974 and 1978, the NIV); the *New Jerusalem Bible* (1985, the NJB); the *Revised English Version* (1989, the REV); the *New Revised Standard Version* (1989, the NRSV); the *New Inclusive Translation* (1995, the NIT); and the *Contemporary English Version* (1995, the CEV) – the last two versions both printed to date only in the States. The list shows how the last two decades have seen major proliferation of other versions.

On the following pages are further examples of translations and paraphrases of Hebrews 1.1–4. Taken together, these illustrate well in contemporary terms the cultural and linguistic influences upon the different theological interpretations of the text.

> In many and various ways God spoke of old to our fathers by the prophets; but in these last days he has spoken to us by a Son, whom he appointed the heir of all things, through whom also he created the world. He reflects the glory of God and bears the very stamp of his nature, upholding the universe by his word of power. When he had made purification for sins, he sat down at the right hand of the Majesty on high, having become as much superior to angels as the name he has obtained is more excellent than theirs.
>
> RSV (1946, 1952, 1973)

> God, who gave to our forefathers many different glimpses of the truth in the words of the prophets, has now, at the end of the present age, given us the truth in the Son. Through the Son God made the whole universe, and to the Son he has ordained that all creation shall ultimately belong. This Son, radiance of the glory of God, flawless expression of the nature of God, himself the upholding principle of all that is, effected in person the reconciliation between God and man and then took his seat at the right hand of the majesty on high – thus proving himself, by the more glorious name that he has won, far greater than all the angels of God.
>
> J. B. Phillips (1958)

> At various times in the past and in various different ways, God spoke to our ancestors through the prophets; but in our own time, the last days, he has spoken to us through his Son, the Son that he has appointed to inherit everything and through whom he made everything there is. He is the radiant light of God's glory and the perfect copy of his nature, sustaining the universe by his powerful command; and now that he has destroyed the defilement of sin, he has gone to take his place in heaven at the right hand of divine Majesty. So he is now as far above the angels as the title which he has inherited is higher than their own name.
>
> *Jerusalem Bible* (1966)

1 Πολυμερῶς καὶ πολυτρόπως πάλαι ὁ
⁵In many ⁶and ⁷in many ways ⁸of old –
portions

θεὸς λαλήσας τοῖς πατράσιν ἐν τοῖς
¹God ³having spoken ³to the ⁴fathers by the

προφήταις **2** ἐπ' ἐσχάτου τῶν ἡμερῶν
prophets in [the] last – days

τούτων ἐλάλησεν ἡμῖν ἐν υἱῷ, ὃν ἔθηκεν
of these spoke to us in a Son, whom he appointed

κληρονόμον πάντων, δι' οὗ καὶ ἐποίησεν
heir of all through whom indeed he made
things,

τοὺς αἰῶνας· **3** ὃς ὢν ἀπαύγασμα τῆς
the ages; who being [the] radiance of the
(his)

δόξης καὶ χαρακτὴρ τῆς ὑποστάσεως αὐτοῦ,
glory and [the] of the reality of him,
representation

φέρων τε τὰ πάντα τῷ ῥήματι τῆς
and bearing – all things by the word of the

δυνάμεως αὐτοῦ, καθαρισμὸν τῶν ἁμαρτιῶν
power of him, ²cleansing – ³of sins

ποιησάμενος ἐκάθισεν ἐν δεξιᾷ τῆς
¹having made sat on [the] right [hand] of the

μεγαλωσύνης ἐν ὑψηλοῖς, **4** τοσούτῳ
greatness in high places, ³by so much

κρείττων γενόμενος τῶν ἀγγέλων ὅσῳ
³better ¹becoming ⁴[than] the angels as

διαφορώτερον παρ' αὐτοὺς κεκληρονόμηκεν
³a more excellent ⁴than ⁵them ¹he has inherited

ὄνομα.
²name.

Figure 16 Hebrews 1.1–4 Greek Interlinear Version

When in former times God spoke to our forefathers, he spoke in fragmentary and varied fashion through the prophets. But in this the final age he has
spoken to us in the Son whom he has made heir to the whole universe, and
through whom he created all orders of existence: the Son who is the efful-
gence of God's splendour and the stamp of God's very being, and sustains
the universe by his word of power. When he had brought about the purga-
tion of sins, he took his seat at the right hand of Majesty on high, raised as
far above the angels, as the title he has inherited is superior to theirs.

NEB (1961, 1970)

Long ago God spoke in many different ways to our fathers through the
prophets [in visions, dreams, and even face to face] telling them little by
little about his plans.

But now in these days he has spoken to us through his Son to whom he
has given everything, and through whom he made the world and everything
there is.

God's Son shines out with God's glory, and all that God's Son is and does
marks him as God. He regulates the universe by the mighty power of his

108

command. He is the one who died to cleanse us and clear our record of all sin, and then sat down in highest honor beside the great God of heaven.

Thus he became far greater than the angels, as proved by the fact that his name 'Son of God,' which was passed on to him from his Father, is far greater than the names and titles of the angels.

Living Bible (1971)

In the past God spoke to our forefathers through the prophets at many times and in various ways, but in these last days he has spoken to us by his Son, whom he appointed heir of all things, and through whom he made the universe. The Son is the radiance of God's glory and the exact representation of his being, sustaining all things by his powerful word. After he had provided purification for sins, he sat down at the right hand of the Majesty in heaven. So he became as much superior to the angels as the name he has inherited is superior to theirs.

NIV (1974, 1978, 1984)

When in times past God spoke to our forefathers, he spoke in many and varied ways through the prophets. But in this the final age he has spoken to us in his Son, whom he has appointed heir of all things; and through him he created the universe. He is the radiance of God's glory, the stamp of God's very being, and he sustains the universe by his word of power. When he had brought about purification from sins, he took his seat at the right hand of God's Majesty on high, raised as far above the angels as the title he has inherited is superior to theirs.

REB (1989)

Long ago God spoke to our ancestors in many and various ways by the prophets, but in these last days he has spoken to us by a Son, whom he appointed heir of all things, through whom he also created the worlds. He is the reflection of God's glory and the exact imprint of God's very being, and he sustains all things by his powerful word. When he had made purification for sins, he sat down at the right hand of the Majesty on high, having become as much superior to angels as the name he has inherited is more excellent than theirs.

NRSV (1989)

At many moments in the past and by many means, God spoke to our ancestors through the prophets; but in our time, the final days, he has spoken to us in the person of his Son, whom he appointed heir of all things and through whom he made the ages. He is the reflection of God's glory and bears the impress of God's own being, sustaining all things by his powerful command; and now that he has purged sins away, he has taken his seat at the right hand of the divine Majesty on high. So he is now as far above the angels as the title which he has inherited is higher than their own name.

New Jerusalem Bible (1985)

Long ago in many ways and at many times God's prophets spoke his message to our ancestors. But now at last, God sent his Son to bring his message to us. God created the universe by his Son, and everything will someday belong to the Son. God's Son has all the brightness of God's own glory and is like him in every way. By his own mighty word, he holds the universe together.

After the Son had washed away our sins, he sat down at the right side of the glorious God in heaven. He had become much greater than the angels, and the name he was given is far greater than any of theirs.

CEV (1995)

Long ago God spoke to our ancestors in many and various ways by the prophets, but in these last days God has spoken to us by a Child whom God appointed heir of all things, through whom God also created the worlds, and who is the reflection of God's glory and the exact imprint of God's very being, and sustains all things by a powerful word. Having made purification for sins, the heir of God sat down beside the Majesty on high, having become as much superior to angels as the name the heir has inherited is more excellent than theirs.

NIT (1995)

This wide variety in the English translations – some using the Hebrew text as their primary source, others the Greek, and yet others the Latin – shows just how much the different theological interests affect the bias of the final translation. Copying a version of Scripture from the same language is one thing; but translating it into another cultural and linguistic form is quite another, where the interpretative element is bound to play a larger part. In some of these examples of the English translations, the underlying concern has been for technical accuracy and for a literal rendering of whatever 'original' has been chosen; and in other cases, the concern has been for a more contemporary and colloquial rendering in the vernacular of the day. Hence again, even with English translations and versions, pluralism is the order of the day.

Towards an Integrated Reading of the Translated Text

The problems raised by the multifarious nature of biblical translations affects all three ways of reading – historical, literary and theological alike. For example, alongside a concern for the social world of the writers and the progressive development of the text and its reception throughout history, there is also the need for informed intuition in understanding the many different styles and structures within the texts. Furthermore, we need to give due weight to the many different theological insights which are found at every level of the reception history of the text. Each approach has its limitations, and needs another in order to hold together a more comprehensive, complementary reading of the whole.

As far as the historical method is concerned, one limitation is that it is impossible to come to any clear conclusions about the actual history of the text. The lapses in our knowledge of the history of the text – at the beginning, the middle and even at the end of the text's formation – create real problems for the historical method. A historical reading should not – indeed, cannot – assume we 'know' what the text really meant in its earliest setting, in another culture and in another language. Our knowledge is limited, and inevitably veiled, on account of the long process of transmission of the text. Hence the historical method cannot become 'historicist', in the sense of making overly confident claims about what can be known throughout the history of the formation of the text. Other ways of reading are needed in order to supplement the gaps in our understanding.

Our own reading of any biblical text is but one small part of a much larger, diverse body of interpreters. Because much of this is contingent upon the culture and language of the readers, there is no way in which the literary approach can make any greater claims about being able to understand the text than can the historical one. The results of readers' interpretations, important as such results may be for their own contemporary discourse, can never be the 'final word', because individual readers are dependent upon the assumptions they bring to their interpretation from their own language and culture. These assumptions are no more and no less significant than the multitude of other languages and other cultures which have interacted with other readers of the text since it was first composed. What is an important emphasis in reading today will almost certainly seem to be less important tomorrow; and so the literary approach itself is also part of a much larger interpretative process. The focus in this chapter on the multifarious nature of the written, translatable text, makes this inevitable. Behind the so-called 'fixed' state of the words we read, a multitude of other processes has been at work, adapting and readapting the text into the thought-form and language of the culture of the day. Just as the historical approach cannot lapse into historicism in terms of reading the bible, so too the literary approach cannot become too 'bookish' in making grandiose claims for its own interpretations.

The theological approach has similar limitations in this respect. For it is clear that, throughout the history of Jewish and Christian tradition, the appropriation of the text into any one linguistic and cultural milieu, has (until perhaps the rise of biblical criticism especially in Germany over two centuries ago) been part of the search for meaning and relevance in a community of faith. Contemporary theological relevance of the biblical texts, and hence their appropriation within a believing community, has always been paramount. Yet even this position has its limitations. There are countless difficulties in assuming too much about the 'final form' of the text on account of the multiplicity of textual evidence. The theological approach, especially one which ties itself to a particular confessional tradition, is apt to assume far too readily that its own belief system offers the most important and the most 'true' interpretation. Yet this just does not face the evidence. There is no such thing as *one* theological way of reading, confessional or otherwise. Rather, we are faced with a myriad of theological approaches, evident within both the Jewish and the Christian communities of faith. The theological approach, on its own, is in fact a highly subjective and selective way of approaching the text – and its frequent claim to be an 'inspired' way of reading simply illustrates this limitation even more fully.

The contextual concerns of the historical approach ('the text as it was then') and the semantic sensitivities of the literary approach ('the text and reader as they are now') are both essential in placing any sort of dogmatic theological interpretation within a broader methodological framework. If the historical approach needs to avoid historicist claims, the theological approach similarly needs to avoid lapsing into a type of fundamentalism – whereby it perceives that it alone has the key to the 'fundamental' meaning of a biblical text. Again, we may conclude that (for the sake of their own wider usefulness) each of the three ways of reading the Bible needs to be supplemented by the others.

It may be that the conclusions of these first four chapters appear to be unduly pessimistic about the nature of the Bible. For instance, we have proposed that there is no such thing as a 'Bible', in terms of there being one coherent book; no such thing as a 'biblical theology' in any uniform sense; no such thing as a 'biblical canon', in the sense of one universally acknowledged collection of biblical books; and finally, now, no such thing as one, standard 'biblical text'. Hence thus far our conclusions have been largely framed in the negative – as an exploration of what Scripture is not. As a result, the limitations (rather than the strengths) of each of the three ways of reading the Bible have been made evident. Whether we look *behind* the biblical text, using the historical method, or look *at* it, using the literary approach, or look *within* it, using a theological reading, the complex, diverse and often fragmentary nature of the text prevent us from coming away from it with the clarity and conviction we would prefer. There are more questions than answers, more uncertainties than affirmations.

But one point of clarification now needs to be made. Thus far we have only looked at the three approaches to reading the Bible in the most general sense, as a means of seeing how each might interrelate to the others in response to the questions raised about the Bible's multiplex form. But as yet we have said nothing about how each of these methods works out in greater detail. The purpose of the following three chapters, hopefully providing a more positive agenda to this book, is to assess in more detail the usefulness of each of the three approaches and then to see how these observations work out with respect to one particular biblical book.

Part Two

PLURALITY IN THE READING
OF THE BIBLE

5

Theological Approaches to the Bible

When a text has a fixed (albeit not final) form, the process of interpretation reaches an interesting stage. Until that point, the interpretation has been at the level of *copying* (from the same language) and of *translating* (across language and culture) and one could argue that the text is still open to new ways of being understood and hence is still developing. Indeed, we noted in the previous chapter just how much this is the case.

Yet to have a text, particularly a religious text, in a fixed form paradoxically allows a greater freedom of use. As it becomes increasingly familiar, through being used in Jewish and Christian worship and in teaching, it is adapted in a variety of ways, often becoming the means of illuminating and interpreting other texts within the same tradition. This process is evident even within the biblical collection itself. For example, in the Old Testament, it is evident in the way that the books of Kings are used by the writer of Chronicles; and within a smaller unit, it is seen in the way that Genesis 1 is used particularly in the Psalms, for example in Psalm 8. The process is continued within the New Testament, in the way that Matthew, for example, uses and reinterprets the prophecies in the Old Testament.

This reworking of the biblical texts goes on long after the formation of the biblical collection, both within the Jewish and the Christian traditions. The study of this process of biblical interpretation is often called 'hermeneutics'. This encompasses a large range of issues, covering both the Jewish and Christian traditions throughout nearly two thousand years of history – hence often making studies of hermeneutics diffuse and rather convoluted. In an attempt to discuss these matters in an organized way, this and the following two chapters will discuss each of the three approaches (theological, historical and literary) in turn, assessing their independent use and worth.

Throughout both Jewish and Christian traditions, the primary concern (until the last two centuries, after the new resurgence of biblical criticism) has been the interpretation of Scriptures in theological terms, with the emphasis on explaining a particular text 'from faith and for faith'. We shall deal with the different sorts of theological interpretations first; this is primarily because they have been a key influence on the other approaches.

One of the most interesting features in the theological approach is the close proximity of interests and of methods used within the Jewish and Christian traditions. Each interpretation has used the diverse theologies within its scriptures as a means of authenticating its own understanding of reality within its present age and, ironically, each tradition appeals frequently to the same texts to make different theological points about their different understandings of that reality. We shall assess first the theological approach to the Hebrew Bible from within the Jewish tradition, and then the theological approach to the Bible from within the Christian tradition.

Theological Approaches to Reading in the Jewish Tradition

Four examples of interpreting the text of the Hebrew Bible within the Jewish tradition, all which have been referred to in the previous chapter, are found in the Samaritan Pentateuch, the Septuagint, the Dead Sea Scrolls and the *Targums*.

The Samaritan Pentateuch

For example, we have seen how the Samaritan community took the book of Deuteronomy, with its interest in Mount Gerazim, and 'rewrote' a good deal of Exodus by inserting into the Exodus text various references from Deuteronomy which then implied that the sanctuary at Gerazim played a formative part in the establishing of the cult and the laws at the time of Moses.

The Septuagint

We have observed how the Septuagint changed the order of some of the books in the Hebrew Bible (for example, Proverbs and Jeremiah) thus giving them a different theological emphasis; and we have seen how the Septuagint (as well as some of the Qumran Scrolls) used the tradition of David's fight with Goliath, in 1 Samuel 17, and added into the Psalter an extra psalm celebrating David's victory as God's anointed king over the forces of evil (Psalm 151) – thus changing the final theological emphasis in the Psalter as a whole, which in the Septuagint focuses on David, rather than on God himself (as in Psalm 150).

The Targums

Furthermore, we saw in the previous chapter how the *Targums* (as well as the Septuagint, at times) paraphrased some of the biblical texts in order to gain a better understanding for their own milieu; and how, in so doing, other theological issues were brought into the basic para-phrase – for example, issues about obeying the law as a means of preserving Jewish identity – and how these were grafted into the text but were clearly not part of the original. One example of this is found in one of the *Targums* on Genesis 2.15 (called *Targum Neofiti*). The verse, taken from the RSV translation, runs: 'And the LORD God took the man and put him in the Garden of Eden, to till it and to keep it.' The *Targums* read: 'And the Lord God took the man and put him in the Garden of Eden, in order to *work in the Torah* (that is, to study the Law) and to *keep its commandments.*' Adam is thus depicted as an exemplary Jew, not as a simple tiller of the soil. His fall from grace is on account of his not having maintained this piety, for he did not attend to the Law in the way God commanded. This is a far more sophisticated theological interpretation of the Garden of Eden story than that presented in the Hebrew original, and is a good example of the ways in which the same text can serve a different end.

The Dead Sea Scrolls

Qumran offers us perhaps the best example of the adaptation of the biblical texts. Several of the scrolls have a theological interpretation of the biblical books which is known quite simply as *pēsher* (from an Aramaic loanword, meaning 'interpretation', and from this, 'commentary'. This is a way of explaining a particular biblical verse from a particular biblical text (the most frequent examples are from Isaiah, Nahum, Hosea, Micah and Habakkuk, and also Psalm 37) by way of identifying a significant event or person referred to in the verse with an equally important event or person in the present writer's day. This means that, before any sense can be made of any one *pēsher* interpretation in Qumran, some prior understanding is required of the beliefs of the community at Qumran.

Several of the writings at Qumran reveal an intense hope for a great figure whose coming would bring in a new age of peace and well-being; such a figure is frequently described as a high priest from the line of Zadok, who would reinaugurate true worship at the Jerusalem Temple.

This would replace the present priesthood (probably referring to the unpopular Hasmoneans) whose presence in the Temple was abhorrent to the Qumran community. Their writings speak of two figures – the one representing the present Jerusalem priesthood, known as 'the Wicked Priest', and the one representing the ideal leader from Qumran, known as 'the Teacher of Righteousness'. Against this historical backcloth, it should now be possible to see how the *pēsher* commentary on fragments of Psalm 37 (verses 21–2, 23–4, 32–3) has used the text to create its own theological emphasis:

> *The wicked borrows and does not repay, but the righteous is generous and gives. Truly, those whom He [blesses shall possess] the land, and those whom he curses [shall be cut off].* (21–2)
> Interpreted, this concerns the congregation of the Poor, who [shall possess] the whole word as an inheritance. They shall possess the High Mountain of Israel [for ever], and shall enjoy [everlasting] delights in His Sanctuary. [But those who] shall be cut off, they are the violent of the nations and the wicked of Israel; they shall be cut off and blotted out for ever.

> *The steps of the man are confirmed by the Lord and He delights in all his ways; though [he stumble, he shall not fail, for the Lord shall support his hand]* (23–4)
> Interpreted, this concerns the Priest, the Teacher of [Righteousness whom] God chose to stand before Him, for He established him to build for Himself the congregation ...

> *The wicked watches out for the righteous and seeks [to slay him. The Lord will not abandon him into his hand or] let him be condemned when he is tried.* (32–3)
> Interpreted, this concerns the Wicked [Priest] who [watched the Teacher of Righteousness] that he might put him to death [because of the ordinance] and the law which he sent to him. But God will not *aban[don him and will not let him be condemned when he is] tried* ...

> (taken from G. Vermes, *The Dead Sea Scrolls in English*, Penguin, 1987, pp. 291–2, from 4 Q 171; square brackets indicate disruptions in text)

Broadly speaking, *pēsher* follows a prophecy/fulfilment schema, whereby the present time is assumed to be the age of fulfilment for the hopes expressed by the biblical writers (in this case, by the composer of Psalm 37) so long ago.

Pēsher and Midraš

For this same reason, it is not surprising that the writer of the Gospel of Matthew is often seen as applying this same sort of *pēsher* technique, in his reuse of Old Testament prophecies, showing how they have been fulfilled in the person and work of Jesus Christ. We have noted this process of interpretation in Matthew before (see pp. 40–2) and the example below (illustrated especially in the italic verses) makes the point clearly:

> Now the birth of Jesus Christ took place in this way. When his mother Mary had been betrothed to Joseph, before they came together she was found to be with child of the Holy Spirit; and her husband Joseph, being just a man and unwilling to put her to shame, resolved to divorce her quietly. But as he considered this, behold, an angel of the Lord appeared to him in a dream, saying, 'Joseph, son of David, do no fear to take Mary your wife for that which is conceived in her is of the Holy Spirit; she will bear a son, and you shall call his name Jesus, for he will save his people from their sins.' *All this took place to fulfil what the Lord had spoken by the prophet:*
>
> *'Behold, a virgin shall conceive and bear a son,*
> *and his name shall be called Emmanuel'*
> *(which means, God with us).* (Matthew 1.18–23)

In addition to the *pēsher* use of biblical texts – exercised not only by the Jewish community at Qumran but also by Jewish Christians such as Matthew – Jewish commentators gradually evolved a much broader and more complex theological approach which became known as *midraš*. Coming from the Hebrew '*dāraš*' meaning to 'inquire', or to 'search out a meaning' (and hence also 'interpret'), this was primarily an oral commentary on the written law, and in the first instance was offered by those who read the law in worship and in teaching; these readers became known as *tānnaitîm* (or 'repeaters', from the Hebrew root *tānâ*, meaning to 'recount', or 'repeat').

Midraš is the product of a tradition that, on Mount Sinai, God gave his people not one, but two laws. The one was the *written* law – the *Tôrâ* – which became fixed in its form, and the other was an *oral* law, which was constantly open to new addition and expansion, provided it always agreed with the written *Tôrâ*. In some ways, this oral interpretation of the law is similar to the way in which the *Targums* emerged; the difference is that the language medium is still Hebrew, and the culture is still Palestinian. This oral law is what is referred to in the Gospels as 'the tradition of the elders', for example in Jesus' debates with the Pharisees in Mark 7.1–13. It is probable that the Pharisees were the successors of the *tānnaitîm*, with their concern for the six hundred and more oral expansions of the law – expansions which are referred to in the teachings of Jesus. The appeal to the oral law is what distinguished the Pharisees from the Sadducees, who held that only the written law was central.

By about 200 CE, this oral commentary, or *midraš*, having passed through many stages, was finally organized into a written collection called the *Mishnah*. This comprised sixty-three so-called 'tractates', or

teaching units, and these were divided into six sections, mainly interpreting Genesis, Leviticus, Numbers and some of Deuteronomy. It is
interesting to note that this was during the period in which the New
Testament writings were also being assembled together. The *Mishnah*'s
primary concern was with ritual cleanliness and ethnic separateness,
and so bears the influence of the stricter Jewish response to the Roman
occupation of the land; it commanded the sanctity of the people in
matters of daily conduct, the sanctity of the priests in matters of
Temple worship, and the sanctity of the scribes in matters of civil law.
Its theological concern was with the establishment of God's rule over
the land and over history, in place of the compromise to faith incurred
by Roman rule. Various supplements, hence expanding the *Mishnah*'s
own expansion of the law, known collectively as the *Gemara*, were added
between 300 and 400 CE. The result was a Palestinian edition, known as
the Palestinian Talmud, ('talmud' meaning 'study', or 'learning') in
about 400 CE, and an edition from what is now Iraq, known as the
Babylonian Talmud, in about 600 CE.

What has this to do with the Jewish theological approach to the
Hebrew Bible? One perhaps oversimplified response would be that, for
the Jewish communities in Palestine and amongst the dispersed
communities east of the Jordan, the *Mishnah* was to their Hebrew
Bible what, for Christian communities in Jerusalem and scattered
throughout Asia Minor and Greece, the New Testament was to their
Old Testament. In other words, the *Mishnah*, like the New Testament,
served as a theological commentary on a sacred tradition, bringing
that tradition up to date to face the new needs and new challenges of
the present community. And yet the *Mishnah* was only the beginning of
the process; further formation took between two and four hundred
years, hence making a further interesting parallel between the shaping
over the same period of this 'canonical' tradition when the New
Testament canonical form was taking shape.

Midraš, as an interpretative tradition, selecting and commenting on
particular biblical texts from the Law, was used before, during and after
the formation of the *Mishnah* and the *Talmuds*, for it served as an open,
continuous tradition of oral commentary and interpretation. This
midrashic tradition took shape in two distinct ways – first, in *haggadâ*, or
story (derived from the Hebrew word *nāged*, which in one form could
be translated 'to tell'). *Haggadâ* comprises lessons to be learnt about
the ways of God with his people by use of stories about exemplary char-
acters; this was thus more narratory and deductive in approach. The
second way was by *halakâ*, or 'teaching' (from the Hebrew *hālak*,
meaning 'walk') which corresponded more with rules, precepts and
laws, being more directly pragmatic and prescriptive in approach. Both

are used in the *Mishnah* and in the *Talmuds*: the Babylonian *Talmud*, for example, comprises almost one-third *halakâ* and two-thirds *haggadâ*. This has further consequences for the Christian tradition of theological interpretation, for this sort of midrashic approach has clear parallels with the Christian tradition of inspiration and interpretation through preaching, in the use of Scripture for the contemporary needs of the community. One might go further still and identify the writings of the church fathers as a type of midrashic activity – where the importance of drawing lessons from the Old Testament setting to the New corresponds with the *haggadâ* and the moral injunctions about Christian behaviour correspond with the *halakâ*.

To summarize: as well as having a written commentary on the Law (the *Mishnah* and the *Talmuds*), which, as part of the Jewish tradition of interpretation of Scripture, has correspondences with the place of the New Testament in the Christian tradition of interpretation of Scripture, there also coexisted an oral commentary (*midraš*) which in the Jewish tradition was mainly the teaching of the rabbis and corresponds in the Christian tradition to the writings of the church fathers. And in both traditions, this oral tradition comprises both a literal, direct application of Scripture (*halakâ*) and a more oblique, parabolic adaptation of the same traditions (*haggadâ*). This twofold approach – one more straightforward and the other more interpretative – is very much part of the Christian practice of interpretation, as we shall see shortly.

Several key thinkers have made significant theological contributions to our understanding of the Hebrew Bible in later Jewish tradition. One example is Rabbi Solomon ben Isaac, known by way of the acronym Rashi (1040–1105 CE), who was a Jewish scholar in Germany, producing his own commentary on the Babylonian *Talmud* and on the Hebrew Bible. His primary reverence was for the literal, halakhic method, which was named *peshaṭ* ('straightforward'), which he contrasted with *dāraš*, which being more enquiring and interpretative was thus more akin to *haggadâ*. One interesting illustration is from Rashi's commentary on Psalm 2. This was a royal psalm, although it had been used many times in the New Testament to refer to Christ as the royal son of God. It occurs particularly in the account of Jesus' baptism and the transfiguration, to point to Christ as the 'beloved Son' in whom God is well pleased. Hence it was a popular psalm in later Christian tradition, because it could be used to point to Christ. In his own commentary on Psalm 2, Rashi writes:

> Our teachers [that is, those of the talmudic-midrashic tradition] expounded [this psalm] with reference to King Messiah, but according to its meaning and also by way of rejoinder to the *minim* [Christians] it is proper to explain it with reference to David himself.

Rashi believed that the elaborate and interpretative approach could give too much credence to the Christian adaptation of texts from the Hebrew Bible. To limit the Christian overlay of these texts, RaSHI preferred the comparative safety of the more literal, historical and straightforward approach. In this task he was followed by another great medieval commentator, Kimchi (1160–1235), known by the acronym Radak, from Narbonne, Provence.

In contrast with Rashi's and Kimchi's more straightforward approach to the biblical texts, another medieval commentator, Abraham Ibn Ezra, from amongst the Sephardic Jews in Spain (1089–1164) appropriated the more elaborate and interpretative approach, especially on the books of Genesis and Isaiah. In many ways, this paved the way for the development of the Jewish mystical tradition, which, although its origins can be traced as far back as the second century, with Rabbi Akiba, was popularized amongst the Spanish mystics between the eleventh and fifteenth centuries CE. This Jewish mystical tradition speaks of four senses by which Scripture can be interpreted: *pešaṭ* (the straightforward, literal reading), *dāraš* (the elaborate interpretation), *remez* ('pointer', 'sign', leading to a more practical and moral interpretation) and *sôd* ('mystery', resulting in the most ambiguous reading of all, because it concerned ultimate truths about human existence).

The two texts which received the most attention for this manner of reading were Ezekiel 1 (the prophet's vision of a chariot-throne in heaven) and the Song of Songs (set out as a collection of love songs between a king and his lover). Each of these texts was given a spiritual meaning. The Ezekiel passage was important because it taught spiritual truths about the kingship of God in heavenly places, and Song of Songs, because it taught about the love of God for his people on earth. The *Zohar* ('Book of Splendour') is an expansive commentary on the Song of Songs used by Jewish mystics, and was as popular as the Hebrew Bible and the *Talmuds* among Sephardic Jews in Spain, for it renewed their faith in God in a time of bitter persecution during the events leading up to 1492, when they were finally expelled from Spain. The *Zohar*, and with it, the mystical way of reading texts was essentially a Sephardic approach to their Scriptures; it was not a popular mode amongst the Ashkenazi Jews in Eastern Europe until the eighteenth century, when groups of pious Ashkenazi Jewis called the *Ḥašidîm* combined this with what had previously been predominantly a more direct, straightforward and hence halakhic tradition.

The more literal and grammatical tradition was predominant amongst Jewish scholars in Eastern Europe; and, encouraged later by the influence of the Renaissance and Enlightenment, they applied this interest in Scripture in terms of textual analysis and Bible translation.

Their contributions correspond with those of Erasmus and the translators of the Bible into English. The interest in classical studies meant a renewed interest in Hebrew language, Hebrew grammar and – at least in a technical, formative sense – in Hebrew poetry. Amongst the best-known Jewish commentators in this tradition were Isaac Abravanel (Abarbanel) (1437–1508) from Spain, whose works mainly concerned the Pentateuch, Obadiah Sforno (*c.* 1470–1550) who taught Hebrew in Rome, and Moses Mendelssohn (1729–86), who was influential in producing a translation of the Hebrew Bible for the Ashkenazi Jews in high German.

In summary, broadly speaking, the Sephardic Jews, especially in Spain, being more open to the culture around them, were similarly open to the more indirect and interpretative way of reading their Scriptures; and the Ashkenazi Jews, living mainly in Eastern Europe, with a self-contained lifestyle which was self-consciously Jewish, were more concerned with a literal, grammatical reading. These two approaches continued in different ways in different places and different cultures until the eighteenth century. Thereafter, in part due to the influence of the *Hasidîm* in Western Europe, in part due to the threats on their Jewish culture from without, and in part due to a Jewish Reform movement in Germany which had some political influence, they became more interdependent. In many ways the history of each of these approaches also corresponds with its history in the Christian tradition, as we shall see in the Christian analysis below.

Theological Approaches to Reading in the Christian Tradition

We have already noted, with reference to the Qumran community's use of *pēsher* as a type of commentary on selected biblical texts, how the writer of Matthew's Gospel uses the same technique, thus showing the way in which the New Testament writers themselves – and they were mainly Jews – worked creatively in the same prophecy/fulfilment mode with their own received texts of Scripture. In addition to Matthew, among other New Testament writers who use the Hebrew Bible in this sort of way are Paul, and the author of the Epistle to the Hebrews.

Paul

Paul seems to have seen himself within the midrashic tradition, for he applies that method of using selected words and phrases (often out of context) in order to make a point of Christian relevance, very much as the rabbis used texts (also often out of context) in order to make a point of contemporary relevance about the Jewish Law. Paul's rabbinical reading should not be surprising. He was brought up as a Jew at Jerusalem at the feet of Gamaliel (Acts 22.3) and was well versed in the rabbinic tradition. Moreoever, he uses the *pēsher* interpretation. This is illustrated in his presentation of Christ as the second Adam and also (in a different passage) as the second Abraham. To show Christ as the second Adam, Paul takes Genesis 2.15 and 3.24, which refer to Adam's disobedience in the garden, and in Romans 5.12–21 and 1 Corinthians 15.20–8 he shows how Christ redeems all that Adam once lost. He also uses the same *pēsher* method when he seeks to present Christ as the second Abraham. Taking Genesis 15.6 and 17.1–8, where Abraham is promised a land and descendants on account of his faith in God, Paul uses the basis of these promises to assure his own audience of Christian believers that, on account of what Christ's faith has achieved on their behalf, they have inherited these blessings in a spiritual sense (Romans 4.1–2 and Galatians 3.6–14). Behind this 'typological' interpretation is the promise/fulfilment interest, typical of the *pēsher* approach, which is also to be found in the Qumran Scrolls and in Matthew's Gospel.

Yet Paul did not only use the Hebrew Scriptures in a typically rabbinic way. In his desire to search the Hebrew texts and find everywhere hidden meanings which pointed towards a fulfilment in Christ, he was also influenced by a more Hellenistic approach which had been used by a Jew called Philo – who was (perhaps predictably) from Alexandria (*c.* 25 BCE – *c.* 40 CE) and who developed an allegorical way of reading the Hebrew Scriptures from earlier Greek writers. Philo found all sorts of hidden insights in the Law and the Prophets. It is this emphasis on what his *hidden* in the texts, in contrast to what is self-evident, which marks of Philo's approach from the *pēsher* readings. For Philo, the hidden meanings of the *names* of the heroes and heroines of faith interested him. Paul's interest in the meaning of Hagar's name and the lessons in it for the Gentiles, outlined for example in Galatians 4.21–31, is very similar to Philo's interpretation of Hagar's name in a work of Philo known as *Leg. alleg.* 3.244. Hidden meanings in *events* are also developed by Philo. For example, in the story of the miracle of the water taken from the rock, described as the work of God through Moses in books of Exodus and Numbers (Exodus 17.1–7 and Numbers 20.2–13) Philo allegorizes the miracle by identifying the rock with the eternal Wisdom of God. Paul finds a hidden meaning in the same way, but in his interpretation, the rock is Christ, and the water flowing out is Christ's gift of life (1 Corinthians 10.1–4). Hence Paul's use of the

Hebrew Scriptures, whether we see his influence primarily from the Jewish *pēsher* tradition at Qumran, or from the more Hellenistic-influence searching for secret meaning associated with Philo, is essentially more interpretative than it is literalistic and textual. It could be said that Paul wishes to extract every ounce of meaning from the Hebrew text and use it Christwards, and in so doing, he is the forerunner of the allegorical way of reading, to be described shortly.

Hebrews

The writer of the Letter to the Hebrews is little different from Paul in this respect; he uses the *pēsher* reading, as well as the interest in implicit meaning associated with Philo's approach. One example of this (rather like Paul's Christianized application of the Old Testament verses which refer to Adam and Abraham) is the use of a figure called Melchizedek. Within the Hebrew Bible, Melchizedek is a shadowy figure, referred to only in Genesis 14 and Psalm 110, and in ancient tradition it was thought he was the priest-king of Salem (later called Jerusalem). In Hebrews 7, Christ is described as a priest after the order of Melchizedek, whose own sacrifice of his life, made in Jerusalem, effected salvation once and for all, and in so doing, brought to completion the Hebrew priesthood which needed to offer sacrifices daily. This theme is developed further in Hebrews 8.10. Some of the themes about the true priesthood have many interesting parallels with the same debate about the Zadokite priests in the Qumran community.

It is interesting to compare this approach in Hebrews with that in Matthew's Gospel. Whereas Matthew used prophecies in order to demonstrate that Jesus fulfilled all that was promised in the Hebrew Scriptures, the writer of Hebrews uses the priestly laws and narratives to illustrate the same idea – that the real meaning of Christ's coming and dying can be found 'hidden' in the Hebrew Scriptures. Hence like Paul's letters, and like Matthew's Gospel, the Epistle to Hebrews is very much part of the elaborative and interpretative approach to biblical texts, and in this way all of them have associations with the haggadic part of the midrashic tradition; few of them have much to do with the textual, grammatical and literal approach of the later writers.

Irenaeus

Yet the more liberal approach certainly made its impression in the Christian tradition. One example is Irenaeus, who, as Bishop of Lyons towards the end of the second century, produced several works which were written to oppose a heretical group called the Valentinians. Like Marcion and his followers, the Valentinians dismissed the Old Testament as inferior to the New Testament writings. Irenaeus defends the significance of the Old Testament by showing how his opponents have misunderstood the context of the passages and so have wrongly dismissed them. According to Irenaeus, they have interpreted the 'obvious' by way of reference to the 'hidden and obscure', and then dismissed the worth of the whole. Hence for Irenaeus, in a very different setting from the New Testament writers, a reading of the Old Testament which was clear, straightforward and uncluttered by too much *pēsher* reading and too much typology was the most appropriate way to present his own particular defence of the Christian faith. Of all the early writers, Irenaeus is the key proponent of this more direct approach, and his teaching on the moral value of Old Testament religion and the practical lessons to be learnt from the texts read in a historical way, takes him close to the halakhic interpretation used in Jewish midrashic interpretation.

Clement and Origen

This approach stands in stark contrast to the allegorical method popularized by Christian theologians writing in Alexandria. Given their openness to Hellenism – as has been illustrated by the translation of the Hebrew text into the Greek Septuagint – and given the influence of Philo, the Hellenistic Jew, their openness to an allegorical reading is hardly surprising. One of the two best-known defenders is Clement (*c.* 150 – *c.* 215) who was greatly influenced by Philo's use of the Hebrew Bible. He set out to defend the prophecy/fulfilment motifs in the typology way that Paul had done (that is, using Christ as the type, and the Old Testament figure as the antitype) and he expanded this approach to include allegorical readings as well. All this was done with the aim of defending in every way possible the centrality of Christ.

Clement's approach is also found in a more systematic form in the work of another Alexandrian, Origen (*c.* 185–254). In one of his chief works called *De Principiis*, Origen defends in theory and practice both the typological and the allegorical approaches. To interpret the Bible in a purely historical, literal way, Origen argues, misses the more important truths which lie hidden. Scripture contains a mystery which cannot be conveyed by words alone, and so points to a reality beyond itself. Taking part of a verse from 2 Corinthians 3.6 ('for the written code kills, but the Spirit gives life') Origen thus proposed that all Scripture has a spiritual meaning. It comprises three senses, which can be understood like human senses. Like the body, there is the physical, literal, historical sense; like the soul (and here Origen's view of the soul may not accord with ours), there was the moral, practical sense; and like the spirit, there was the spiritual, prayerful, mysterious, 'analogical' sense. In many ways this threefold approach corresponds with the four ways of reading proposed by the medieval Jewish mystics (that is, the literal reading, the elaborate reading, the moral reading and the mysterious reading). For Origen, this was an attempt at balancing a variety of approaches to reading Scripture, where the spiritual is the most important meaning, but the literal is an essential starting point. Such a view undoubtedly influenced other Christian commentators in medieval and Reformation times.

Theodore of Mopsuestia and John Chrysostom

Not that this view went unchallenged, for it was seen to be too open to external cultural influences without the necessary constraints; it allowed the various dissidents to dismiss biblical figures and events as having little to do with actual history. Hence this was opposed by a different school of theologians, from another influential church tradition, but this time in the north – in Antioch in Syria. The Antiochenes believed that the allegorical approach made nothing more than symbols of every biblical event and character from Adam to Daniel. A typical piece of polemic runs as follows:

> People ask what the difference is between allegorical exegesis and historical exegesis. We reply that it is great and not small; just as the first leads to impiety, blasphemy and falsehood, so the other is conformed to truth and faith. It is the impious Origen of Alexandria who invented this art of allegory ...
>   (quoted in Grant and Tracey, *A Short History of the Interpretation of the Bible*,
>   SCM, rev. ed. 1984, p. 64)

Two supporters in the Antiochene tradition were Theodore of Mopsuestia (c. 350 – c. 428) and John Chrysostom (c. 347 – c. 407). Theodore, Patriarch of Mopsuestia from 392 CE, interpreted the entire Old Testament in a straightforward historical way. For example, the Psalms were psalms of David, not prophecies about a coming Messiah, and the Song of Songs was a collection of love songs from the time of Solomon, not poems about God's love for his people. John

Chrysostom, Patriarch of Constantinople from 398, wrote a work stating that Paul never actually used allegory himself, and almost never even used typology (the Adam/Christ and Abraham/Christ discussions would therefore be exceptions rather than the rule). According to Chrysostom, the coming of Christ cancels the need for too much elaboration of meaning, in the same way that a painting is deemed to have less symbolism when one has encountered the reality of what is painted.

The divide between the Alexandrian School, preferring the hidden meanings in Scripture, and the Antiochene School, preferring more straightforward readings of the same texts, was in danger of polarizing two potentially complementary approaches. What the Jewish tradition gained in holding both the straightforward and the explanatory approaches together in their midrashic interpretation, the Christian apologists seemed to lose. Ironically, it was the Christocentric emphasis in the Christian tradition which pulled the different schools of interpretation apart. Jewish tradition could afford to be more eirenical, because it had a less focused point of contention.

Nevertheless, some Christian writers did try to hold together the best of both theological methods. Many would argue that Origen himself tried to achieve this, in his threefold approach, although others would say that he stressed theological truth as mystery and ambiguity at the expense of a necessary historical medium which could then result in more clarity and simplicity. Setting Origen aside, perhaps the three greatest thinkers who embrace both views, and in so doing contributed to a more balanced reading typical of later Medieval theology, were Jerome, Augustine and Gregory the Great.

Jerome

Jerome (*c.* 342–420), a contemporary of Theodore of Mopsuestia and of John Chrysostom, moved from an allegorizing method to the more literal one. His time in Antioch, and his interest in *Hebraica veritas* – the truth expressed through the Hebrew language and through the history of the Hebrew people – caused him to appreciate more the literal approach to reading biblical texts. Putting the emphasis in a different way than did Origen, according to Jerome the medium for the spiritual was always through the literal. We have already seen the influence of Jerome in his Latin translation of some of the Hebrew Bible, known as the Vulgate. And it was this literal principle which Jerome applied in his translation of the Vulgate. For Jerome, both approaches were important; but the literal came first.

Augustine

Augustine of Hippo (354–430) by contrast, was more influenced than was Jerome by Origen and Philo and the Alexandrian School: his time at the University of Carthage and later in Milan (where he came under the influence of another great allegorical thinker, Bishop Ambrose) furthered his interest in allegorical reading. However, unlike Origen, he saw that a fuller interpretation of Scripture could not rest primarily on allegory. Augustine, following Ambrose here, affirmed the complementariness of the two main theological approaches to the text – the literal/physical/historical and the allegorical/mystical/spiritual. His ʿ main reason for affirming this was in order to propose a viable way of interpreting the Old Testament in the light of the New. Rather like Irenaeus' polemic against the Valentinians, a balanced use of the Old Testament was an essential part of Augustine's defence of Christianity against a heretical group called the Manichees, whose view of the origins of evil from two opposing powers caused them to deny the worth of all the Old Testament (with its monotheistic tendencies) and, for the same reasons, most of the New. Augustine's affirmation of the literal worth of the Old Testament was thus a means whereby it could be preserved in the face of those who dismissed it out of hand.

Gregory the Great

The concern to hold together both the straightforward and the hidden readings of Scripture is also evident in the work of Gregory the Great (540–604). Taking up Origen's view of the three modes of interpretation, while also affirming the more traditional view of the modes of reading as used by Augustine, Gregory adapted and popularized a 'four-sense approach'. Although not necessarily the product of Gregory himself, this is summed up in Latin verse known to be in existence in the sixth century:

> *Littera gesta docet, quid credas allegoria,*
> *Moralis quid agas, quo tendas anagogia.*
> The letter shows us what God and our fathers did;
> The allegory shows us where our faith is hid;
> The moral meaning gives us rules of daily life;
> The analogy shows us where we end our strife.
>   (quoted in Grant and Tracey, *A Short History of the Interpretation of the Bible,*
>   SCM, rev. ed., 1984, p. 85)

The correspondence of this and the much more developed 'four-sense approach' in the medieval Jewish tradition cannot be missed, with the same emphasis on the straightforward meaning, the elaborate meaning, the moral meaning and the mysterious meaning, named here as 'anagogy'. Although this may appear to increase the variety of theological approaches to the text, and thus complicate the issue further, the first and third approaches might be seen to relate to each other, corresponding with the literal (and, in Jewish terms, the halakhic) approach, while the second and fourth relate together and are a part of the interpretative (and, again in Jewish terms, the haggadic) approach. The most important sense is perhaps the fourth; this reflects the concern for ultimate meaning, and the mystery of truth which is hidden with God (also evident in the work of Origen, it may be noted) and hence places allegory in a wider context. The movement towards this analogical sense was a gradual one, finding an increasing number of levels of meaning: first, the more detailed analysis of a text using the *pēsher* approach; second, a search for the hidden meaning in a text; third, the use of typology; fourth, the use of allegory; and then fifth, the use of analogy.

We noted earlier with respect to the Jewish theological tradition that it was in the late medieval period that the mystical reading of Scripture really began to become popular, using a variation of the four-sense approach above. In the earlier part of the medieval period, the mystical and contemplative reading of Scripture became increasingly used in the Christian tradition. The monastic tradition had a good deal of influence in this respect. *Lectio divina* was the term used for meditating on Scripture in a more spiritual, prayerful sense. John Cassian (*c.* 360–435) was one of the first monks to teach the reading of Scripture in this way; Benedict of Nursia (*c.* 480 – *c.* 550) drew from this teaching for the Benedictine Rule. Similarly Cassiodorus (*c.* 485–580), a Roman writer and a monk, drew from this same tradition, writing a commentary on the Psalms which used a literal reading, with its emphasis on matters grammatical and textual, but which focused especially on the spiritual meaning, by using the poetry to search out hidden meanings and relate them to Christian beliefs. A further example of someone who used Scripture in this prayerful, meditative and spiritual way was Bede (623–735) who used several of his old English translations of the Bible as a vehicle for this approach.

Up to the time of the Middle Ages, it would therefore appear that any sort of theological reading of Scripture was undertaken in an attitude of belief, whether for the purpose of private meditation or the public defence of faith. We termed this approach earlier a 'confessional stance', and noted how very different this can be from the more open-ended, critical and analytical approach required for undertaking biblical studies as an academic discipline today. Yet, when looking back at the influence of the synagogue and the church in Jewish and Christian study of the Bible even up to the Middle Ages, we must be careful that all we see is the influence of religious experience and liturgy. Important as this confessional context may be (and the purpose of this book is not to denigrate this as such, but rather to concentrate on a more academic view of the Bible), even from the very first use of theological approaches, from the New Testament onwards, this faith-centred approach was nevertheless also dependent upon the culture around it. Greek philosophy, for example, played an enormous influence indirectly in the popularizing of the typological and allegorical approaches.

Aquinas

Graeco-Roman philosophy certainly played a very large part in the further formation of the four-sense approach to Scripture in the later Middle Ages. It is not surprising, therefore, that a more rationalistic and less faith-orientated view of Scripture gradually began to emerge, alongside the more prayerful and contemplative use of the texts. In no small way this was due to the influence of scholastic writers such as Thomas Aquinas (*c.* 1225–74), who, in addition to his philosophical works, wrote commentaries on the Gospels and Epistles and on Isaiah, Jeremiah, the Psalms and Job, emphasizing the distinctive activities of reason and faith. By this time, the fourfold approach was capable of being used as a technique whereby the reader was able to have some objective means of interpreting Scripture; faith came through the rational process of understanding the text.

One could argue that this was in fact the beginning of study of the Bible in terms of academic discipline. It is certainly the case that, although study was still at this time undertaken within communities of faith, reason was beginning to inspire that faith and, given that the source of that reason was inspired as much by secular culture as it was by belief, a faith-inspired, faith-orientated view of the Bible was no longer the only way to read it. There was an alternative approach. The reality of this gradual shift in terms of the study of Scripture took some time before it was fully recognized. One could argue that it was not made explicit until after the time of the Reformation, although the real recognition of some separation between academic study and devotional study of the Bible did not come about until the nineteenth and twentieth centuries. Nevertheless, it is important to note that it was in the medieval period that the seeds of separation between the faith and reason began to take root.

Although the earlier Reformation theologians wrote important works in matters of doctrine, their use of Scripture has little variation from the methods we have already outlined above. Bible translators such as Wycliffe and Tyndale, with their emphasis on philology and textual analysis, demonstrated the value of the literal approach in practice. The Christological concerns of Luther and Calvin necessitated an emphasis on the typological approach, whereby the Old Testament could be used to bear witness to its completion in Christ. The New Testament writers, especially Paul, were taken up as important examples whose own defence of the gospel legitimized a more interpretative approach. But overall Luther and Calvin resisted the extensive use of allegory, and preferred as far as was possible to use *sola Scriptura* ('Scripture alone') in its most straightforward and direct form of appeal.

Richard Hooker

Richard Hooker (1554–1600) was among the first in England to write about the use of reason in the interpretation of Scripture. In his five-volume *Treatise on the Laws of Ecclesiastical Polity*, he distinguished between three different resources – 'what Scripture doth plainly deliver'; 'what any man can necessarily conclude by force of Reason'; and 'after these, the voice of the church succeedeth'. In this, Hooker was doing little more than develop the implications of first, the more rationalistic legacy of medieval exegetes such as Aquinas; second, the emphasis on the faith of the Church and the authority of the traditions of the fathers of the church, made at the Council of Trent; and third, the emphasis on 'Scripture alone' advocated by Reformation theologians. Hooker was opposed to the pietistic view of Scripture which saw it as a code of rules (exemplified, for instance, in the teaching of the Puritans, which Hooker mistrusted). He preferred instead to see matters of natural justice and commonsense morality as the medium through which Scripture could address his own day. This resulted in a much more reasonable, rationalistic understanding of Scripture – neither specifically literal, nor allegorical – and so paved the way for the independent use of reason and analysis in approaching a biblical text.

Seventeenth-century Approaches

From this time onwards, the new confidence in reason, fired further by the spirit of the Enlightenment, resulted in a renewed appreciation of autonymous reason in informing faith. Key seventeenth-century figures who implicitly contributed further to the understanding of the Bible in this way include Thomas Hobbes (1588–1679), whose publication of *Leviathan* in 1651 showed how the Bible could be used not so much as a mode of inspiration but rather as a vehicle for political philosophy; Baruch Spinoza (1632–77), a Dutch Jewish philosopher who, enquiring whether the Bible and philosophy were compatible, concluded that the Bible was in no way able to answer any of the questions set up by philosophy, and hence by implication placed rational belief outside the sphere of Scripture; R. Simon (1638–1712), a French priest, who was one of the first to write denying Moses as the author of the Pentateuch, and thus encouraged critical and rational enquiry into the Bible.

Eighteenth-century Approaches

Among the important eighteenth-century figures who influenced a more critical approach to the Bible are David Hume (1711–76), who questioned whether one could still believe in miracles and the supernaturalistic world which presupposed them, in the way they had been taught by the Church from the Bible; Immanuel Kant (1724–1804) who advocated a self-sufficiency in matters of commonsense morality rather than any subjection to the imposed ethical teaching of the Bible through the Church; and Georg Hegel (1770–1831) who taught that the history of the Bible was but a small part of the history of world affairs, thus questioning the sense of Israel's pride in her special election and special protection. By the end of the eighteenth century, a most significant German theologian, Friedrich Schleiermacher (1768–1834) could advocate interpreting the Bible in the same way as one would any other book, and thus the specially privileged hold which religious tradition had had on its sacred text was severed still further. From this period onwards, biblical study was not only a discourse from the Church and to the Church; the growing concern for the place of reasonable analysis and the importance of critical detachment marked the real beginnings of the approach to biblical studies as an academic discipline.

Obviously, the more confessional way of reading the text 'from faith and for faith' continued in Church and monastic circles. The mystical and contemplative traditions were particularly important towards the end of the nineteenth century, when there was a resurgence in the monastic movements. Yet at the same time, throughout the nineteenth century, the more critical and rational theological study of the Bible continued apace.

Karl Barth

It is interesting to see that even within these last two decades of this twentieth century, both approaches continue to make their own claims on the study of the Bible. Of those who believe that any theological approach to the Bible is primarily 'confessional', in that it relates to questions of faith and of belief, and so can only be properly undertaken in the context of a religious tradition (for this is the only context which can be properly sympathetic to the religious traditions which have brought about the gradual growth of the biblical text) a key exponent is F. Watson, most recently in *Text, Church and Word* (1994). In the other category are those who, without denying the validity of Watson's arguments for those who have a believing faith, would defend as primary a rigorous intellectual study of the Bible, whereby the legitimacy of a theological assessment takes place within an academic institution. This, they would argue, is a necessary setting for gaining independence from the constraints which are imposed by a confessing community. On this side of the divide are R. P. Carroll and A. G. Hunter, in *Words at Work* (1995) and P. R. Davies, in *Whose Bible Is It Anyway?* (1995).

Yet from the time of Schleiermacher in the early nineteenth century up till the publications of the above works, the separation of academic theology from its earlier confessional base has by no means been clear-cut. One of the most difficult issues has been the value different theologians give to other academic disciplines which shed light on the study of the Bible – for example, archaeology, social sciences, anthropology, comparative religions, psychoanalytical studies and philosophy of language. Some would see that such approaches collectively undermine the cause of faith, by making the reader more dependent on the tools of reading than on the text itself. A typical example of this is the work of Karl Barth (1886–1968), who stressed that the Bible was first and foremost the Word of God which was communicated to us through the words of men. Foreshadowing many of the writers of the biblical theology movement, Barth defended the Bible's message as a coherent whole which centres on God's final word to us in Christ. Because of this, Barth argues, the theological truth of the Bible concerns first and foremost God's thoughts about us and not our thoughts about God. Hence for Barth, the Bible is unique, the confessional approach is primary, and philosophical and historical aids to understanding compromise the true and direct spiritual communication God sets before us. Whether this approach might be called pre-critical or post-critical is a moot point, but it is clear that Barth could not follow those for whom reading the Bible was essentially an academic process.

Rudolf Bultmann

In contrast to Barth, other writers welcomed the use of other disciplines (very much along the same lines that the early Church in Alexandria embraced the Hellenistic philosophy of its day), recognizing that an interdisciplinary approach not only enables us to read the Bible in the way we do any other text but also offers new ways for enabling us to understand its message and purpose a good deal better. Perhaps the best example of this position is the German scholar Rudolf Bultmann (1884–1976), who was committed to understanding the historical growth of the text, although at the same time he was highly sceptical about what could be known in detail about it. For example, Bultmann stressed it was important to know *that* (German: *daß*) Jesus had lived on earth, but he also stressed it was impossible to know a good deal of *what* (German: *was*) he actually said and did from some two thousand years' distance. This sort of agnosticism at one time encouraged Bultmann to adopt a position more like Barth's: that to understand the Bible as the Word of God was more a helpful way of circumventing the uncertainties.

In his later days, Bultmann compromised this Barthian position by turning to the existential philosophy of the German thinker, Martin Heidegger. Through this Bultmann thought he could understand the text better, because it was easier to find a tool for understanding by starting with human existence (which we all know a good deal about anyway) rather than starting, as did Barth, with divine existence (which will always be a mystery and so will always evade us). In Chapter 2, where we looked at New Testament theology, we assessed the ways in which this philosophical method and an experienced-based approach became too much of a system imposed upon the text rather than emerging from it, so in its own way this was as restrictive a method of reading as was Barth's God-centred approach. But nevertheless, Bultmann's approach was very much an influence on later thinkers and on biblical scholars who were concerned about biblical hermeneutics as an academic discipline.

Biblical Hermeneutics

The term 'biblical hermeneutics' usually implies the use of an open-ended approach, undertaking theological study of the Bible without assuming any believing, faith-centred concerns. This is not to say that biblical hermeneutics denies a faith-centred approach. It is simply that a faith-centred approach is seen as only one way of reading among many; it certainly does not mean that this is the only way of reading the Bible. In this way, contemporary biblical hermeneutics has several correspondences with the more rationalistic approach we noted earlier with respect to the Middle Ages; but it is also quite different from it, in that it no longer necessarily works from the Church, or for the Church, in its theological task. The academic community is the central focus for its interpretation. Three examples of proponents of this sort of hermeneutical approach to the Bible will suffice.

H.-G. Gadamer, born in Germany at the beginning of this century, defended the need for a culture-orientated reading of the text. This challenged the reader to recognize not only the critical differences between the worlds of the writers and the worlds of the readers, but also to appreciate what may be held in common between the two worlds in spite of the differences. This sense of a critical historical awareness of the text had a good deal in common with Bultmann's approach, and also indirectly supported a literal, straightforward way of reading the Bible.

P. Ricoeur, born in 1913 in France, used the same culture-centred approach, and noted in addition the need for a 'pre-understanding' of the text – a term also used by Bultmann. This pre-understanding, for Ricoeur, is not only about trying to gain some awareness of the history of the text, but also involves an awareness of the language in which the text is communicated. In this way this allows some sort of discourse between the text and the reader. However, it is not necessarily a text-affirming process, for the discourse sometimes results in what might be called a 'hermeneutics of suspicion' on the part of the reader, who may eventually have to recognize a dissonance and distance between themself and the text.

Another German, J. Habermas (b. 1929), works on two levels. The first is a critical recognition of the particular social system in which the text has taken shape (somewhat like Gadamer in his historical approach), while the other level concerns what might be called a 'transcendental framework of reference'. Seeking for continuity where Ricoeur noticed dissonace, this framework (which may be ethical, or experiential) is a vital means by which a text can be understood and used *beyond* its own social system, as well as within it.

Broadly speaking, Gadamer uses a critical historical approach as the main resource for his theological method; Ricoeur uses a more linguistic approach; and Habermas more that of the social sciences. One might argue that these represent just three of the modern-day equivalents of the 'four-sense approach' of the Middle Ages. Reading the texts theologically, then as now, certainly requires a multi-disciplinary approach, and the use of reason is as important a tool as the recourse to faith. There are of course many other approaches which illustrate even more what is happening in biblical hermeneutics in this century: R. Morgan and J. Barton look at other examples in the final two chapters of their book, *Biblical Interpretation.*

In addition to the examples of scholarly exegetes referred to above, another mode of reading requires some attention, in part because it is very recent (much of its popular development can be traced to the early 1970s) and in part because it is a very specific response to present-day cultural issues, and hence illustrates the increased split between a more confessional study of the Bible (which is done essentially for the Church and within the Church), and theological study which is done for secular culture and within secular culture. The broad term for this sort of theology might be 'praxis', and it falls into several different concerns. On the one hand this includes the complex debate about the use of the Bible in ethics, whether with respect to the larger sphere of international politics, warfare and ecology, or to the more personal familial sphere of divorce, abortion and euthanasia. Another entirely different approach (yet related on account of its pragmatic concerns) is a reading of the Bible using a psychoanalytical approach: the poetic passages (not least the Psalms and prophets) are most apposite in this respect. Yet another related approach is that of using the Bible with the help of the social sciences – the narratives being particularly useful in this respect.

To illustrate some of the issues which are involved, and not least how these issues also make use of the more recent literary approaches to the Bible, two other examples of theology from praxis will be discussed in some detail. These have been selected because they relate to two very particular issues, namely gender and social class. They are particularly useful because they appropriate a good deal of the biblical hermeneutical material referred to above, but yet at the same time use a number of the literary approaches to be discussed in the following chapter. Furthermore, both examples offer various insights concerning two complementary ways of reading the text. On the one hand, they both engage critically with a selected text, using the 'hermeneutics of suspicion' approach, being critical to the presuppositions and ideologies of the writers. Yet on the other hand, both are also concerned about using a 'transcendental framework of reference', whereby a text is seen to have some continuity between the past and present, and so is capable of addressing the issues with which they are concerned. These two examples of theology from praxis have been termed 'liberation theology' and 'feminist theology'.

LIBERATION THEOLOGY

In liberation theology in particular, the 'transcendental framework' which gives the Bible any relevance at all today is the theme of justice and of righteousness which could be said to run right through Scripture; and the cultural context which gives this theology its cutting edge is the impoverished communities in the Third World (particularly in Asia and in Latin America) and depressed urban communities in the First World. Hence whatever use the Bible may be in these settings, it is clearly more to do with the praxis than the theory. It is about changing the way people act as much as the way they think; and in this way liberation theology in particular is quite different, in its stress on praxis, from the other theories of using the Bible which were looked at earlier.

Furthermore, because of its practical nature, it involves the use of the Bible from within the Jewish tradition as well as the Christian one. Indeed, a good deal of the material used in liberation theology is from the stories in Exodus of the escape from Egypt, or from concern for justice in the teaching of the prophets and of Jesus himself. And because it is about the importance of faith as well as about the importance of the eradication of the unjust structures in society, it is one of the few examples of a theological approach to the Bible which often works creatively and constructively at attempting to integrate confessional theology on the one hand with political and social concerns on the other. Liberation theology has as its ultimate concern the well-being of the poor; hence its use of the Bible. Especially because the biblical tradition has itself clearly emanated from those in positions of power (kings, priests, prophets, scribes, church leaders), modern biblical theology has to be as critical of the ideologies found within the biblical texts as it has to be of the ideologies expressed in the unjust and oppressive societies of our own day. In this respect, liberation theology is a multifaceted discipline, which works both within the Church and outside it, both with the Bible and against it. Some of its proponents offer most important insights about what it means to 'do' theology today and to 'use' the Bible as they do so. C. Rowland and M. Corner state the issues as follows:

> When we use the Bible in wrestling with the contemporary problems of Christian discipleship we find that our exegetical efforts frequently have not been matched with the skills necessary for the provision of illumination from the Bible on the exploration of those questions which our generation is asking ... The reconstruction of that past world in which the texts originated can therefore enable the contemporary reader to view present prejudices in a fresh light ... What such biblical interpretation dramatically reminds us is ... there must be a continuous dialogue between that present

story told by the poor of oppression and injustice, and the ancient stories they read in the Bible. Indeed, the knowledge of the past story is an important antidote to the kind of unrestrained fantasy which then binds the text as firmly to the world of the immediate present and its context in the same way that the historical-critical exegesis bound it to the ancient world ...

(*Liberating Exegesis: The Challenge of Liberation Theology to Biblical Studies*, SPCK, 1990, pp. 35, 37, 40–1)

It is interesting to note that these authors affirm that good reading is essentially about the staightforward, direct and the practical way of approaching the text. Overall, the liberation approach is less concerned with theoretical allegorizing of Scripture, and more concerned with the praxis of how a text, properly understood, can be used in the life of the community of the poor today.

FEMINIST THEOLOGY

Feminist theology is closely related in some of its concerns and methods to liberation theology. Feminist writers have been similarly concerned about the issue of oppression, not so much in terms of social status as in terms of gender, although, unlike liberation theologians, most feminist theologians write for themselves, rather than in defence of others who are often less equipped to write for themselves. But in terms both of offering a strong critique of the patriarchal ideologies of the biblical writers and of responding to a present-day cultural issue, feminist theology – like liberation theology – has to face the twin task of working between the world of the Bible and the world in which we live. It is, therefore, another example of hermeneutics in practice. Like liberation theology, it has a role in both Jewish and Christian traditions, for patriarchal elements pervade both collections of Scripture.

Also like liberation theology, feminist theology works both within the Church, yet also very much outside it. Being essentially another voice of protest (expressed by different writers in different degrees), it studies the biblical texts with the same 'hermeneutics of suspicion'. Phyllis Trible, writing in the late 1980s, describes the relationship between 'feminist hermeneutics' and biblical studies as follows:

Born and bred in a land of patriarchy, the Bible abounds in male imagery and language. For centuries interpreters have explored and exploited this male language to articulate theology: to shape the contours and content of the Church, synagogue and academy; and to instruct human beings – male and female – in who they are, what rules they should play, and how they should behave. So harmonious has seemed this association of Scripture with sexism, of faith with culture, that only a few have even questioned it.

Within the past decade, however, challenges have come in the name of feminism, and they refuse to go away. As a critique of culture in light of misogyny, feminism is a prophetic movement, examining the status quo, pronouncing judgement and calling for repentance. In various ways this hermeneutical pursuit interacts with the Bible in its remoteness, complexity, diversity and contemporaneity to yield new understandings of both text and interpreter.

... Thereby understanding of the past increases and deepens as it informs the present.

(from 'Feminist Hermeneutics and Biblical Studies', in A. Loades (ed.), *Feminist Theology: A Reader*, SPCK, 1993, pp. 23–9)

Again we may note the interest in the history of the text and on the practical consequences for our understanding of that history (often in a negative sense) within modern culture. Like liberation theology, the reading is little concerned with the allegorical and analogical methods of reading, for these presume too much continuity between the text and the reader. Feminist theology, like liberation theology, is essentially a theology of protest against the accepted values of the status quo, both within biblical culture and within our own.

There are, of course, different shades of this theology of protest. At one end of the spectrum are feminist theologians who take a more cautious revisionist approach, wishing to clear the text of some of its irregularities, and to go for the deeper meanings within the texts (that 'transcendental framework of reference') which avoids too much polarization of gender opposites; while at the other end are those who have rejected the coherence of a biblical faith altogether, on account of its irredeemable patriarchy, not only because of the male-centred structures of faith but also because of its interpretation of the character of 'God'. Examples of the various revisionist approaches include popular feminist writers such as P. Trible and A. Loades, as well as E. Moltmann-Wendel, M. Bal, A. Laffey, L. Russell, R. Radford Ruether, P. Bird, A. Brenner, E. Schüssler Fiorenza, C. Exum and C. Meyers; examples from their works are to be found in the Bibliography at the end of this book. By contrast, the works by M. Daly and D. Hampson suggest a more rejectionist approach to biblical culture.

Within this spectrum, it is interesting to note that the different methods of reading the biblical texts put forward by feminist theologians illustrate accumulatively the need for a pluralistic approach in the theological debate about using the Bible. Furthermore, the feminist debate as a whole is a very useful illustration of just how far theological study of the Bible has developed – from the early Church up to the Middle Ages, and from the Middle Ages up to the present day, with

142

its greater emphasis on the importance of present-day culture in determining approaches to biblical study, and hence its greater stress on the secular community as well as the confessional community in determining the rules of the game.

Conclusions and Implications

This discussion on the theological approaches to the Bible has covered a wide range of concerns, and has moved a long way from noting the initial stages of theological reflection on Scripture which took place within a closed circle of faith, to these latter stages of theological reflection whereby the community of faith is by no means the only context in which to read the Bible theologically. This is not to say that the context of faith and belief is to be rejected; quite the opposite. It is vital, particularly if a pluralistic approach is to apply. Indeed, throughout the history of interpretation, prayerful and contemplative approaches to studying the Bible have in many ways contributed to the survival of the Bible as a constant spiritual resource throughout a time of change, and illustrate well the importance of continuity as well as discontinuity between the world of the reader and the world of the Bible.

But times *have* changed, and other approaches are fitting as well; and academic study is a vital means of ensuring the survival of the use of the Bible in another way. Again, theological pluralism holds the key. There is too much to be gained from the main different approaches to reading the Bible theologically to allow for the primacy of one mode of reading above any other. And it is the same pluralism which holds the key to the more recent historical and literary ways of reading Scripture, as will be demonstrated in the following chapters.

6

Historical Approaches to the Bible

Our previous survey of the theological approaches to the Bible has already indicated just how much historical issues are tied up with theological ones. One could argue that the 'literal' reading, described in the previous chapter, with its emphasis on the direct, straightforward reading of the text (and hence setting itself against any superimposed allegorical meaning), is an early example of reading with a historical bias. Certainly by the time of the Middle Ages, when the 'four-senses' approaches prevailed, the concerns of the 'literal' approach are quite close to the 'historical' approach; both emphasize the straightforward meaning of the text *as it was*. This compares with the three other approaches – the moral, allegorical and analogical readings – which all include a more interpretative theological element.

When (at about the time of the Enlightenment) rational study was an important means of understanding the biblical text, it became far more questionable as to whether one could in fact read the text 'as it was'. Our last section drew attention to seventeenth- and eighteenth-century Enlightenment thinkers such as Hooker, and Hobbes, Spinoza, Simon, Hume, Kant, Hegel and Schleiermacher. These were significant influences on the way that study of Scripture was seen as an entirely rational enterprise, when the text came to be examined in the same way as one would examine any other text. This in turn had critical implications on a historical reading of the Bible.

As well as the thinkers and commentators listed above, three other eighteenth-century thinkers are most important in the ways in which they too influenced historical approaches in biblical studies. G. F. Lessing (1729–81) made a critical assessment of the Gospel-writers as historians rather than as theologians – and was thus duly disappointed with them. J. von Herder (1744–1803) read the Bible from what became known as a 'psychology of nations' approach, whereby each nation – Israel included – was seen to possess its own distinctive characteristics (evident as much in its poetry as in its stories). According to

144

von Herder, the study of biblical literature required a sensitivity to those 'national' settings which had inspired them, and so one needed to view the literature from the point of view of the ancient 'historical' awareness which had given rise to them. J. G. Eichhorn (1752–1827) was an early influence on that later group of writers called the 'History of Religions School', who believed that to a great extent other ancient religions had informed the world of the biblical writers. Eichhorn's views about the borrowing of ancient myths in these biblical stories foreshadowed the work of several later biblical scholars.

Although each of these three scholars had a very different view of the history of the Bible, they each cohered in that they began and ended their own observations with the view that it is impossible to read these texts with the historiographic assumptions of our *own* age.

Different Historical Approaches

In the early part of the nineteenth century, and especially in Germany, the rational study of Scripture was encouraged by the introduction of theology as part of the syllabus in (secular) universities. As may be evident from our above discussion, with reference to the debate in the previous century, this had two entirely different consequences as far as the historical method was concerned.

On the one hand, and somewhat paradoxically, such a secular and academic approach resulted in a renewal of confidence in what could be achieved by means of historical criticism. Seeing this as a kind of scientific study of the text, it was deemed possible that modern historiography could gain new insights into the ancient context. And by the end of the nineteenth century, the growth of other related disciplines – for example, the comparative study of the religions and the literature of Akkadia, Egypt, Canaan, Assyria, and Babylon; the new interest in archaeological studies in the land of Palestine; the growing interest in the philology of the Hebrew language and its borrowings from other cultures; and the beginning of studies in the social sciences – all these added fuel to a greater confidence that the historical method could indeed solve some of the enigmas of the past, if only by building up a broad historical framework in which the biblical works were seen to be a typical part.

But, on the other hand, there was also the inevitable ongoing scepticism about what could really be achieved by the sort of historical enterprise outlined above. As far as the study of the Bible was concerned, this spilled over into at least five problematical areas. We shall assess each of these in turn.

The Problem of Myth

One particular problem was raised by a new awareness of the biblical writers' adaptation of myth. This began with the assumption, like that of Herder and of Eichhorn expressed somewhat earlier, that our understanding of history, and with this our use of the historical method, were so at variance with ancient times that there was a danger of recreating biblical history in our own image. The findings in the studies of comparative religions (and the rise of the History of Religions School) did little to silence this view. It became clear, for example, that the ancient mind freely expressed itself in mythical categories, whereby great stories of myths were played out in the rituals at various festivals in different cultic sanctuaries, and these were eventually transmitted into the biblical literature. This in turn created a good deal of scepticism in viewing the stories of the Bible as 'historical' in any way at all.

Through comparative studies of the nineteenth century, it became apparent that not only did the Israelites borrow a good deal of mythical material from their neighbours, in order to describe the activity of their God working in history, but also that this mythical material was especially evident in the more liturgical books, of which the Psalms are the best example. For instance, in the Psalms we find myths about God presiding over a heavenly council with other deities (e.g. Psalm 82), myths about God being a heavenly warrior fighting a battle in heaven above for his people below (e.g. Psalms 93 and 96), myths about God dwelling on a holy mountain called Zion (e.g. Psalms 46 and 48) and myths about God fighting and slaying a sea-monster typifying chaos (e.g. Psalms 74 and 89). This meant that many of the psalms – and along with this, many of the prophets who also adopted a good deal of liturgical material for their own purposes – had to be seen as communicating truths on a mythical rather than on an historical level.

The view that the books of the Bible included a good deal of mythical material did not stop, however, at the Psalms and the prophets. The book of Genesis received this same treatment. One of the greatest contributors in this respect was H. Gunkel, who had been influenced by Eichhorn and had himself been part of the History of Religions School at Göttingen. Although Gunkel wrote first on the importance of understanding the early cultural context of the New Testament, his main area of interest was in Genesis (where he focused especially on the use of Babylonian mythology within the stories of creation and flood in Genesis 1—11), the Psalms (where again he was interested in Babylonian influence, as well as in the importance of mythology in liturgy) and the prophets (which he saw also used references to Babylonian and Canaanite chaos mythology).

One might argue that one could forgive mythical expression in the Old Testament which, the work of a primitive people, would be more likely to use mythical categories of expression. But the idea or the pervasion of myth spread from the Old Testament to the New, not least to the Gospels. A seminal work in this respect was *The Life of Jesus Critically Examined* (1835) by D. F. Strauss from Tübingen. The book acknowledged the success of the historical method in undermining the credibility of the Gospel accounts as historical works (following on from Lessing), and proposed instead a different way of reading the Gospels. They were to be seen as expressions of religious concepts, rather than as records of historical events. Put briefly, Strauss believed that the New Testament is about theology and not about history. Thus the Gospels can best be understood through the category of myth (and one can see here the allegorical interpretation of the Alexandrian School stretched to its limit) which was the vehicle of 'truth' used by the early Christian communities.

Hence, according to Strauss, it is possible to see the virgin birth and incarnation as a type of a 'heavenly redeemer myth' similar to the myths expressed in Greek mystery religions. So too, the death and resurrection stories suggest the same mythical categories of suffering, dying and rising figures which were known to have been popular at that time. Whether one speaks of miracles, or of the birth stories, or of the death and resurrection accounts, everything is part of a mythical story, and so conveys eternal truths relating to an ideal Christ-figure beyond. Strauss acknowledged that the historical Jesus may be a necessary part of the process of understanding such truths; but because our knowledge of the historical Jesus is defective, we have to focus on a far greater theological truth – what Strauss called 'the Christ of faith'. One of the key influences on Strauss was the philosophy of history put forward by Hegel, which developed the idea of an ideal realm of truth over and above the contingencies of human history. For Strauss, that ideal realm of truth was Christ; and the expression of that truth was through the category of myth, of which the stories about Jesus form a critical part.

It is not surprising that Strauss met a good deal of opposition for this view, and was accused of following an early second-century heresy called 'Docetism' (denying that Jesus entered our history in human form, and saying that he only appeared to do so). Strauss' views nevertheless influenced many other New Testament commentators, who were similarly convinced that myth was an important vehicle of truth for the ancient mind, both with regard to the New Testament as well as the Old, and that the biblical writers – including the Gospel-writers –

were little different from the Greeks and Romans in this respect. Two further well-known proponents of this view after Strauss were A. Schweitzer (referred to in Chapter 2, concerning the formation of New Testament theologies) and F. C. Baur (1792–1860). Baur was also at Tübingen, and was also influenced by Hegel. He continued this same idea of the 'Christ of faith' not only with regard to the Gospels but beyond them, within the teaching of both Peter and Paul.

Hence confidence in the value of the historical method was in this way actually undermined by the emphasis that the historical awareness of the biblical writers was not like our own; it resulted in acknowledging that one of the key differences was the ability to convey spiritual truths in mythical categories. In response to this, it could be said that myth certainly was used in the biblical accounts, but the question is whether everything may be described as myth. This 'pan-mythical' view can become as false an estimation of the world-view of the biblical writers as can the 'pan-historical' view. But the positive consequence of writers such as Strauss was a proper caution in assuming that the biblical material could ever be used as a record of historical events for the benefit of the modern-day mind.

The Problem of Contradictions in the Accounts

Any confidence in the assumption that biblical material *is* historically reliable is made no easier by the recognition of the number of contradictions in the biblical accounts. Referring to the Old Testament alone, and beginning, as it were, at the very beginning, even in the first two chapters of the Bible, Genesis 1.1—2.4a and Genesis 2.4b–25, we read of differing ordering of creation. For example, the accounts speak quite clearly of the different ways in which man and woman were created. In the first account, in Genesis 1, 'man' is created as the pinnacle of God's world, in the image of God, after the creation of the natural order and the animal kingdom; and in the second account, in Genesis 2, man is created first out of the dust of the earth, to be followed by the animal kingdom, and then last of all (out of the rib of man) woman is created. And in the flood stories (Genesis 6—9), on the one hand (Genesis 7.1–10; 8.6–14, 20–2) we read of seven pairs of unclean animals and two pairs of clean animals being taken into the ark, and the flood's duration being forty days, before receding after two periods of seven days, while on the other hand, only a few verses later, we read that Noah took only one pair of each animal, and that the flood lasted 150 days, receding in another 150 days (Genesis 6.9–22; 7.11–24; 8.1–5, 15–19; 9.1–17).

It could be argued that because the category of myth rather than history best describes the purposes of chapters such as Genesis 1—11, the evidence of contradictions may say something about the nature of the literature but it says nothing about the nature of history, because the account is not intended to be read that way. However, moving further into the Old Testament story, we come across doublets (correspondences) and repetitions on several different occasions. For example, the Joseph story (Genesis 37) narrates how Joseph was sold first to the Ishmaelites and then to the Midianites and so sold in different ways into slavery in Egypt. Another example is found in the accounts of how the people entered the promised land: Joshua 1—12 speaks of a sudden conquest, and Judges 1.1—2.5 of a difficult and protracted settlement. Or again, in the accounts of Judean kings, figures such as Hezekiah, Manasseh and Josiah are presented in a different light in 2 Kings 18—23, compared with the accounts in 2 Chronicles 29—35.

One might then want to argue that in the Old Testament, the literature is 'different' and the problem matters less. But there are discrepancies in the New Testament as well. For example, although the variations are often subtle and occur for theological purposes, within the four Gospels we read of different accounts of miracles, different records of parables, and different emphases (and often variant chronologies) of the events in the life of Jesus. The most significant by far is the different accounts of the resurrection appearances. Cumulatively, this raises critical questions about the reliability of the history which is being examined.

Most of these contradictions were very much part of the ongoing discussion in the nineteenth century about the role of the historical method. One of the key proponents, J. W. Colenso (1814–83), the first Anglican Bishop of Natal, caused concern when he stated publicly that, particularly on account of the contradictory elements in Genesis, he could not possibly teach his Zulu converts that the Bible was a 'matter-of-fact historical narrative'. Like Strauss, but for different reasons, Colenso's courage to speak openly about his doubts (the seven-volume work, *The Mosaic Authorship of the Pentateuch* was written between 1862 and 1879) created some controversy in England as well as on the Continent. But in many ways, Colenso was right. If we read all the contradictions above as 'matter-of-fact historical narrative', and then see this is a historical narrative which contains mistakes, the historical method flounders. On the other hand, if the examples are not to be read as history – but rather as myth, legend, story – then the historical method no longer applies.

The Problem of Miracles

One of the most significant genres to be reassessed on account of the problems of a historical reading has been the miracle stories, particularly within the Gospels. One of the very earliest commentators to question the miracle accounts was H. S. Reimarus (1694–1768). As a deist, he believed in God, but not in any supernatural explanations for events in the Bible. Reason was paramount, and the idea of any supernatural interference with the world was therefore unacceptable. He argued that Jesus' origins were no different from those of any other great figure in Judaism, and that they did not need to be explained by recourse to the miraculous. Reimarus examined the internal content of the Christian revelation, and found the key tenets which had miraculous overtones (the resurrection, the idea of atonement and the second coming) were all contradicted by the facts of history. Furthermore, on examining the external evidence for the Christian revelation – and here Reimarus always emphasized the necessary medium of history for our understanding of such events – he found wanting any supernatural explanation of the origins and growth of Christianity.

Much of his work corresponds with what his contemporary Hume was also arguing, although in Hume's classical *a priori* and *a posteriori* rejection of miracles, he used more general philosophical arguments than New Testament exegesis. (Here we may see why Strauss tried to find a positive way forward after Reimarus and Hume, by stressing that eternal truths could still be expressed through the content of the Christian message. Ironically, Reimarus took biblical history *too* seriously, whereas Strauss perhaps did not take it seriously enough.)

Hence a real tension emerged between a historical understanding of events and a miraculous explanation of them. And yet again, the problem took on a different significance when it moved out of the Old Testament literature and into the New. For example, it was just about possible to find an explanation for the nature miracles in the Old Testament (for example, the plagues in Egypt, the parting of the Red Sea, the provision of manna and water from the rock, all in Exodus and Numbers); but – for theological reasons brought to the text – it was far more difficult to do this with the nature miracles of the Gospels (for example, the stilling of the storm, the walking on the water, the feeding of the five thousand, the changing of the water into wine, the miraculous catch of fish). Yet, as Reimarus in part implied, could it be that the New Testament miracles were in fact *invented* to add more weight to the idea of a prophecy/fulfilment schema? Were they thus no more than a theological device to show Christ was better than Moses? This sort of questioning shows that the New Testament miracles provide even more problems for the historical approach than do Old Testament ones.

We can develop this in another way. It was possible to question the validity of the more personal miracles in the Old Testament. This could be applied to healing miracles, and to the stories of the raising of the dead (these occur mainly in the stories about the prophet Elijah's powers in 1 Kings 17—19, and the parallel stories about Elisha's powers in 2 Kings 1—6). It also includes the accounts of miraculous escapes (for example, Daniel's escape from the lions' den in Daniel 6). The legendary nature of this material makes such a sceptical approach to the miraculous element quite feasible. But this then raises more critical implications when it comes to other personal miracles in the Gospels and in the Acts of the Apostles (the healings, and the raising of the dead performed by Jesus, and, in the Acts of the Apostles, the miraculous escapes of the apostles from shipwreck and from prison). Does one again see the New Testament miracles as part of a prophecy/fulfilment schema at work? And so must we also conclude that their worth is more theological than historical?

Furthermore, if one is to explain away the miraculous in these stories, one has to be consistent. It is then legitimate to explain away the miraculous elements in the birth and resurrection accounts as well. This is, of course, possible – not least give the absence of a birth narrative in Mark and John, and, as we have already noted, the conflicting reports of the resurrection in all four Gospel accounts – but the consequences for any distinctive, supernatural faith are even more severe with respect to the beginning and end of Jesus' life than with the isolated stories which record events in between. Either the stories offer some way of preparing us for the greater miracle, and so they all need to be viewed in the same light; or the stories show us the impossibility of assenting to any supernatural explanation, and so the whole realm of the miraculous disappears altogether, and one resorts to the Strauss-like explanation of myth throughout the entire Gospel story. Once one has become overly critical about the use of miracle in relation to the life of Jesus, the consequences are that the figure of Jesus becomes increasingly different from the way the accounts portray him, as the rigorous use of the historical method erodes the miraculous details, one by one.

The Problem of Religious Language

One other issue which has been influential in a critical and cautious view about the historical nature of the biblical accounts – Old and

New – has been a new understanding about the nature of religious language. Much of Scripture is couched in different kinds of religious language, and the recognition of the kind of language which is being used (for instance, whether it is descriptive or prescriptive) can often suggest whether the material in which it occurs is to be understood historically or not. Given that, by its definition, religious language has a reference point beyond this world order alone (insofar as it is trying to mediate not only earthly realities but also a transcendental reality) then, in many instances, it may be best to assign some biblical texts which use this language with particular intensity (for example, in the apocalyptic imagery used in the Gospels and in Revelation) into a category which goes well beyond history. We are brought back again to some form of mythical explanation, in that this can indeed be an important vehicle for religious insights.

However, as well as myth, the use of metaphor can be equally important in this respect. As a figure of speech, in religious language it is often used to describe a reality or truth which is non-literal, spiritual and transcendental by means of using in part language which is literal, physical and material. A good deal of work on the use of metaphor has been done in more recent literary critical studies, particularly with respect to the New Testament. (N. Perrin's study of the metaphorical language of the kingdom of God is a case in point, but at this stage we are trying to assess the importance of religious language as it affects our understanding of a work being 'historical'.) For example, when one takes well-known biblical descriptions of Christ, such as the Lamb of God, the Prince of Peace, the Living Water, the Alpha and Omega, the King of Kings, and the Wisdom of God, it is quite obvious that they are metaphors, used to convey a religious and spiritual insight beyond that which is literal and historical.

Biblical material abounds in metaphorical expressions, and cumulatively they reveal that a vast proportion of the biblical material is more about theology than it is about history. Yet one could take this argument further still. For, as well as referring to titles for Jesus Christ (and the list above was only a brief selection) what is to prevent us from reading the narrative accounts in a metaphorical way as well? This takes us close to the mythical approach to the text, or, at the very least, to the allegorical way of reading which was popular in the Middle Ages. But, in terms of metaphor, it is quite possible to take a 'metaphorical interpretation' from the story of the expulsion of Adam and Eve from the Garden of Eden in Genesis 3; or similarly from Jacob's fight with the angel in Genesis 28; or again from the call of Moses by the burning bush in Exodus 3; or from the account of Daniel's friends in the fiery furnace in Daniel 3. These are all ways of conveying hidden spiritual truths through a story form. They are not history, nor even myth, but – and here the emphasis is undoubtedly on what hidden truths we can learn from the stories – rather, they serve as metaphors pointing to a reality beyond the historical. Such an interpretation may well undermine a historical reading yet further, but it at least provides us with an alternative theological meaning. This is, of course, what Strauss was saying; by referring in his case to the use of myth rather than the use of metaphor, he showed how the theological meaning is far more important than the historical fact.

And what if, following Strauss with his use of myth, the range of metaphor is carried over to the New Testament stories? The account of the temptations, the baptism, the transfiguration, the ascension and the account of Christ coming again could all be seen as a way of using literal and physical pictures to depict spiritual and transcendental truths. The issue here is that metaphor is even more of a slippery term than myth. Categories of myth can at least be given some form of classification which relates them back to the cultures from which they may have borrowed their ideas, but the appropriation of a metaphorical reading can be so ambiguous that it becomes difficult to know whether there is anything more than just story and meaning, and no history and fact. When texts are read in this sort of way, metaphor creates another problem for the historical method. In brief, if one is to accept metaphorical readings of the poetry of the psalms, and the prophets, and in apocalyptic literature, then one has to ask why one does not do so with the narrative accounts as well; and if one does so, any 'historical' reading of these texts is deemed to be redundant.

The Problem of the Historical Jesus

It is small wonder that, throughout the latter part of last century and in a good part of this, questions have arisen repeatedly about how much we really can know about the historical Jesus. On the one hand, one could take the Reimarus line, and by rigorous use of the historical method, see Jesus as no different from any other Palestinian Jew of his day. Or, on the other hand, one could follow Strauss, and by circumventing the historical method, declare that the real truth of the Christian message did not hinge on a historical Jesus at all, but on the Christ of faith – an ideal figure known only through the preaching of the Church. The 'quest for the historical Jesus', as it has been known, has broadly followed one of these two lines.

On one side of the divide have been those who have focused on the Jesus of history, in spite of the increasing lack of confidence that we could actually know much about him. This has been very much part of a German debate, and has included scholars such as A. Ritschl (1822–89), W. Wrede (1859–1906), W. Bousset (1865–1920) and J. Weiss (1863–1914), all of whom had some associations with the history of religions school, and in different ways stressed the moral and pragmatic side of Jesus' message, seeking to understand the Jesus of history by way of reference to Jewish ideas and Jewish religion of his time.

On the other side of the divide have been those who have emphasized most the Christ of faith: among these we find, following Strauss, F. C. Baur (1792–1860), A. von Harnack (1851–1930), M. Kähler (1835–1912) and W. Herrman (1846–1922), who in different ways, stressed the importance of *meaning* in history (the *Geschichte*, or 'story') rather than the importance of knowing the brute facts themselves (the *Historie*). These writers have emphasized the importance of faith found not so much in the facts of the Gospel story as in the meaning of the Christian message, expressed through the preaching of the Church. This emphasis on 'knowing Christ through proclamation' has become known as kerygmatic theology (from the Greek *kerygma*, meaning 'proclamation', and from this, 'preaching'). It was one of the key tenets in Bultmann's theology in this century. Bultmann, like Strauss and company, circumvented the problem of mythical categories and historical difficulties by emphasizing instead the Christ of faith who could be encountered through the preaching of the Church, even though he could not be found from the processes of history.

Against this backcloth, it is now possible to see in a different light the emphasis on 'the activity of God in the history of his people' which we noted to be the watchwords for the biblical theology movement referred to in Chapter 2. By advocating that the key uniting theme around which biblical theology coheres is its view of God acting uniquely in human history, we may now see how precarious this was, and how it was a view which was swimming against the tide of its day. Eichrodt, von Rad and Wright were among the chief exponents to whom we referred in our discussion of Old Testament theologies, and Cullmann, Richardson, Hunter and Jeremias in our discussion of New Testament theologies. Being confident of what could in fact be known about the history of the Bible, and rejecting the observations of historical critics, many of these writers then staked their theology on dubious historical claims.

The works of these writers were published in the early and middle parts of this century, as changes were taking place in biblical scholarship. But then the tide which had brought in an increased scepticism regarding what could be known about the historical Jesus began to turn, initially in Germany, beginning in the 1950s. In part this was an anxiety that if one so divorced the Jesus of history from the Christ of faith, one would be left with little more than a Docetic heresy – a detached spiritual Christ-idea – for our own time. Hence there was a good deal of continuity between the concerns of those involved in the 'New Quest for the Historical Jesus' (as it became known) and those who, in the 'Old Quest', sought to understand the historical Jesus in his own time, whether through the lens of Judaism or through Graeco-Roman religion.

The New Quest resulted in a renewed interest in studies of the Jewish Law – for example, the extent to which Jesus could be seen as a kind of Jewish rabbi, closer to the Pharisees than had once been thought, but giving the Law new meaning. New work was done on Jewish apocalyptic thinking at the time of Jesus, again to show that Jesus was closer than had been thought to the Judaism of his day, and that he was simply giving it new meaning. Similarly, the titles used for Jesus were looked at in a new light – not so much as metaphors as to ascertain what insights this might offer in the Gospels' interpretations of how Jesus saw himself in relation to God, and how this too fitted with the Jewish ideas about God in his day. E. P. Sanders, in his *Jesus and Judaism,* is representative of these concerns in the English-speaking world by the late 1970s.

Another aspect of the New Quest was its attempt to get behind the kerygmatic preaching of the Church communities, in order to place more emphasis on the Jesus (Jewish) history than on the proclaimed faith of the (Christian) Church. The key proponents included were E. Käsemann (b. 1906, *Commentary on Romans*), G. Bornkamm (b. 1905, *What Can We Know about Jesus?*), J. Jeremias (1900–79, *The Parables of Jesus*), E. Fuchs (1903–83, *Studies of the Historical Jesus*), G. Ebeling (b. 1912, *The Nature of Faith*); from America, N. Perrin (1921–76, *Rediscovering the Teaching of Jesus*) and J. M. Robinson (b. 1924, who was responsible for the publication of the Nag Hammadi Library); and somewhat later, from the UK, J. A. T. Robinson (1919–83, *The Priority of John*). Most of these scholars wrote commentaries on New Testament texts to set out their theories in the practice of reading.

The New Quest had its problems, and in many ways they were the same as those of almost a century earlier, for the proponents tried yet again to use more modern aids to enrich an understanding of the biblical background. By focusing so much on the *human* Jesus, for the history of his own day, it became difficult to understand how and why any kerygma should evolve in relation to such an ordinary Jewish figure. In other words, the human and earthy interpretation of the Jesus of history created as many problems in achieving a full explanation of the Gospel accounts as did the over-ethereal and abstract interpretation of the Christ of faith.

This New Quest has resulted in one particularly interesting offshoot, from a movement which started in the 1980s. Known as the 'Jesus Seminar', the participants in this movement realized the implications of the New Quest. They observed how it is possible to focus on the historical Jesus and to find little more than a revolutionary peasant, resisting Roman occupation; or a Jewish cynic, subverting traditional Jewish wisdom; or perhaps instead a simple Galilean preacher of justice. Given these particularly human interpretations, some seventy-five academics, centred mainly in California, attempted to take this further. Their founders include J. D. Crossan and R. Funk (who himself was once part of the 'New Questers'), and their goal has been to establish more clearly and conclusively this 'historical Jesus' by means of dividing up the Gospel material into authentic and inauthentic passages. The problem has been that, in aiming to mark out the uncontroversial units, one is left with the lowest common ruling by the group at large. The project thus becomes, rather like that of Reimarus, historically orientated, but increasingly reductivist. The results which were published in the early 1990s on the sayings of Jesus, which were termed the 'fifth Gospel', included one verse from Mark, nothing from John, and less than 20 per cent of Matthew and Luke. The Lord's Prayer, the sayings from the cross and the claims of Jesus to divinity were not included. The group as a whole shows again the problem which emerges when one takes the historical Jesus out of the context of the Christ of faith. The two emphases, one historical and the other theological, belong together and when they are split apart, a real problem of interpretation arises.

Thus far we have discussed the different views about the historical method in general, showing how the different moods of confidence and doubt had their ebb and flow. Such an overview should have helped us to see how those who used the historical method fell roughly into two groups. One group, being ultimately confident about what the historical method could achieve, upheld that new light could always be shed upon the historical settings of the texts. The other group, working in a more abstract and conceptual way, has argued that, overall, the historical approach has often been more foe than friend when it has come to establishing the validity of the biblical accounts. These two approaches will be seen below, as we discuss the practical outworking of the historical method in terms of reading the biblical texts.

The Diachronic Approach: Six Examples of the Historical-Critical Method

Amidst this flux and change, it is not surprising that historical criticism of the actual biblical texts, from the middle of the last century onwards, has slowly grown into a discipline which has several sub-groups, each with a different concern about the nature of the text and each with a different level of confidence as to what might be achieved – theologically and historically – as a result of each method. The six most significant are outlined below, before attending to them in more detail.

The earliest subdivision is characterized by its interest in the historical context of the purported *author*, as well as in the date and provenance of the work alongside this. A second group may be discerned by its greater interest in the *sources* which the author may have used. A third group may be determined because of its interest in the *forms* (oral and written) which the author has chosen in order to convey his message. A fourth group is evident because of its interest in the *traditions* (in this case, theological beliefs) which may have influenced both the author and other editors who have adapted the text. A fifth division is seen in the interest in the influence of the final stage of revision – the *redaction* – of a whole work. And a sixth group is characterized by its interest in the way that a work has been collected and set alongside other works which eventually made up Scripture – an activity which has become known as '*canon criticism*'. Obviously, these interest-groups overlap each other. The first acts as baseline, insofar as it asks questions about the actual author, while the second and third look at the processes which were influences upon the author. The fourth, fifth and sixth focus on progressive influences upon the text after its earliest stages of composition. We shall now deal with each of these interests in turn.

Biblical Criticism

HIGHER CRITICISM

The overall interest in the author, and in the date and provenance of a text by way of this author, was originally known as 'literary criticism'. Although today this is a misleading term because it has a very different connotation in modern literary studies, it certainly serves in biblical studies to explain a method which is essentially about trying to understand the literature through a historical lens. But, to avoid confusion, today it is more generally known as '*biblical criticism*'. This approach is most obviously linked back to the 'literal' way of reading a text, and so could be said to have been a method of reading from very early times, both in Jewish and in Christian tradition. It developed in the eighteenth and nineteenth centuries as a recognizable discipline; in part, as we have just seen, this was due to the rise of interest in the historical reading of texts during this period. Another influence (and one which is certainly found in the work of scholars such as Herder and Eichhorn) is the Romantic movement, which was interested not only in the aesthetic quality in a text, but also in the biography of the poet and writer by whose inspiration the text had been written.

As we have already noted, biblical criticism was marked initially by the confidence that we can indeed know something about the original setting of a biblical text. The importance of the personality inspiring the work was the most important issue; the movement was from text to author. Hence the laws were by Moses, the psalms were by David, wisdom was by Solomon, and the prophetic works were by those whose names had been given to the books. So too the Gospels were by those whose names headed each work; and following from this, the Epistles were by Paul, and Revelation by John. The importance of naming the authors was, of course, inextricably bound up with other more confessional issues about the theological validity of Scripture, its authority and claims about its inspired nature. The assumption was that the coherence and reliability of Scripture was more effective if it could be traced back to single names and inspired personalities. The idea of a number of 'editors' working on a text, or 'schools' offering some influence on the writers seemed to compromise the essential theological premise of believers, namely that Scripture is an inspired book. In this way, biblical criticism, when it was able to affirm the unity of authorship and assured knowledge of context, served the concerns of the Church well. In many respects this was continuous with the way this straightforward, historical approach had been part of the literal reading of Scripture from earliest times. Given the enormity of the task, it is small wonder that, in time, this enterprise became known as 'higher criticism'.

LOWER CRITICISM

Only when biblical criticism began to question the integrity of 'one author' and 'one book', and when it became increasingly agnostic about the knowledge of the provenance and dates of books did the separation from confessional theology begin. As should now be obvious from the previous survey, this process took several decades, and the reasons for this split may be found within the nature of the method itself. For biblical criticism really comprised two parts: the interest in the author and the date and provenance of the text was called, appropriately, 'higher criticism'; and the interest in the text itself, albeit still in relation to the author, was called 'textual criticism', or 'lower criticism'. Textual criticism, as we have seen in Chapter 4, was capable of causing havoc with respect to the integrity and wholeness of the text. Concerned about the comparison of biblical texts with other cognate languages (Ugaritic, Akkadian, Arabic, Aramaic), it pointed out the many discrepancies within the text. And its work concerning copyists, manuscript variations, versions, misspellings, repetitions, omissions and punctuation did much to undermine the appeal to the concept of the unity of a whole text as the work of one personality from one place at one point in time. Hence while higher criticism tried very hard to use the historical method for positive ends – in attempting to establish the identity, date and provenance of a biblical author – lower criticism, because of its textual concerns, often ended up drawing more negative conclusions about how the historical method could show us anything in detail about the identity, date and setting of a given biblical writer.

Source Criticism

Near the end of the nineteenth century, when the discomfort with the results of the higher criticism was beginning to be felt, along with the discomfort about the historical method as a partner for the theological enterprise in biblical studies, another approach emerged. This focused in part on the text and in part on the author, and was a method which could be applied to the entire range of biblical texts. This was called 'source criticism'. Its origins were really as early as the eighteenth century with respect to the Old Testament, and the cause for this began with the problem of the contradictions in the biblical accounts – for example, those which we noted earlier in the accounts of creation and flood in the book of Genesis.

A French scholar, J. Astruc (1684–1766), proposed that these contradictions, or 'doublets', had once suggested that the author (Moses) was making use of at least two different earlier documents. But it gradually became clear that one of the documents, which went beyond Genesis into Exodus, Leviticus and Numbers, and which had priestly interests (and hence was often called quite simply 'P'), must have post-dated Moses. Furthermore, another document ('D') found especially in Deuteronomy, was probably not completed until the late monarchy and so it too was much later than Moses. Hence it became increasingly difficult to see how these five books (the Pentateuch as a whole) could both contain separate documents and yet still claim Mosaic authorship.

At the very beginning of the nineteenth century, W. M. L. de Wette, defended the late dating of the P source, and the later dating still of a D source, and hence affirmed – against centuries of popular religious tradition – that the author of the Pentateuch could not be Moses. This view was refined by W. Vatke, who in 1835 (the same year as Strauss published his *Life of Jesus*) published his own book, *Biblical Theology*. His thesis was that P, with its advanced view of priesthood and ritual, was likely to have come last of all, in post-exilic times, and hence after D. For Vatke, this demonstrated how the Pentateuch represented the three key phases in Israel's religion. It had its origins in the early 'primitive' period (developed in a source called 'J', because of the name 'Jahweh', or more often transcribed, 'Yahweh', which was used for God throughout it); this was developed later during a period of great reform (found in the source D); it was finally brought together at a later period still, after the Exile, when Judaism began to develop (found in the source P).

Hence it became clear that at least three sources, later comprising one collection of five books called the Pentateuch, or the Law, or *Tôrâ*, were all fed into the material at different stages by different compilers. It was against this background that J. Wellhausen (1844–1918) wrote, developing a theory which was later known as the 'documentary hypothesis', which was expressed in part in his *Prolegomena to the History of Israel* (1878; 1883). More influenced by de Wette than Vatke, and also by K. H. Graf (1815–69), Wellhausen argued that *four* sources were to be found in the Laws of Moses from Genesis to Deuteronomy. This continued to take the emphasis away from Moses as the author (a necessary distraction, one could argue, at a time of scepticism as to what could be known about the author anyway), and placed new emphasis on the compiler of the sources or documents (the term 'document' is often used to emphasize that this is already a written account). Here we have the beginning of the idea of a 'scissors-and-paste' process for understanding the growth of biblical books – from different sources to the greater whole.

Genesis and Exodus were obvious places to start; sources could be proposed where there were repetitions and double accounts. These included the accounts of creation, of the flood and of the beginning of the story of Joseph, already referred to. In addition there are other double accounts – for example, in the stories of Abraham (Genesis 12—25) and in the accounts of Moses and the plagues in Egypt (Exodus 1—11), the stories of the origins of the Passover and the crossing of the Red Sea (Exodus 12—15), and the account of God's appearance on Mount Sinai (Exodus 19—24). Wellhausen wrote clearly and succinctly about the times and places of each of the sources he believed had been used, by a much later editor, in the Genesis and Exodus accounts. The first source, which mainly used the name Yahweh for God, was called J; the next source, which mainly used the name Elohim for God, was E; the next – less evident in Genesis but more so in Exodus and certainly in Deuteronomy – which was interested in obeying the covenant, was called D; and the final source, with a repetitive (liturgical) style and an interest in priestly matters, was called 'P'. Wellhausen's dating of these sources – here following the views of scholars before him – was J-E-D-P. Hence the Pentateuch was a combination of all four sources, developing from as early as the time of Solomon (J) to as late as the time of the restoration of the people after the Exile in Babylon (P).

The implications of this source-critical approach for other books of the Bible were monumental. For in every biblical book, one could now take the emphasis away from the author, and place it instead on an (unknown) editor. For example, in the Old Testament, the differences in the settlement accounts in Joshua and Judges could be explained away in terms of a compiler, who used at least two key (variant) sources for the framework of this account. So too the prophets were assessed in this way. Jeremiah, for example, was seen to contain two or three sources: the poetic oracles of the prophet himself; a narrative about the prophet's sufferings compiled by the prophet's secretary, Baruch; and prose homilies and didactic explanations which were either seen as a separate source (like D in the Pentateuch) or seen as the work of a final editor (similar in style and theology to the editor of Joshua-Judges-Samuel-Kings, who became known as the Deuteronomist).

Within the New Testament, the interest in sources focused initially on the Gospels, with a hypothesis that a shared 'sayings source' called 'Q' was used by all three Synoptic Gospels. The debate about the Synoptic Problem (the extent to which each of the first three Gospel-writers shared common material or borrowed from separate sources, and the extent to which Mark might have been used as the 'source' for Matthew and Luke) is very much related to this same issue, and one sees here many of the issues which were raised in the documentary hypothesis. At a time when questions were being asked about the historical Jesus, it again took the weight off the quest for the persona of Jesus and put the emphasis on the Gospel-writers as editors instead.

Source criticism in the New Testament went beyond the Gospels alone. Whenever it was seen that the material shared some correspondences (to use the Old Testament term, 'doublets') with other New Testament passages – for example, Ephesians with Colossians, and 2 Peter with Jude – the issue was about perceiving which 'source' had been used, and hence which work was primary. And where a narrative was seen to contain double accounts, the same proposal about sources was made. For example, in the Acts of the Apostles, there might have been a possible source containing the accounts of Paul's visits to the churches, or a purported autobiographical memoir source which became the basis of the 'we' passages used by the editor (possibly Luke) of the Acts of the Apostles. Hymns were also assessed as if they were sources which had been adapted by later editions – for example, Philippians 2.5–11 and Colossians 1.15–20 within these two epistles, and smaller liturgical pieces in the book of Revelation. And within John's Gospel, the question arose as to whether there had been a particular source used for John's seven miracles, described as 'signs' of God's presence in the midst of his people (and hence the source was termed the 'signs source'), around which the editor fitted later discourses which related to the inner theological meaning of each of these 'signs'.

Although source criticism is not used in exactly the same way in the Old and New Testaments, in both cases this is still very much about the historical background to the text, and everything is focused away from the originality of the purported writers. Source criticism is still interested in personality, in the way it proposed different theological concerns of the various sources, but this involves looking at the writers as editors and not as authors. Yet the results of source criticism are nevertheless hypothetical. We still have to come to terms with how little we really know with any precision about the growth of the text, whether through authors or through editors. The historical Moses, as the historical Jesus, still eludes us.

Form Criticism

The interest in form criticism runs parallel to the interest in sources, although it is more closely related to the rise of the History of Religions School, and the interest in trying to understand more about the particular settings of particular religious ideas. The key difference when compared with source criticism is that the analysis of the different forms used by different writers takes us down to much smaller units of material than is the case with the analysis of the different sources. This was an attempt to classify – albeit often subconsciously – the material into particular genres so that one could then propose a common life-setting for the groups of particular genres (hence the influence of the History of Religions approach). It goes without saying that, for those who first put forward this approach, myth is an important contribution to the whole debate.

162

In Chapter 1, on the library of the Bible, we looked at the various forms which are found within the Old Testament material (see Table 5 on p. 24 and the discussion on p. 22) as well as the forms in the New Testament material (Table 6 on p. 24 draws this together, and the discussion on p. 23 fills this out). Typically again, the work on the Old Testament was done initially on the books of Genesis and Psalms. We may note here the influence of Gunkel, and the interest in myth as a form-critical category. In the New Testament, the most work was done initially on the Gospels – M. Dibelius (1883–1947), a pupil of Gunkel, being noteworthy in this respect.

The work on Old Testament form criticism took a slightly different turn in the earlier part of the twentieth century. This was due to the different value given to oral and to written forms. Scandinavian scholars were particularly interested in the oral forms within the Old Testament – the myths, but also the hymns, blessings, curses, laments, proverbs, oracles and love songs found throughout the biblical books – proposing a liturgical setting as the means through which many of these forms were preserved. English and German commentators have written much on the literary forms of the Old Testament – again its myths, but also the law codes, short stories, the letters, archival records, genealogies, tractates, legends, parables, as well as others listed also as oral forms – and noted the importance of the various groups which have preserved this material – prophets, priests, scribes.

The division between oral and literary forms is somewhat different when we examine the New Testament material. Putting it simply, the Epistles were more obviously written compositions from the outset, and the Gospels were more dependent upon a long oral tradition which went before them. It has always been difficult to classify precisely the Gospels as literature; there is nothing quite like them in another ancient literature. The shorter forms within the Gospels have correspondences with other ancient literature – the parables, sayings, discourses, short stories, miracles and riddles – but as a whole, the Gospels are a distinctive type. Much of this may be due to another factor which illustrates their lengthy oral nature – their use in the preaching tradition of the Church and the importance of the *kerygma*, which commentators such as Bultmann emphasized, for example in his *History of the Synoptic Tradition*. This basic 'kerygmatic' form is probably what lay behind the formation of the Gospels, according to form critics; smaller forms were preached in various Church communities, and were adapted and expanded over a period of time. Hence in the New Testament, the interest in form criticism originally lay mainly in the Gospels, on account of their long and distinctive oral tradition; and the interest was as much in the life-setting which had given rise to the forms (especially the setting within the preaching life of the Church). Although the liturgical influence in the preservation of forms is thus as apparent in the New Testament as it is in the Old, and hence the interest in the early life-settings of the material is the same, the analysis of forms in the New Testament is really quite different when compared with the Old.

Perhaps one of the greatest difficulties in the form-critical method is the emphasis it places on the way in which different communities gave rise to so much of the biblical material. Moving away from the focus on the author, as in biblical (higher) criticism, and even away from the focus on an editor or compiler, as in source criticism, the emphasis is now on the community as the great preserver and inspirer of tradition. One wonders whether the community (itself such a nebulous and complex unit) can bear all the weight that form critics choose to place on it. Although the personality of one author as the creator of biblical texts is a difficult hypothesis to maintain, the personality of a community as the creative element in this process is by no means any easier to assent to. Form criticism has within it a strange anomaly: it claims to be interested in the details of the smaller (often oral) parts behind the greater whole, but makes grand sweeping statements about the typical and shared nature of these parts. It presumes, for instance, that because one finds a lament form, or a hymnic form, this evidences a setting in liturgy, rather than assuming instead that a creative writer may well choose to use a lament or a hymn in a non-liturgical way (thinking here of the non-liturgical use of hymnic material in Amos and Job, and the non-liturgical use of lament material in Jeremiah and Job).

In brief, form criticism is certainly not, as it was once apt to claim, a scientific way of reading texts, but it is often very much an intuitive art; and it is certainly not able to produce any more assured results just because it stresses the importance of the community and representative types and settings. It could be argued that more assured results come from affirming instead the creative role of individual writers and collectors, even though their precise historical setting is often unknown. Form criticism has thus not taken us much further down the road towards historical clarity.

Tradition Criticism

Tradition criticism, like form criticism, is interested in the context in which an idea is expressed, and, like form criticism, it bears the mark of the influence of the History of Religions School. It has two distinct concerns. On the one hand, it emphasizes the theological influences on the writers themselves. This presumes that the writer has absorbed the thought-world of his day and, as well as borrowing from the forms in which those thoughts were expressed, he also borrows from the key religious ideas prevalent at the time. (Here more than anywhere we see the mark of the History of Religions School.) These theological traditions could either be used in some oral form (assumed to be more the case with Scandinavian scholars such as I. Engnell and E. Nielsen) or could already have been established as literary works (more popular with German commentators, for example, G. von Rad and M. Noth).

Applying this to the Old Testament, these traditions may be, for example, the tradition of the Exodus – in its recital of what God had done in redeeming the people from slavery in Egypt; or it could be the tradition of creation – a tradition expressed in many different ways, whether with respect to God's greatness, in his bringing the whole cosmos into being, or with respect to God's love and kindness, in his bringing each human life into being. It could be the tradition of Zion, which recalled God's defence of the city in times of distress and his dwelling in the Temple there in order to protect his people in their hour of need. Or it could be the tradition of King David, which recalled God's promises that he would always be with his people through an anointed figure, who would lead the people in justice and mercy on his behalf. A tradition need not be an overarching theological theme, but may more simply be a theological statement in a word or phrase such as 'God reigns', or 'Blessed be ...' or 'justice and righteousness'. Whichever tradition one might presume to have been used by a particular writer, one concern in tradition criticism is the influence of various theological beliefs on the mind of the writer, and in this sense the approach concerns the substance of the message rather than the form taken by the message.

But there is a second way in which tradition criticism is understood. This is to see the influence of any of the above traditions upon the development of the text at various stages in the history of its transmission. In this sense, rather like form criticism, this view of tradition puts more emphasis on the role of the community in shaping the tradition (again, as with form criticism, probably through liturgy). Within the worshipping community, priests, prophets, scribes, apocalypticists would have all played their part. This is therefore more of an interest in the theological developments of the text – working 'from faith for faith'.

Tradition criticism in the New Testament has followed roughly the same line as in the Old. On the one hand, the debate has been about the long process of an oral tradition of preaching and teaching. Yet again we may note the kerygmatic theology of Bultmann, whose influence on the New Testament in this respect can be compared with Gunkel's on the Old Testament. On the other hand, the discussion has been about the assent to the importance of accepted literary traditions (not least those from the Septuagint which were used for prophecy/fulfilment purposes). The importance of liturgy and creeds as the contributions of different Christian communities is one example of this. Examples of creeds might be found in 1 Corinthians 15.3ff., concerning the resurrection of Jesus, and in 1 Timothy 3.16, concerning the value of the received Scripture. Liturgical elements may be found in the hymns in the opening chapters of Luke on the birth of Jesus, and in 1 Corinthians 11.23ff., which suggests an early liturgy of the institution of the eucharist. The larger traditional themes may be found mainly in the Gospels, especially in Matthew and in Luke. Working from the largest to the smallest examples, these would include: the birth and passion narratives; the references to prophecy being fulfilled, especially seen in Matthew; the references to the kingdom of God breaking in, for example in Luke 17 and 18; the hope for some future culmination of history, for example in Luke 24; and the allusions to God's intimate care for his created order (Matthew 6.25–34). These examples usually imply the effect of the received tradition on the mind of the 'author', rather than the importance of the tradition in the mind of the 'community'.

In this way, tradition criticism, although significant on a far larger scale in the Old Testament, is nevertheless used both within the Old and the New Testaments. It is in many ways a method of compromise. It deals with theological substance as well as outward form, with oral units as well as literary works, with the effect on the writers as well as on the later communities, and with theological themes. These theological themes are on the one hand distinctively part of the biblical world-view (Zion, David, Exodus, in the Old Testament; and the birth of Christ, the kingdom of God, and the resurrection, in the New), yet on the other hand may be borrowed from the non-Jewish world beyond it. Although as a methodological approach tradition criticism is perhaps the most difficult to define, for those drawn to a pluralist way of interpreting the biblical texts it is also perhaps the most attractive to use.

Redaction Criticism

Redaction criticism could be said to have been minted in Germany, coined in the UK and used in America. It emerged at about the same time as the New Quest – where there was a renewed concern in establishing as much as possible about the Jewish background to the stories of the historical Jesus, and hence when it was important to have renewed confidence in the final editors and collectors as those through whom the traditions of Jesus had been mediated.

In many ways redaction criticism is the most clear and obvious of the methods of historical reading, because of its concern with the final stage of the text. It has a theological bias, in that it is concerned with what the final editors of texts actually believed, in order to assess the influence of their voice – the ultimate voice – within the texts. Hence with the prophet Isaiah, for example, the concern is with the theological intentions of the editor who 'sewed together' the other three major prophetic works in Isaiah 1—39, 40—55, and 56—66. Or with Genesis 1—11, it is with the final editor who joined together the J source and the P source and brought about one larger theological unit which begins with the ordering of the cosmos and ends with the dispersion of the nations. The more complex the growth of the work, the more significant the role of the redactor. This is made most clear when it comes to looking at the influence of the final editor and commentator on the long history from Joshua to 2 Kings, or the final voice in the large unit comprising Chronicles–Ezra–Nehemiah.

This method, which in some ways follows naturally out of tradition criticism, developed mainly in the post-war years. Its main exponents, in this case, have more often than not been within the sphere of the New Testament: for example, G. Bornkamm (on Matthew), W. Marxsen (on Mark) and H. Conzelmann (on the Acts of the Apostles). The work on the Old Testament has been mainly on the narrative material (for example by more recent writers such as R. Alter, R. C. Culley and P. D. Miscall) where it is very close indeed to the literary approaches, to be discussed in the following section.

Within the New Testament, the main area of interest has again been the Synoptic Gospels, and has its roots in a much earlier approach associated with F. C. Baur and the Tübingen School, called *Tendenzkritik* (tendency criticism), which is concerned with identifying the overall theological tendencies of the writers of the Gospels. Here a particular problem soon becomes evident. When we speak of the importance of redactors, are we in fact referring to the Gospel-writers themselves as the creative influence upon the texts in their own names, or are we referring instead to another, later, unknown hand whose final theological influence is more important than that of the earlier writers?

Whichever view one takes, redaction criticism works on difficult ground because it attempts to discover what is the Gospel-writer's (or Gospel-editor's) distinctive contribution within the complex mass of inherited material. Sometimes this influence is traced back to the material which the Gospel-writers appear to have arranged in a distinctive way. In Matthew, this would include the Sermon on the Mount (chapters 5—7) or the sevenfold group of parables about the kingdom (Matthew 13) or the collection of woes against the scribes and Pharisees (Matthew 23). In Luke, it might be the way that the author uses 4.16–30 as an introduction to the whole manifesto of Jesus and in so doing anticipates the reasons for his ultimate rejection. In Mark, it might be the way the writer interweaves two stories together to intensify the theological meaning – for example, the cleansing of the Temple is broken up with the cursing of the fig tree in Luke 11.12–20. In John it might be the placing of the account of the raising of Lazarus in the heart of the book (John 11) in anticipation of the future suffering, rejection and ultimate victory over death by Jesus himself.

Whether we assume this to be about the personal contribution of the actual Gospel-writers, or of the editors and compilers of the Gospels in a later generation, the major significance of redaction criticism is that its emphasis is very much on the contributions of individuals rather than of great communities. It is as if the pendulum has swung back to the earlier concerns of higher criticism. The only difference is that one approaches the issue of individual contributions with greater caution about what we can actually know historically.

Canon Criticism

The sixth historical approach, canon criticism, really developed some time after the rise of redaction criticism (having more influence in America than in Germany). This approach asks the questions of the text the other way round. Instead of asking about the essential contributions of the writer, it asks questions about the overall theology of the entire book. Hence, as compared with the individual focus of redaction criticism, this assumes instead the importance of the community as the guardian of the received traditions expressed in the whole book.

In many ways, canon criticism is more of a theologically orientated method than a historical one, for (rather like tradition criticism, which is also theological in its concerns) it asks questions about the ideas expressed in the text, rather than about the intentions of the earlier writers. We have noted already, at the end of Chapter 2 and again in Chapter 3, that canon criticism has had a major influence in supporting the idea of biblical theology, because it emphasizes a belief in the ultimate theological uniformity of the books in the Bible and in the Bible as a book. Yet in other ways, canon criticism belongs to more recent literary critical discourse, for it is concerned as much with the text as a unit of communication as it is with the community of faith which preserved and transmitted it.

We have already examined one example of how canon criticism works, in our discussion of the works of B. S. Childs; for example, in his *Old Testament as Scripture*. But of course other writers have made their mark in this area as well. One star scholar in this field is J. A. Sanders, whose best-known work is perhaps *Canon and Community: A Guide to Canonical Criticism*. Like Childs, Sanders' main concern is to seek to redress the problems inherent in other historical methods, which were apt to result in a splintering and fragmentation of the biblical texts into ever smaller parts. Certainly fragmentation had been the problem inherent in source criticism and in form criticism, and it had also been a difficulty in some of the ways it was used in the tradition criticism as well. Given that the rise of canon criticism coincides with growing criticism about the actual success of a New Quest, it offers an alternative approach, being as concerned with things theological and also literary, as with things particularly historical. In this way, it prepares the way for some of the literary approaches to the Bible, as we shall see in the following chapter.

Summary

Figures 17 and 18 (p. 170) are a means of describing visually how the historical approach 'works'. We might view the historical method overall rather like an archaeological dig. Operating at the many different levels which are present in a text, it is a way of looking *through* a text rather than simply looking *at* it. (Hence the term 'diachronic'; taken from the Greek, this is about reading a text 'through [the processes of] time'.) Figure 17 illustrates within this diachronic process the relationship of the six different methods to each other; Figure 18 shows how this might be applied in relation to one Old Testament passage we have referred to several times throughout this survey – namely Genesis 1—11. The purpose of presenting these figures at the end of this survey is not only to summarize all that we have discussed in terms of the six most common historical methods which have been used in biblical studies. It is also to prepare the way, by a form of comparison and contrast, with the six most common literary methods used in biblical studies to be discussed in the following chapter.

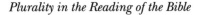

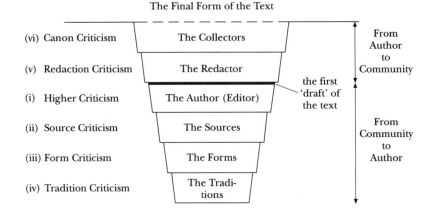

Figure 17   Historical Criticism: A Diachronic Reading of the Biblical
Texts

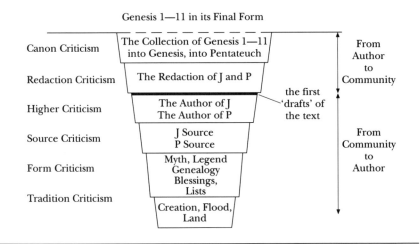

Figure 18   A Diachronic Reading of Genesis 1—11

7

Literary Approaches to the Bible

A different approach is called for ... if the Old Testament is to be given its due theological weight as Christian (as well as Jewish) scripture, and not relegated to the historical presuppositions of Christian faith and theology. Literary study, which is less tied to the author's original intentions, may prove more important than historical exegesis in the theological interpretation of the Old Testament ...

Theological preferences have long favoured historical research and hindered the development of a secular literary criticism of the Bible. It was the relaxation of these theological pressures that encouraged the change, but theologians have begun to recognize that it also has considerable potential for their own purposes.

(R. Morgan and J. Barton, *Biblical Interpretation*, OUP, 1989, pp. 113, 200)

The historical approach was, in the main, a response to the rationalistic spirit in the eighteenth and nineteenth centuries; yet in theological circles it was seen as bringing new illumination about the origins and development of the Bible. In the light of this, it is interesting to observe that, in this century, the literary approach to the Bible, itself a response in the early 1920s to the rise of secular literary studies ('New Criticism'), was also hailed in theological circles as shedding new light upon our reading of the Bible. Whether it will be worthy of such confidence has yet to be seen. For of all three approaches, literary criticism of the Bible is undoubtedly the most recent and, on that account, the least fully tried.

Different Literary Approaches

As we noted in the previous chapter, historical criticism is often known as the diachronic approach, looking through the different layers of interpretation and editing which have brought the text into its present

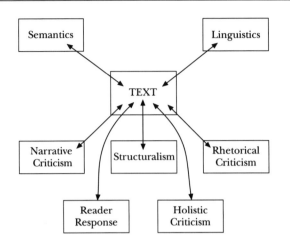

Figure 19 Literary Criticism: A Synchronic Reading of the Biblical Texts

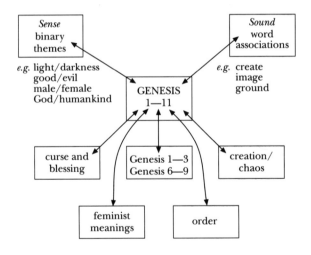

Figure 20 A Synchronic Reading of Genesis 1—11

form. By contrast, literary criticism is known as the synchronic approach, for it works alongside (from *syn* meaning 'together with' or 'alongside' in Greek) the present form of the text. It is not interested in the shaping of the text through the process of history; rather, it asks questions about the shape of the text in the here and now. In historical criticism, the dialogue is within the text throughout its past history. In literary criticism, the dialogue is with the text with the present concerns of the reader foremost in mind.

In order to understand this in a pictorial way, Figures 19 and 20, which illustrate the synchronic approach, should be compared with the figures illustrating the diachronic approach at the end of the last chapter. Whereas Figures 17 and 18 correspond to an archaeological dig, because of the stratification through the many different levels in the text, Figures 19 and 20 correspond to a series of interconnected squares, indicating that the synchronic approach is not so much about the depth of a text as about the interrelationships of the parts with each other. As with the two earlier diachronic figures, the synchronic figures both show first how the various methods work in general terms, and then how they work out in relation to the text of Genesis 1—11. (More will be said about Genesis 1—11 in relation to literary criticism in the next section of this chapter.)

In spite of these contrasts, an intriguing aspect of the recent development of literary studies of the Bible – for it has developed as an academic discipline only over the last twenty-five years or so – is that there are several clear correspondences with the 'criticisms' applied in the historical approaches to the text. The previous chapter has already looked at the different branches of historical criticism; Table 12 lists these branches alongside the major branches of literary criticism. It can be seen how the correspondences between the two methodologies show parallel concerns.

Table 12 A Comparison of the Historical and Literary Methods

Historical Critical Method	*Literary Critical Method*
Biblical Criticism:	Literary Criticism:
Higher Criticism	Semantic Readings
Lower Criticism	Linguistic Readings
Source Criticism	Narrative/Poetic Criticism
Form Criticism	Structuralist Criticism
Tradition Criticism	Rhetorical Criticism
Redaction Criticism	Reader-Response Criticism
Canon Criticism	Holistic Criticism

For example, in historical criticism, the concern is with the meaning of the text, understood through the concerns of the ancient author; in literary criticism, meaning is found in the language and style and form of the text itself, understood through the concerns of the present-day reader. Or again, in historical criticism, the interest in how the text was brought together is evident in source criticism, in form criticism and in tradition criticism; in literary criticism, this same question of how the text 'works' – for the readers, not for the writers – is answered under the categories of poetic and structuralist criticism. Yet again, in historical criticism, the interest in those who formed the text in its final stages is demonstrated in redaction criticism and in canon criticism; in literary criticism, parallels are to be found in the interest in the part the readers play in giving new meanings to the text, albeit after its final form. These points will become clear in the discussion in the next section; Table 12 makes the contrast clear at this initial stage.

In spite of its evident youth as a discipline in its own right, several aspects of the literary approach can be found in the very early period of the biblical tradition, and so link it not only with historical criticism but also with the theological approach. For example, an interest in style and meaning had to be paramount when undertaking any translation work, be it from the Hebrew to Greek, or Hebrew and Greek into Latin, or Greek into Syriac. Furthermore, the interest in texts as self-contained units was also important in the organization of materials into the different canonical collections. The interest in 'plot', 'characterization' and 'narrative' was very much also a part of the Jewish haggadic tradition, and this found its way (with a good deal of theological colouring) into the Christian allegorical tradition. The interest in the response of the reader (or perhaps as was more often the case, the listener) was evident in the preaching and apologetics of the exegetes of the second century onwards. Thus for centuries, many of the characteristics of the literary approach (the interest in the style and meaning of biblical texts, the interest in the canonical acceptance of those texts, the interest in the stories and the characterization exhibited in those texts, as well as in the response of the recipient) have always been present in the way the Bible has been read, translated and used in different theological traditions. To put it as simply as possible, the literary approach has always been used, often unconsciously, as an aid to our theological appreciation of the text, within both the Christian and Jewish traditions.

Not only in early times, but also in the latter part of the twentieth century, the literary approach has had a close relationship with the theological approach as well. One very good example of the vital relationship between them both is found in two more recent approaches to the Bible discussed in Chapter 5 – namely liberation theology and feminist theology. These two provide interesting examples of how the theological approach in praxis draws from literary critical approaches. The most obvious examples from literary studies are the 'reader-response theories' and 'rhetorical criticism', where the reader enters into discourse with the text, asking questions about its assumptions and its ideologies, and from this also asks questions about the intended audience (the ancient one) and the actual audience (the contemporary one). From this, the reader then asks further questions about the theological meaning of the text today.

One might ask, when did this literary way of reading the Bible, with both its historical and its theological associations, eventually become an independent academic discipline in its own right? It was not until the 1920s that the aesthetic interest in classical literature for its own sake ('New Criticism') was beginning to find its voice. I. A. Richards and T. S. Eliot were perhaps the most popular proponents of this new wave of literary interest. However, it is surprising that, on the level of literary studies of the Bible, these writers made little impact at the time. This may be because within biblical studies, the biblical theology movement and the history of religions school were still very much in vogue. In this way, the biblical text itself was thus still viewed as a means to another end, rather than, as literary criticism emphasized, an end in itself.

One critical publication which did in fact influence a literary approach to the Bible was a book by N. Frye called *The Anatomy of Criticism*, published in 1957. This recognized more overtly the different ways in which literary criticism, as an academic discipline, might be more rigorously applied to the Bible. Interestingly, this publication coincided with the then disillusionment about what the history of religions school could ultimately achieve. Furthermore, Frye's publication also coincided with a growing dissatisfaction with the biblical theology movement on account of its imposition of a particular system of ideas upon the text. And the 1950s marked the beginning of more attention being given to the final form of the text, illustrated best in the growth of redaction and canon criticism as more appropriate ways of reading the Bible as a whole. Hence the time was ripe for defending literary criticism as a distinctive academic study of the text – not detached from theological study, but by no means dependent upon it. Certainly some time between 1957 and Frye's publication of *The Great Code* (1982), literary criticism in biblical studies began to make its mark in short articles in journals and in a few major publications.

Frye's 1982 publication is typical of this later development in literary studies. It seeks to apply what may be termed a 'structuralist' approach to the imagery of the Bible, codifying the repeated use of related paired images such as gardens and cities, mountains and rivers, bread and wine. This literary criticism of the Bible goes beyond reading it just as 'good inspired literature', or as an aid to faith, or as a conscious correction of the scepticism of the historical method. 'Structuralism', in Frye's use of this term, is not only an analysis of the language but also of the social systems which have influenced it. We shall examine this further in the next section. At this stage, the main issue is that this represents literary study as a more secular account of the biblical text. Hence gradually the vocabulary of biblical studies expanded to use terms such as linguistics, social anthropology, social sciences and reader-response theory.

Between the 1950s and the 1980s, much of the influence was from France and Eastern Europe, as well as from the United States. By the time of the publication of *The Great Code*, writers such as M. Sternberg, T. Henn, R. Alter, F. Kermode, A. Berlin, R. M. Polzin and A. N. Wilder had produced serious literary-critical studies of biblical literature, both of its prose and its poetry. The journal *Semeia*, begun in 1974 as part of this literary-critical approach to the Bible, marked another stage along the way. By the 1980s, literary studies was no longer an appendage to the theological method, but a separate discipline in its own right.

Thus it can be seen that literary study of the Bible has been linked both to the historical approach, in its corresponding methods of reading, and with the theological approach, in its shared concerns about the application of the text in the present day, yet has now become a method of reading on its own merits. The following section will therefore assess its effectiveness by using the six subsidiary branches of criticism referred to at the beginning of this chapter (see especially Table 12).

The Synchronic Approach: Six Examples of the Literary-Critical Method

Literary criticism works well with some parts of the biblical literature, and yet quite badly with others. Within the Old Testament, it is obviously suited to the narrative sections, where a good deal of work – for example, on the irony and the dramatization of the story – can take place. A cursory glance at the composition of the biblical library

176

should reveal just how great a proportion of the Old Testament this is. Examples of the use of this approach are works by Alter and Kermode. In terms of the discerning of structures, and the aesthetic appreciation of language, poetry also is obvious literature to use – not only the liturgical poetry of the psalms, but the poetic forms used by the prophets and the wisdom writers, as well as poems which occur frequently within the narrative literature. Among the most significant works in this area are books by Alter and Berlin.

However, there comes a point where the literary approach creates as many problems in some parts of the Old Testament literature as does the historical method in other parts. One most obvious example where the literary approach is more limited is in the Law – the legal codes especially – and in the proverbs and aphorisms in the wisdom literature, where issues of a more historical nature, about context and purpose, usually also need to be addressed. Questions about presentation and context get in the way. Similarly in the New Testament, the narratives of the Gospels and Acts are ideally suited for a literary approach; but, given that there is so little poetry in the New Testament, there is very little scope for this sort of literary approach in this respect. And the Epistles suffer the same limitations as does the legal and proverbial material in the Old Testament.

Literary Criticism

SEMANTIC READINGS OF THE TEXT

Semantics (concerning the analysis of the *meanings* of words) has to do with the interpretation of the different biblical terms used in texts, asking why one term has been used and not another. Whereas in higher criticism this involved the attempt to discover a meaning through the discovery of the context of the text – the date, place and author – in the study of semantics, the interpretation of terms is by way of reference to the setting of the contemporary reader rather than to the world of the ancient author. Hence both higher criticism and semantic readings are concerned to interpret the meaning and the purpose of a text; the difference is that, in the historical approach, meaning comes from the context of the purported writer, and in the semantic approach, meaning arises out of the text itself, without giving any reference to the interests of the biblical writer. In many ways, this approach is closely related to various kinds of structuralist approaches, which are also very much concerned with the patterns of the language.

LINGUISTIC READINGS OF THE TEXT

In textual (lower) criticism, the study of language was closely related to the study of the context of the text (higher criticism). This involved understanding comparative philology in the ancient Near East, and the origins and development and use of Greek and Hebrew as the 'original' languages of the Bible. A concordance, lexicon and dictionary are all tools of the trade for textual criticism. By contrast, the importance in the linguistic approach in literary study is the relationship between one word and another. The focus is not so much backwards – tracing origins and the earliest meanings of words in their ancient settings – but the focus is rather sideways – looking at the ways in which choices of vocabulary and the associations of words in relation to each other affect our understanding of the translated text. Hence words like assonance (repetitions of sound) and parataxis (the way that parallel clauses fit together) and paranomasia (plays on words which sound alike) are more important than strict grammatical technicalities. To put it as starkly as possible, the tool for reading in this way is better served by a thesaurus than by a lexicon.

Nowhere is the contrast of these two approaches to language more evident than in the coincidental publication of two entirely different resources to help the Old Testament student use the Hebrew language. One is *The Dictionary of Classical Hebrew* (D. J. A. Clines (ed.), 1993—). This comprises an anticipated eight volumes from Sheffield and is a linguistic aid. The other, published first in Germany and now being translated into English as *The Hebrew and Aramaic Lexicon of the Old Testament* (comprising four volumes in all; L. Koehler, W. Baumgartner and M. E. J. Richardson (tr. ed.), 1994—) is a philological aid. The Sheffield publication looks at a word through the lens of its contemporary meaning (for example, where the word occurs elsewhere, in all its different literary settings and its different parts of speech, working from the English into Hebrew) whereas the German translation looks at a word by way of its historical development, in its comparison with other cognate languages, in all its different grammatical constructions, working from and in the Hebrew.

Already in the analysis of the most basic of the literary-critical methods, the differences between the diachronic and synchronic approaches should be evident. As in historical criticism, the concern is with the meaning and purpose of the texts. But in historical criticism, meaning is inevitably tied up with authorship and origins; and language is tied up with ancient usage and comparisons with other ancient cultures. And in literary criticism, meaning belongs to the text as it is (synchronic – working *with* the text in its present mode): it has nothing to ask of the text in the past. The language belongs to the relationship of words alongside one another (synchronic – words *with* each other) and has no need to ask anything initially of the use of that language, nor of the language from which it might have been translated. The text, read and interpreted by the reader in their own contemporary setting, is the paramount concern in the literary approach.

Narrative Criticism and Poetic Criticism

Although prose and poetry cannot produce exactly the same results, the methods involved in narrative and poetic criticism have many aspects in common, and the general points can therefore be included in the one discussion.

The first and most important feature of this approach is that it looks at the whole unit, whether of prose or of poetry. Thus the doublets, repetitions, contradictions, gaps and inconsistencies in the translated text are included as part of the whole; they are an effective mode of enabling us to understand the variety and balance in the text, and they enrich our knowledge of the text as a whole. It is possible from this 'holistic' view of the text to create a theology which unites the whole – a theology however created by the text, and not by the author. But the emphasis is on the whole poem, or the whole story – there is no concern here for the smaller parts which may have made up the whole.

The comparison of this approach with source criticism should be evident. Instead of sources, discernible previously because of the repetitions and contradictions in the text (thinking here of how source criticism in the Pentateuch and in the Gospels was first established) this approach takes whole units and works across the sources. For example, instead of reading the story of Genesis 1—2 in two parts, as two different creation stories from different sources and from different points in time, the emphasis is on the story of creation as a whole. Or again, instead of reading the flood story in Genesis 6—9 by dividing it up according to the doublets, one reads the text as it is, looking for a larger structure evident in the text as a whole, thus allowing all the differences (for example, concerning the number of animals and the durations of the flood) to be seen within a larger whole. Or, taking this time a poetic composition such as Psalm 89 – which has often been seen to comprise three different sources, using the forms of a hymn, a royal psalm and a lament – one ignores the subdivisions and looks instead for a unity of structure within the psalm as a whole. Finally, instead of reading Luke in terms of its dependence on Mark and its use of Q and its associations with Matthew, one reads the entire Gospel – looking for an overall theme and a structure within the whole.

Source criticism divided up passages by way of reading the stylistic differences and making decisions about the development of the text in all its stratification, through (*dia*) the process of history. Narrative and poetic criticism take the unit they have chosen on its face value, working with (*syn*) the differences. The variations in the text contribute towards a part of the final whole, and not, as we noted earlier, as a number of smaller parts.

Structuralist Criticism

One of the hallmarks of structuralist theory is its interest in classification. This in part has its roots back in F. de Saussure's studies in linguistics in the early 1920s, when it was clear that the study of language could no longer be about the history and development of particular words (what might be called the study of *langue*), but was also about the communication of language, and from this, an ability to study the words in their relationship to each other (what might be called the study of *parole*, or discourse). The concerns of Gadamer and Ricoeur, with their combined interest in culture-centred readings and in the importance of discourse between the text and reader, are obviously important in this respect. The interest in the structures of language in literature was furthered by writers such as V. Propp, who wrote a classification of the common linguistic themes in Russian folktales, and C. Lévi-Strauss, who made a similar analysis of the common underlying structures of biblical myth. (The differences between this approach and that of the other [unrelated] Strauss to the role of myth in the Gospels is significant in this respect: D. F. Strauss was more concerned about the origins of myth and its function in the culture of first-century Judaism, and Lévi-Strauss is more interested in the overarching corresponding features between mythical stories and their communication now as much as then.) One other major influence outside biblical studies was A.-J. Greimas, whose classificatory work on narratives resulted in the observation that myths and fairy-tales had within them one unifying structure, which was varied in a number of ways. This structure consisted of six features in three pairs: the subject and object; a sender and a receiver; and a helper and an opponent. Many of the stories about the patriarchs in Genesis (12—36) could be seen as conforming – albeit loosely, at times – to this pattern.

One of the first to apply to the Bible these theories of the discourse and communication of language, and from this the structures and patterns in which this discourse takes place in narrative form, was R. Barthes. One of the most important points made by Barthes was that structuralism no longer required any specific, creative author. The structures are given; no author can add meaning to or subtract it from what already exists. From the mid-1960s onwards – in an age when biblical criticism had all but declared the search for specific authors of specific texts null and void – this was indeed welcome news, for it avoided a problem and provided another means of reading, using the text as it *is* rather than the text as it *might have been understood*. Some of the points of contention about the historical nature of the miracles gain from such an approach; likewise, the Gospel parables too.

However, there is a problem in this approach. This has been clearly developed by A. Thistelton in his *New Horizons in Hermeneutics: The Theory and Practice of Transforming Bible Study*. He notes that the interest in classification of language evident within the text, the understanding of discourse emanating from the text itself, and the importance of the reader in discovering the deeper structures in the text, *all* take one no further than the text itself. The end result is that there is little perspective from anywhere other than the discourse between the text and reader, and, whether reading the Gospels or the book of Genesis in this way, one is left with little more than *self*-discovery. This problem of subjectivity and a closed circle of reference is perhaps one of the greatest issues with regard to structuralist readings of biblical texts.

Perhaps one of the most important aspects of classification of language is the identification of the binary opposites within the text, in the combination of words such as light/dark, chaos/order, death/life, blessing/curse, war/peace. Genesis 1—11 fits this type of approach very well. Within each of the sources (J and P) there is a notable amount of repetition of words such as earth/land, blessing/curse, light/dark, evil/good, God/humankind, male/female, life/death, and so on. By taking each of these binary ideas in turn, and seeing where they are found in the text and what interest they serve, the unity of purpose within Genesis 1—11 overall becomes more in focus. The same approach could be used with the prophets. For example, in the book of Amos – which is believed to come from several hands from at least three different stages, thus indicating the more disparate nature of the text – the structuralist reading can attempt to put back together texts which might otherwise be seen to be far apart. Binary 'catchwords' such as justice/righteousness, house/strongholds, burn/devour, Nile/Egypt and lion/bear all yield interesting results about the unity of the text of Amos overall. The purpose is still to focus on the tensions in the text, but to see these by way of some balance between two opposites, and hence to find some basic structure in the text as a whole.

One further application of structuralism, and a most useful one from the point of view of biblical studies for it takes the emphasis away from subjectivism and self-discovery, is linked not so much to linguistics as to social sciences. The concern here is to assess how much the text informs us, through its use of language, about social structures presupposed within the text. One apposite use of this theory is with regard to feminist theory – the assessment of gender difference in the text, the discourse between the text and reader by way of either agreeing or disagreeing with the world-view presented, and the response of the reader to what has been read. Political readings of the text – not least those of the liberation theologians referred to earlier – also fall into this category. So too do readings which apply psychoanalytical studies.

It may seem strange to connect structuralism with form criticism. But there are at least two themes in common: first, the interest in classification (whether of forms, or of patterns and structures of language), and second, the interest in the social world which is reflected through this classification. Form criticism does this by way of its emphasis on the cult as the ancient, social context for many of its forms, and structuralism does this by its emphasis on the discourse between the contemporary social context of the reader and the apparent concerns of the text.

Rhetorical Criticism

Rhetorical criticism offers a way of looking at the text as a vehicle of persuasion. It asks questions about the arrangement of material and the choice of the discourse; it also asks whether or not there is an affinity between the reader and the text in this respect. It looks for silences in the text – the gaps in the discourse, the bias expressed implicitly – and from this it either seeks to turn the text into a vehicle of communication which supports the interests of the reader, or to upturn the text (this marks the beginning of what is often called 'deconstruction') so that the gaps and silences in the text are filled out with what the reader feels to be a necessary balance. Any unwelcome bias which is expressed, either explicitly or implicitly, is restated so that it serves the reader's interests rather than works against them. Hence this is as much about the imposition of the rhetoric of the reader as it is about the discovery of the rhetoric of the text. In the first instance it is about asking questions (that is, about discovering the rhetoric of the text) and then, second, it is about giving answers (that is, about filling in what is lacking the rhetoric of the text). This is why rhetorical criticism has been used as an important tool by feminist scholars, of whom P. Trible in *God and the Rhetoric of Sexuality* is probably the best example.

In many ways, affinities between this reading and tradition criticism can be seen. Each is interested in the ideas within the text, and in what can be learnt on account of how those ideas are communicated. Tradition criticism is in fact more receptive and more conservative, insofar as it does not seek to impose its own ideas on the theological traditions which are already there, but simply looks for an explanation of how they came to be there in the first place. But the concern about the substance of the text – communicated in the case of tradition criticism through the medium of the writers and communicated in the case of rhetorical criticism through the medium of the text – is a factor common to both of these methods.

Reader-Response Criticism

Rhetorical criticism focuses in part on the role of the reader, although the text is paramount in the process. 'Reader-response' indicates exactly what it signifies: the reader is to supply the gaps which are in the text, to iron out the repetitions and the doublets and the inconsistencies, whether by way of harmonizing them, or by way of offering an alternative explanation. In this way it is very closely related to rhetorical criticism, although the emphasis here is even more on the active role of the reader. The assumption is that there are many possible responses to one single text – in fact, the text has as many ways of reading as it has readers.

Reader-response criticism is a close ally to feminist theology and liberation theology, which have their own critique and explanation of the texts when it comes to criticism of patriarchy or of ideologies of power. Both a gender-orientated and a politically motivated reading may find a reader-response approach the only creative way of reading which is open to them, because it frees them to disagree with the text as it is written. Certainly in liberation theology, liberationist (often here also called 'materialist') readings of the Gospels in particular make good use of the reader-response approach. Of these, C. Myers in *Binding the Strong Man*, which is a materialist/liberationist reading of Mark, provides one of the best examples.

This approach is in fact quite close to redaction criticism. In the case of redaction criticism, the interest in the 'response' to the text is through the contribution of the redactor; in the case of 'reader-response', the reader actually 'becomes' the redactor. Both approaches are concerned with the text in its final stage; neither is interested in asking questions about its composition or development up to that stage. And both approaches seek to ascertain what the final concerns of the text might be. In the case of redaction criticism, these are about the concerns in the text as it used to be, and in the case of reader-response theory (also known as reception theory) these are about the concerns in the text as it affects life today.

Holistic Criticism

The term 'holistic criticism' signifies what it really means – an approach to the whole text, rather than a fragment of it. This means looking at the whole of a prophetic book, rather than at just a chapter of it, and the whole of a Gospel, rather than a parable or miracle from it. In terms of its application to the Bible, it is thus concerned with theology, too – the theology of the whole book, and how this theology affects our understanding of each part. For example, the book of Job comprises a prose prologue and epilogue, and the middle part is poetry. Historical criticism would see this as the work of two hands, with two styles, two theological agendas, writing at entirely different times, and would seek to find the message of the whole by comparing the different parts; but literary criticism would see Job as one book and would seek to find an approach which understood its theology and purpose in a more uniform way. A similar example could be found in the Gospel of Luke. Rather than extricating parts (such as the infancy stories, the passion narrative, the Q material, and so on) holistic studies would look at the Gospel as a uniform whole, asking only questions which concerned the text in its entirety rather than in the breakdown of its smaller parts.

It should not be difficult to see how close this is to the canonical approach – not only its interest in the final collected form, but in unifying theology within that collected form. The difference is that, whereas the canonical approach has within its agenda the interest in the ancient community which brought the final collected form into being, a holistic reading of the text is more concerned with the way in which the text makes sense within the life of the community in the present day, and is therefore more actively engaged with the contemporary communication of the text. Whereas canonical criticism is more descriptive, holistic criticism – because it is more interested in praxis – is inclined to be more prescriptive.

Conclusions and Implications

This chapter has given a wide-ranging survey of complex material covering many disparate themes, and we must now try to draw some conclusions from the many approaches to reading the Bible which we have covered. Another observation from *Biblical Interpretation* is helpful:

> This pluralism of possible interpretations allows scripture to illuminate the great diversity of human experience. The price to be paid is that it then becomes more difficult for rational argument to exclude unacceptable interpretations ... [I]t is necessary to be aware that a radically pluralist society has spawned a variety of understandings of literature, and opinions about how it should be read.
>
> (R. Morgan and J. Barton, pp. 198, 218)

It should now be clear how many different ways there are of approaching the biblical text, and how many of them come within the sphere of academic study as within the context of a believing community. However, what is important in this fragmentation is the place of the disparate parts within the greater whole.

Let us take an analogy. Think of the Bible and a historic ('listed') building. The historical approach looks at the building by offering several limited (but nevertheless, in general terms, important) insights about the social and political life of the occupants since the time when it was built. The literary approach offers us different (but nevertheless related) possibilities of assessing the edifice in the way one might approach an architect's plan for future development; properly devised, this would still be sensitive to the history of the building, the concern being for its future use for the sake of posterity. And finally, the theological approach, with its interests in memories, recollections, ideas and experiences associated with the place through the centuries is close, by analogy, to those paintings and photographs which portray the life-histories of those who have lived in the building, both past and present, capturing them in a particular way, and yet doing so for all time.

All analogies, not least those relating to biblical hermeneutics, fall short when attending to the details. Nevertheless, the purpose of this one is to show that, in the light of the pleas for pluralism, the integration of all three approaches offers some control and constraints on such open-ended pluralistic readings.

Just how this works in practice remains to be seen, and the Psalter is as good a place to start as any. The last two chapters will thus seek to show how a pluralistic approach to reading, with the three main emphases outlined here, working *with* rather than *against* each other, can enrich our understanding of the Psalms, rather than limit it. The first of these two chapters looks at the Psalter as an entire 'book'; the second is a close study of Psalm 8, which is a short hymn of praise.

8

The Many Voices in the Psalms

It is commony recognized amongst theologians that the Psalter contains in microcosm the problems that are found throughout the Bible as a whole. Taking first the issues set out in our first four chapters, the Psalter illustrates extremely well the issues of diversity – as literature, in theology, as a canonical collection, and as a biblical text.

Plurality in the Making of the Psalter

The Psalter as a Collection of Smaller Parts within a Greater Whole

Although the term 'library' cannot really be applied to a work which consists entirely of poetry, the Psalter is undoubtedly a book of miscellaneous compositions. The term 'anthology' is the closest one can get, although the liturgical influence on most of the psalms is undervalued if we use this more literary term. The Psalter is in fact part hymn book, part prayer book and part anthology – all three terms together thus indicate its literary and liturgical elements, and its public and private concerns. The following discussion is an illustration of this diversity, using examples first of the public, processional and liturgical psalms, then of the private, reflective and didactic psalms, and then of the two remaining most familiar forms – the laments, and the praises.

Almost all of the public poetry is associated with liturgical use. Psalms 15 and 24, as liturgies for accession to the Temple, fit this well:

> Who shall ascend the hill of the Lord?
>   And who shall stand in his holy place?
> He who has clean hands and a pure heart,
>   Who does not life up his soul to what is false ...

> (Psalm 24.3–4)

So too does an early processional psalm, 68:

> Thy solemn processions are seen, O God,
>   the processions of my God, my King, into the sanctuary –
> the singers in front, the minstrels last
>   between them maidens playing timbrels:
> 'Bless God in the great congregation,
>   the Lord, O you who are of Israel's fountain!
>
> (Psalm 68.24–5)

Other obvious examples include later psalms which have been composed as recitals of the nation's history – some in order to express praise to God, others in order to elicit confession from the people – such as Psalms 105 (praise) and 106 (confession), and Psalms 135 and 136, both hymns of praise. We might add to this list another group of psalms which were composed for festival occasions, probably for the prophets to use in their exhortations for greater loyalty to their God. The best examples are Psalms 50 and 81:

> Hear, O my people, while I admonish you!
>   O Israel, if you would but listen to me!
> There shall be no strange god among you;
>   you shall not bow down to a foreign god.
>
> (Psalm 81.8–9)

By contrast, the private concerns evident in other psalms suggest that overall they are less obviously bound up with liturgical occasions, being more personal reflections of an essentially literary kind, bearing more the influence of the wisdom tradition in style and in theology. The clearest examples are Psalms 1, 19 and 119, all of which reflect the importance of keeping the law, suggesting a later period when the Law was an authoritative collection:

> The law of the Lord is perfect,
>   reviving the soul;
> the testimony of the Lord is sure,
>   making wise the simple ...
> Moreover by them is thy servant warned;
>   in keeping of them there is great reward.
>
> (Psalm 19.7, 11)

Other examples include those which reflect on the tension between human suffering and the justice of God, such as Psalms 37 and 49:

> Why should I fear in times of trouble,
>   when the iniquity of my persecutors surrounds me,

188

men who trust in their wealth
  and boast in the abundance of their riches ...
Their graves are their homes for ever,
  their dwelling places to all generations,
  though they named lands their own.
Man cannot abide in his pomp,
  he is like the beasts that perish.

(Psalm 49.5–6, 11–12)

In addition to the different public/liturgical and private/reflective aspects of psalmody, two other important categories are important. First, the prayers of complaint composed from situations of distress, commonly known as 'laments'; and second, the prayers of thanksgiving composed as 'praises', offered at times of celebration and well-being. Both these types of psalms would have been composed originally for occasions of worship, either at the Temple or at local sanctuaries; in later times they would have been used, like a private prayer book, by individuals or even by synagogue communities. Although the two basic forms of lament and praise are found in other liturgical collections outside Israel – for example, Babylonian laments and hymns follow a very similar basic pattern to the laments and hymns found in the Psalter – the adaptation of these forms by different psalmists reveals a good deal about the diverse and creative use of established patterns.

The basic form for the lament – whether individual or communal in orientation – would be a cry of despair or plea for help, a description of the distress, and a vow of trust in God's care. The adaptation of this form may be seen in a lament by an individual, such as Psalm 22; verse 1 is the cry, verses 2 to 21 essentially the description of distress, and verses 22 to 31 the vow to trust God's care. The same adaptation can be seen in laments composed for the community, such as Psalm 44: verse 1 is the cry, verses 9 to 25 the description of distress, and verses 2 to 8 the vow of trust (thus a good illustration of the use of the same motifs, but in a different order). There are many variations of this threefold format for the laments; the moods of the psalmist appear to control the ordering of the motifs. Perhaps the most extreme is Psalm 88, a psalm about the fear of death and of dying, where the whole psalm is one long description of distress with no expression of trust or faith uttered at all.

The basic form of the hymn is a call to praise God, a description of the reasons for offering praise – either specific in the life of the psalmist, or general in the character of God – with the vow of confidence – or another call to praise God – at the end. A clear example of this basic form is Psalm 113: verses 1 to 3 are the call to praise, verses 4 to 8 the reasons for offering praise, and verse 9 is the vow of confidence. But there are many variations of this basic form. Psalm 145 is different because it uses an acrostic form, whereby the first letters used for each of the stanzas are in some form of alphabetic order, and this is therefore a good example of the blend of liturgical and literary skills. Psalm 100 is different because it includes a sixfold antiphonal arrangement, probably for use by a leader and a choir.

It could be argued that it would be strange not to find in such a collection of hymns and prayers polarities of human experience; and the very fact that the prayers cater for both the heights (in the hymns) and the depths (in the laments) of human existence explains why they were preserved, for they address most aspects of the human condition.

But the issue of diversity does not stop here. Another most important observation is the way these two most familiar forms of lament and praise have been arranged within the Psalter overall. The laments occur predominantly in the first part of the Psalter, and the hymns increasingly so towards the end. For example – and here we are being specific only in order to show the pattern overall – of the laments, both communal and individual, we may note Psalms 3—7, 9—10, 12—13, 17—18, 20—2, 25—6, 28, 31, 35—6, 38—9, 42—4, 51, 54—7, 59—61, 63—4, 69—71, 74, 77, 79—80, 82—3, 85—6, 88—90, 94, 102, 106, 108—9, 120, 123, 126, 130, 137, 140—4. And of the hymns, we may note 8, 19A, 29, 30, 32—4, 47, 65—8, 92—100, 103—4, 107, 111, 113—18, 124—5, 129, 134—6, 138 and 145—50. This distribution is made clear in Table 13.

Table 13   The Distribution of Hymns and Laments throughout the Psalter

Book One	Psalms 1—41	25 laments 7 hymns
Book Two	Psalms 42—72	17 laments 5 hymns
Book Three	Psalms 73—89	10 laments no hymns
Book Four	Psalms 90—105	2 laments 11 hymns
Book Five	Psalms 106—50	12 laments 21 hymns

As Table 13 indicates, the Psalter is subdivided into five books, imitating the five books of the Law. Psalms 41.13, 72.18–20, 89.52 and 106.48 form the 'markers' at the end of each book, by way of additional ascription of praise to the name of God (called a doxology), the common features being broadly the same between one doxology and another. For example:

> Blessed be the Lord, the God of Israel,
> from everlasting to everlasting!
> Amen and Amen.

(Psalm 41.13)

The hymns and laments, as well as other public and private psalms, are thus scattered throughout the five books of the entire collection.

Hence in terms of its origins and purpose, the start of the process of the formation of the Psalter reflects very different forms – some liturgical and other literary, some as compositions for public use and others for private use, some reflecting individual concerns and others reflecting more corporate ones. Looking at the middle of the process, such diverse forms must point to a diverse number of authors – some in the cult and writing for liturgical occasions, and others more independent of cultic concerns and writing from a more didatic and reflective point of view. And looking at the end of the process, we may note the deliberate arrangement of the miscellany of material into five books (in fact, it is more than likely that the first three books came into existence as collections before the final two), and the spread of the different forms – here we noted especially the lament and the hymnic/thanksgiving forms – with a deliberate movement towards the predominance of praise at the end of the Psalter as a whole. The end result is a 'collection of collections'.

Hence the Psalter in microcosm illustrates the issue of diversity which we discussed in relation to the Bible as a whole in our first chapter.

The Psalter as a Diverse Collection of Theologies

Not only the diversity of material, but also the sheer extent of time over which the Psalter took shape must suggest that the Psalter contains a large number of different theological outlooks. For the composition of psalmody begins at the time of the monarchy, and ends (as far as the canonical collection is concerned) in the late restoration period. (The extent of cultural and social changes throughout this whole time is illustrated by way of a brief overview on p. xvi.)

For example, those psalms written during the time of the monarchy, and hence during the establishment of the state, must have been composed to reflect the pro-royal and pro-Zion/pro-Temple theologies. Put simply, most of these psalms would have been composed for use at state occasions to support the status quo. Examples of this include the royal psalms (Psalms 2, 18, 20, 21, 45, 72, 89, 101, 110, 132, 144) which would have been used for the king's accession to the throne (Psalms 2, 72, 110, 132), at times of military victory or defeat (Psalms 18, 20, 21, 89, 144), or even for a royal wedding (Psalm 45). Other examples include the Zion hymns (Psalms 46, 48, 76, 84, 87, 122) which support the idea of Jerusalem and the Temple being at the heart of God's concerns for his people. The 'establishment theology' should be clear:

> 'I have set my king on Zion, my holy hill ...
> Ask of me, and I will make nations your heritage,
>   and the ends of the earth your possession.'
>
> (Psalm 2.6, 8)

> Give the king your justice, O God,
>   and thy righteousness to the royal son! ...
> May he have dominion from sea to sea,
>   and from the River to the ends of the earth!
>
> (Psalm 72.1, 8)

> Great is the Lord and greatly to be praised
>   in the city of our God ...
> Walk about Zion, go round about her,
>   number her towers ...
> that you may tell the next generation
>   that this is God,
> our God for ever and ever.
>   He will be our guide for ever.
>
> (Psalm 48.1, 12–14)

By contrast, psalms written during the time of the exile must reflect the disappointed hopes of a people deprived of land and statehood, now questioning the justice of God in it all. Examples of this include psalms which speak of the desecration of the Temple site (Psalms 74 and 79) and a lament which refers to Babylon as the land of exile (Psalm 137):

> O God, why dost thou cast us off for ever?
>   Why does thy anger smoke against the sheep of thy pasture? ...
> Direct thy steps to the perpetual ruins;
>   the enemy has destroyed everything in the sanctuary!
>
> (Psalm 74.1, 3)

By the waters of Babylon,
   there we sat down and wept,
   when we remembered Zion ...
For there our captors
   required of us songs,
   and our tormentors, mirth, saying,
'Sing us one of the songs of Zion!'

(Psalm 137.1, 3)

It is likely that the 'song of Zion' referred to in Psalm 137 is in fact a psalm such as 46, which is itself a Zion hymn, and which was used in better times, probably before the Exile, to celebrate God's protection of his city.

As a further contrast, another group of psalms, composed during the time of the restoration to the land, reflect different uncertainties and hopes. Without the restoration of the monarchy but nevertheless with the Temple rebuilt, and the priesthood reinstated, albeit under Persian governship, the returned exiles (packed into a tiny corner of Judah) had to set about building a new future – not now as a nation, but as a religious community. Two clear questions are evident from other literature composed at this time. First, individual questioning of faith was more commonplace; Job and Ecclesiastes are good illustrations of this. Second, another great issue concerned the relationship the restored people should have with the Gentiles (and here the different attitudes in Jonah and Ruth, and in Ezra and Nehemiah, illustrate this well). Hence psalms which wrestle with issues of God's justice in more personal terms (for example, Psalms 37, 49, 73, 91, 133) and psalms which reflect tensions of party-strife between the righteous few and the impious enemies of the people (for example, Psalms 56, 58, 59, 60, 62) also suggest theological reflection from this later time. Two examples must suffice:

Be still before the Lord, and wait patiently for him;
   fret not yourself over him who prospers in his way,
   over the man who carries out evil devices!

(Psalm 37.7)

For God alone my soul waits in silence;
from him comes my salvation ...
How long will you set upon a man
   to shatter him, all of you,
   like a leaning wall, a tottering fence?
They only plan to thrust him down from his eminence.
   They take pleasure in falsehood.
They bless with their mouths,
   but inwardly they curse.

(Psalm 62.1, 3–4)

193

Obviously one cannot be too categorical about presuming a context for the psalms and then proposing a psalm which fits best with it. There is a danger here of circularity; it may be that a psalm composed at an earlier time, for example concerning the threat of the enemies of the people in a more national sense, was reused to described party-strife in a more social sense. But what is clear is that the Psalter comprises many contrasting – even apparently opposing – theological themes. The concern for God's establishment of the nation in pre-exilic times (for example, in the Zion hymns, such as 46 and 48) has to be set alongside the belief in God's world rule and hence his concern for all peoples (Psalms 47, 93). The sense of living in an age of well-being (expressed, for example, in individual terms in Psalm 40, and in a hymn such as Psalm 100) has to be set alongside the experience of God's anger and judgement when all lay desolate and destroyed (as in Psalms 74 and 137 referred to above). The interest in cultic worship – the rituals, sacrifices, processions and festivals – was vital when the Temple was standing, both before and after the Exile (as in the Temple liturgies in Psalms 15 and 24, and the only psalm referring explicitly to the role of the ark, a royal psalm, 132). But this had to be complemented, after the experience of the Exile and the temporary end of the Temple and its sacrificial system, by a different emphasis on individual acts of personal piety, where integrity of spirit, an attitude of prayer and individual moral responsibility were viewed as pleasing God as much as Temple worship (for example, Psalms 26, 32, 51, 69). And the God who was seen to protect those in power and authority in earlier times – the king, the priests, the prophets, the scribes (noting Psalms 2 and 72 quoted above, as well as Psalms 45 and 110) – was seen (especially after their demise) as the God who also cared for the 'powerless' – the righteous poor, the saints, the meek and humble of heart, and the physically downtrodden (Psalms 86, 109, 139, 140).

Hence the Psalter is not so much about one theology as it is about many. It is as difficult to speak of the theology of the Psalter as a whole as it is to speak of the theology of the Bible as a whole. There is a danger of imposing one great overarching theme upon the whole, and trying to force the smaller parts to fit into it. For example, the theme which was proposed as a central tenet of Old Testament theology, the theme which is best summarized as 'God who acts particularly within the history of his people', is evident in some of the psalms, including several of those referred to above; but it is by no means evident in all of them, and it would be wrong to impose such a theology upon them.

As with the theology of the Old Testament as a whole, it is equally possible to unite the whole Psalter under a theme which is so vast it says very little (and even then, some psalms may not be included within it).

Examples include 'the kingship of God' (proposed by B. S. Childs), 'God's presence in Zion' (H.-J. Kraus), and 'God's making and remaking of the covenant with David' (so G. H. Wilson). But even here, there are some psalms which simply do not fit these concerns; several of them have been referred to already. It is far more appropriate to see the Psalter as a blend of diverse theologies loosely bound together into a disparate whole. Hence again the Psalter provides an ideal illustration of what was said at the end of Chapter 2 about the theology of the Bible as a whole.

The Psalter and the Diversity of Canonical Collections

We referred in the previous section to the likelihood that the Psalter developed slowly, and that at one time it only comprised Books One to Three, with a number of additional collections (for example, Psalms 93, 95–9, on the theme of the kingship of God, and Psalms 120—34, collected for use by pilgrims going up to worship at the Temple). There might even have been a time when Psalm 119 was the final psalm of the Psalter, before the addition of Psalms 120–34 and the other psalms following this collection, representing the second stage in the process after the formation of Books One to Three (Psalms 1–89). This would make the first and last psalms of this collection reflective wisdom psalms, and would make the Psalter more like a didactic prayer book than a Temple hymn book. Whether this is the case or not, the addition of Psalms 120–34, and of Psalms 145–50, with other additions integrated in between, created the opportunity for subdividing the whole collection into five books. This was on account of the importance of the number five in the laws of Moses. Hence the canonical collection of the five books of the Psalter came about; that this took place by the second century BCE is clear from the fact that this is what was translated into the Greek.

Unlike Ecclesiastes and Esther, and other disputed books in the Writings, once compiled, the Psalter's acceptance into the canonical collection was never disputed. The most obvious reason for this was its foundational place in the liturgy of the Temple and in readings in synagogue worship. What *was* disputed was its actual order within the Writings. It was normally placed at the head, and then followed either by Job and then Proverbs, or by Proverbs and then Job. But there is evidence from the Palestinian tradition of an order whereby Chronicles headed up the Writings, with the Psalter coming second. This was later used, for example, by the Sephardic Jews in Spain. But the *Talmud* refers to yet another order, whereby the book of Ruth headed up the collection, because Ruth was the grandmother of David and hence chronologically first. The order which exists in Protestant and Catholic Bibles today is taken from the Vulgate: Job is first, the Psalms second, and Proverbs next. But the early disputes about the actual place of the Psalter in the Canon overall illustrates that, initially, this was a variable tradition.

Another indication of a different canonical tradition is the numbering of the psalms within the Psalter as a whole. Here the Greek and Hebrew traditions diverge. Basically, the Greek translation unites together Psalms 9 and 10 (Psalm 10 has no heading, so could be combined with Psalm 9 anyway), as also Psalms 114 and 115. This translation then splits up Psalms 116 and 147, so the total number is 150, although the numbering is different. (Catholic Bibles follow the Greek numbering, from the Vulgate, but Protestant Bibles follow the Hebrew.) Table 14 shows the differences.

Table 14   The Psalms in the Hebrew and Greek Versions

Hebrew	*Greek*	*Hebrew*	*Greek*
Psalms 1—8	**= Psalms 1—8**	Psalms 116.10–19	= Psalm 115
Psalms 9—10	= Psalm 9	Psalms 117—46	= Psalms 116—45
Psalms 11—113	= Psalms 10—112	Psalm 147.1–11	= Psalm 146
Psalms 114—15	= Psalm 113	Psalm 147.12–20	= Psalm 147
Psalms 116.1-9	= Psalm 114	**Psalms 148—150**	**= Psalms 148—50**

As Table 14 shows, only the first eight psalms and the last three psalms of the whole collection have the same numbering in the Greek and Hebrew versions.

Psalm 151, which uses part of 1 Samuel 16—17 for its account of David's victory over Goliath, is added at the end of the Septuagint, but it is called 'supernumerary'. Hence the decision to maintain the same number, in spite of the different order, is an important indication that the Psalter's canonical tradition, albeit not final, was at least fixed for the Greek translators in the second century BCE. This was not always the case, however. A rabbinic text, *Ber*ᵉ*ḵoṯ* 9b–10a, from some two centuries later, has a text which contains not 150 psalms, but 147. This is because of the combinations of Psalms 1 and 2, 14 and 15, and 117 and 118; that this was a deliberate liturgical practice is clear because 147 is a number subdivisible by seven, thus creating twenty-one lectionary readings.

But, more importantly, what the existence of Psalm 151 does show is that a good deal of psalm-writing was still in progress at this time. There are other imitations of psalms preserved elsewhere in the Septuagint, the Psalms of Solomon and the Odes of Solomon being the best examples. The Syriac versions have other psalms, too; a twelfth-century manuscript has evidence of five such psalms, including Psalm 151. Most importantly, Qumran gives us particular evidence of other psalms not included in the Psalter, as well as several psalm-like compositions, the most significant collection being the Thanksgiving Hymns (1QH), which comprises thirty or so other thanksgiving psalms, imitating the canonical psalms in form and in style, concerned with the twin themes of salvation and knowledge of God.

The practice of imitating psalmody is also found in the New Testament. The most clear examples are in the hymns and thanksgivings purportedly sung at the time of the birth of Christ, as Luke 1—2. It is thus often difficult to know the boundaries between the psalmic imitations and canonical psalms, except that most compositions (with the exception of Qumran) were not in Hebrew, and the Hebrew language was a firm criterion with regard to the acceptance of a text as canonical.

On this account, Qumran perhaps offers us the best insights regarding the status of the Psalms from the second century BCE to the first century CE or it offers us insights which at the very least reveal there were exceptions to the rule. As we saw in Chapter 3 on the Canon, Qumran offers as many insights on the Psalms as it does about any other Old Testament book, with the exception of Isaiah. Over thirty psalm texts (or commentaries on psalm texts) have been found in the eight Qumran caves since 1947. Eighteen of these are from Cave 4, all dating from the first two centuries BCE. 4 Q Ps a joins together Psalms 38 and 71. This may be because of the similar phraseology in each psalm ('make haste to help me' as in 38.22 and 71.12, and 'those who seek my hurt' in 38.12 and 71.13), but as these formulae are found in other psalms, this could not be the only reason for combining them together. All that can be known is that the Qumran lectionary did not use the psalms in the traditional canonical order, for it connected together different psalms even from different books in the Psalter.

Other significant Qumran discoveries are from Cave 11, dating from the first century CE. For instance, 11 Q Ps b contains many psalms in Books One to Three, following overall the order as in the MT. But 11 Q Ps a contains mainly Books Four to Five, and takes an entirely different order: from this particular scroll, it would appear that the greater variations occur predominantly within these two latter books, affirming our observations that these were the two latest books to become part of a fixed tradition. For example, Psalms 106—8 and 110—17 are missing, but thirteen other psalms are found in an entirely different sequence (Psalms 109, 118, 147, 146, 148, 119, 145, 139, 93, 133, 144, 140, 134). Psalm 145 has an additional refrain after each verse. And although in the Psalms of Ascent (Psalms 120—34) the first thirteen are in order, this changes as the order progresses. In addition, poems (hymns and laments) not found in the Psalter are interspersed with several psalmic texts. 2 Samuel 23.1–7 is included, as also Psalm 151 (in a longer and a shorter form) as well as Psalms 154 and 155 (so-called because of their place in the Syriac Psalter), Ecclesiasticus 51.13ff., as well as additions named 'The Apostrophe to Zion', 'The Hymn to the Creator' and 'Davidic Compositions'.

There are in fact two possible views on the Canon as a result of these discoveries at Qumran: either it demonstrates that the Canon was not in any complete state at this time (so J. A. Sanders and G. H. Wilson) or it illustrates an entirely different tradition being accepted at Qumran (so P. Skehan), although it could be argued that in the end this comes to the same thing. Whichever emphasis one takes, the Qumran scrolls undoubtedly show the diversity in the canonical tradition of psalmody at least up until the first century CE.

The titles used for the Psalter throughout this same period simply serve to confirm these observations. On the one hand, it would appear that the Hebrew-Aramaic tradition used the title *Tᵉhillîm*, 'songs of praise'. This was an inappropriate enough title, given the proportion of hymns dispersed throughout the Psalms as whole, although even this title fails to do justice to the other psalms in the collection – for example, the large number of laments as well. In other traditions, the term *Tᵉphillôṯ*, 'prayers', as used in Psalm 72.20 is evident. This has the advantage of including both praises (prayers of thanksgiving) and laments (prayers of complaint) within the same category. The Greek translation evident in the codices of the Septuagint diversifies this understanding. The designation '*psalmoi*' in Codex B (also in Luke 20.42) is a translation of the Hebrew word '*mizmôr*', which occurs as a title in fifty-seven psalms and takes us back to the overall classification as 'hymns'. Another title, evidenced in Codex A, is '*psalterion*'. This is a translation of the Hebrew '*nēbel*', which denotes a musical instrument like a harp or lyre, and hence the designation that this is a collection of hymns and prayers to be sung to such a six-stringed instrument.

Within the first three centuries of the canonical life of the Psalter, it was not at all clear what was the predominant form – praise or lament. Nor was it clear what purpose the Psalter as a whole served – whether liturgical or reflective. More likely it was of course part of each, and the emphasis depended on the geographical location of that particular collection of psalmody. Psalms of Palestinian origin would be more likely to be tied to Temple usage until 70 CE, and psalms composed in communities further afield, centred more on lectionary readings in synagogues, would be more tied to a very different liturgical setting because of the differences between synagogue and Temple worship. Diversity of usage thus resulted in a diversity of the canonical traditions.

The Diversity of the Psalter Evidenced through Manuscripts and Versions

The term 'intratextuality' is a popular one in biblical studies today. But it need not imply contemporary usage. The variant tradition of psalms being copied and used for different purposes and then being preserved in different places within the same overall collection is evident in the Psalter itself.

There are three obvious examples. Psalms 14 and 53 are identical psalms, although the Hebrew text offers some variations when comparing the two. The clearest illustration is in the two different names each psalm uses for God. Psalm 14 uses 'Yahweh' every time (verses 2, 4, 7) while Psalm 53 uses 'Elohim' in the same parallels (verses 2, 4, 6). Psalm 53 is believed to be the later, more developed text of the two. For example, 53.5 and 14.5 have a very different grammatical construction and that in Psalm 53 is the more complex. Psalms 40.13–17 and 70 offer another example of pairing, and again the texts are not identical. In Psalm 40, 'Yahweh' is used, except in verse 17b; and in Psalm 70, 'Elohim' is used instead, except in verses 1b and 5b, showing again a different tradition for the use of the names of God in each psalm. Psalm 108 is an amalgam of Psalms 57.7–11 (108.1–5) and 60.5–12 (108.6–13) and the same illustration of a small amount of textual variation applies here too; one brief example is 57.7 which has an additional phrase ('my heart is steadfast') not found in 108.2.

In addition, there are two other examples of psalms within the Psalter which have parallel texts elsewhere in the Bible. Psalm 18 and 2 Samuel 22 are the best examples. Here there are many more differences; the Hebrew text even uses a different system of pointing in the two poems. The key differences, using Psalm 18 as the base, are found in verses, 1, 2, 4, 6, 11, 12, 14, 28, 32, 35 and 41. These are almost all small words and emendations, but there are enough of them to indicate a variant tradition rather than copyists' slips. The other example is from 1 Chronicles 16, which uses parts of three psalms (105, 95, 106 in that order). This illustrates two variant features: first, that of the different canonical tradition in terms of the organization of the collection, and second, a small but nevertheless noticeable, different textual tradition.

Hence if even in the more closed circle of the Hebrew Bible, such variations can take place, how much more so is this likely to be the case when it comes to translations and versions outside it? The Septuagint translation, albeit one of the more literal translations of the Old Testament books, has many divergences from that Hebrew text which eventually became known as the Massoretic Text. One problem here is that of the lack of complete early manuscripts of the Psalms. *Codex Alexandrinus* from the fifth century CE does not have Psalms 49.19—79.10, and *Codex Vaticanus* from the fourth century CE lacks Psalms 105.27—137.6. Only *Codex Sinaiticus* (also fourth century CE) has the complete Psalter.

The difficulty in making comparisons between the Greek and the Hebrew texts is not only that of interpreting different translations, but also that of making sense of the disagreements between one Greek manuscript and another. Two examples only must suffice, although there are many more illustrations. Psalm 95.6 reads (from the Hebrew), 'O come … let us kneel before the Lord our maker.' The Greek, reading the Hebrew for 'kneel' (*nbrkh*) as one consonant less (*nbkh*, meaning 'weep') thus reads 'O come … let us weep before the Lord our maker.' Or again, Psalm 20.9 reads (from the Hebrew), 'Give victory to the king, O Lord; answer us when we call.' The Greek, perhaps more sensibly, reads, 'Give victory, O Lord, let the king answer us when we call.'

Three Latin versions of the Psalter are evident by the fourth century CE. The oldest in *Vetus Itola* – a translation of the Septuagint, made in North Africa in the second century CE. Some two centuries later, this was revised by Jerome (in about 383) and was known as the Roman Psalter. Jerome then made another Latin translation based on the Greek, and not the Latin, probably taken from Origen's *Hexapla*, known as the Gallican Psalter. Jerome's final Latin version of the Psalms (made between 390 and 405 CE) was based on an entire Old Testament translation from the Hebrew, known as *Psalterium juxtu Hebraeos*. Although all the other Old Testament books translated were accepted by the Churches and became known as the Vulgate, the only work not to be accepted was the Psalter. This was because the Gallican Psalter had already achieved a good liturgical reputation. But Jerome's three Latin translations from three different language media – the Latin, Greek and Hebrew – says a good deal about the diverse textual tradition of the Psalter, even by the fourth century CE.

One very obvious point to make here is that the English translations of the Psalms have used the variations and the differences between the various versions to full advantage in gaining better clarification of the meaning of uncertain texts. Recognizing that there is no such thing as one definitive text, most translations indicate where use has been made of Jerome, or of the Greek, or of the *Targums* (*Tg*), or of the *Peshitta* (Syriac) in preference to the MT Hebrew. The RSV, for example, is full of references by way of footnotes to the variant translations from different texts. In Psalm 24.9, *Tg* is deemed the better translation: not 'lift up, O ancient doors', but 'be lifted up, O ancient doors'. So too in Psalm 11.1: not 'flee to the mountain, O bird' as in the MT, but 'flee like a bird to the mountains', following the Greek, Syriac, Jerome and the *Tg* in preference to the MT. In Psalm 16.2, the footnote reads that the meaning of the Hebrew (MT) is uncertain; hence the translators follow Jerome and *Tg*, 'I have no good apart from thee.' Psalm 31.10 reads, 'my strength fails because of my misery.' This too follows the Greek and Syriac; the Hebrew reads 'iniquity' instead of 'misery', Psalm 50.11 reads, 'I know all the birds of the air'. This follows the Greek, Syriac and *Tg*, for the Hebrew reads, 'I know all the birds of the mountains'. Psalm 69.10 offers a more simple translation by using the Greek and Syriac: 'When I humbled my soul with fasting'; the Hebrew reads 'I made my soul mourn (weep) with fasting.'

These are of course very minor variations, but they are useful in helping us to see the ninth/tenth-century CE Hebrew text against an earlier linguistic background. There is no doubt that the comparisons with the different versions reveal that small corruptions and catch-words are very much in evidence. Hence it should not be surprising that, within the Hebrew text itself, at least seventy examples are to be found in the Psalms of the Massoretic practice of correcting the text by way of $k^e th\hat{i}bh$ ('it is written') and $q^e r\hat{e}$ ('to be read'). The mistakes of the MT – in terms of missing letters, exchange of letters, miscopying, and even making sense of an archaic and corrupt text – are inevitable. Yet, in spite of this, it is the MT text (taken mainly from the tenth-century Aleppo Codex and the eleventh-century Leningrad Codex) which is the norm for most translations, and, as the footnotes above indicate, the versions are seen to complement and illuminate the MT, rather than the reverse. To take us back to the conclusions at the end of Chapter 4: the Psalter illustrates well that there never was such a thing as any normative, definitive text of the psalms – and this in spite of the central role of the Psalter in both Jewish and Christian tradition.

Plurality in the Reading of the Psalter

The Psalter and Theological Approaches

In terms of reading the Bible as a whole, the two most significant theological approaches discussed in Chapter 5 were the literal and the allegorical. While the literal reading is concerned with the direct, straightforward sense of a text, the allegorical reading emphasizes different levels of interpretation, being more concerned with hidden meanings than with plain sense. As far as the Psalter is concerned, there are essentially four different ways in which it has been interpreted theologically throughout Jewish and Christian tradition, and in these four ways the combination of the literal and allegorical readings can be seen in different measures.

From earliest times, the most predominant use of the Psalter in both Jewish and Christian tradition has been the liturgical one, and this has continued up to the present day. This starts with the plain sense, but moves on to find a deeper, 'hidden' interpretation, on account of the need to appropriate what is said in ancient times to a contemporary setting. A second use of the Psalms, common from the post-exilic period onwards, and used by both Jews and Christians alike, is the didactic reading; this is closer to the literal, direct sense of a passage than any of the other three. A third use, beginning from about two centuries before the time of Christ and also evident in early Christian tradition (and from time to time also in later Jewish and Christian movements) is what might be termed a prophetic interpretation. This is very close to the allegorical interpretation, for it places a good deal of emphasis on the hidden meanings in various important psalmic texts. A fourth use, and really running parallel to the liturgical interpretation but different from it insofar as this is as much about private as about public reading, is the spiritual interpretation. Like the liturgical approach, this too is a combination of the literal (the importance of the plain sense of the prayer in question) and the allegorical (the importance of applying that ancient sense into present-day life).

THEOLOGICAL APPROACHES TO THE PSALMS IN THE JEWISH TRADITION

The liturgical use of the Psalter is self-evident. Many of the psalms were composed for the royal liturgy and annual festivals of the first Temple, while many others were composed for the liturgy of the second Temple. The use of such psalms, even after the Temple's first destruction in 587 BCE, has been within a liturgical context, whether in the Temple itself or perhaps in a synagogue setting. (The reference to the exiled community 'singing songs of Zion' 'by the waters of Babylon' in Psalm 137.1–3 may well suggest the very earliest formation of a worshipping group in exile, probably imitating the later use of the psalms in synagogue practice.) After the final destruction of the Temple in 70 CE, the psalms were used entirely in synagogue worship, as had been an increasingly regular practice in Jewish communities dispersed in different lands to the north, east and south even before this time.

Gradually, as the dispersion continued – into Spain, southern France, mid-Germany, Poland, west Russia, North Africa – and as synagogue worship became the focus of religious unity for all such Jewish communities, lectionary reading (and singing) from the psalms played a large part in synagogue services. Almost half the Psalter would have been regularly used in readings for daily services, for Sabbath services, and for the three great annual festivals – the Feasts of Passover, Weeks and Tabernacles. The *siddur*, or the Jewish prayer book, is known to have been in existence by the ninth century at least. As well as using the Ten Commandments, and some credal texts from Deuteronomy 6 and 11, and blessings from Numbers 15, the group of psalms most in use are the psalms of praise, 113—18, known as 'the Great Hallel' (the Hebrew '*hallel*' means 'praise', and this is a common theme in the Psalms), but over a third of the Psalter is known to have been used in this collection.

Furthermore, the *Mishnah* instructs the use of psalms at regular times on regular days: Psalm 24 on Sunday, 48 on Monday, 82 on Tuesday, 94 on Wednesday, 81 on Thursday, 93 on Friday, and 92 on Saturday. Interestingly, this corresponds in large measure with the Septuagint headings for each of these psalms, concerning their use on these same days. This again serves to show the daily use of psalms, and this would have taken place in synagogue worship, alongside the other collections of psalms (for example, 113—18) used in the annual festivals and alongside selections of other psalms used in Sabbath services. (This practice is of course evident in Jewish prayer books to this day.)

In his book, *The Psalms through Three Thousand Years*, W. L. Holladay concludes that from the first century CE up until the twentieth century, some fifty-seven psalms played a regular and significant part in Jewish liturgy. Many of these are hymns and thanksgivings, as well as liturgies and the prophetic exhortations. In this way, the psalms played a vital part in providing a continuity of tradition, not only within Jewish communities dispersed throughout Europe in the Middle Ages but also in the Reformed, Orthodox or Conservative Jewish communities established over the last two centuries. Indeed, it could be argued that the place of the Psalms in liturgy was second only to the Law.

The didactic use of the psalms is similarly clear. This may well have been part of a very early practice in psalmody, whereby a suppliant, upon recovery from illness or upon any other sort of restoration, used a psalm as a means of edifying the community about God's goodness and graciousness and exhorting them to trust God as well. Certainly this is a feature of many of the thanksgiving psalms. The suppliant turns from addressing God in praise to addressing the community in instruction, for example:

> O Lord, thou hast brought up my soul from Sheol
>> restored me to life from among those gone down to the Pit.
> Sing praises to the Lord, O you his saints,
>> and give thanks to his holy name.
> For his anger is but for a moment,
>> and his favour is for a lifetime.

(Psalm 30.3–5)

There are many examples of this feature. Examples include Psalms 32.10–11, 40.9–10, and the whole of Psalm 34.

In addition to this feature in the thanksgivings, other psalms also seem to have been composed for the purpose of instruction from the start. Psalms 1 and 119 are good examples and, as noted earlier, these may well have formed an instructional introduction and conclusion to an early edition of the Psalter, whereby the user was reminded of the importance of keeping the law as a means of achieving inner piety and blessing from God. Psalms 120 to 134, all bearing the title 'Songs of Ascents', may well have been another type of collection for instructing Temple pilgrims in lessons of piety.

Clear didactic elements are also found in the several psalms which have been composed using an acrostic style (whereby the first letter in each line serves to create a sequence of letters, usually alphabetic, throughout all the lines). This is clear in Psalms 111 and 112, where the pattern is created through single line-forms; in Psalms 25 and 37, where the pattern is between one verse and the next; and in Psalm 34, which has both the instructional element and the recurring alphabetic pattern throughout the entire psalm. Psalms 9 to 10 also has some linking alphabetic structure, although several letters are missing, and it too has a didactic element. Psalm 145, where the acrostic form seems in the middle to spell out the Hebrew word for king (*melek*) by inverting the letters k-l-m to m-l-k, is similarly didactic in its teaching on the kingship of God. But the best example of an acrostic form in an instructional psalm is Psalm 119. Here the pattern is in the use of the same letter at the beginning of a line, repeated eight times to create a full stanza, in which there are also eight references to different words for

204

the law; the stanzas are repeated twenty-two times, so that the acrostic works 8 x 22 = 176 verses, using every letter of the Hebrew alphabet eight times, and synonyms for the law, eight times.

One other way in which this didactic use of psalmody was validated was by giving psalms titles which referred to David. As the memory of the Davidic monarchy continued in post-exilic times, in spite of the absence of the king, so an increasing number of psalms was assigned to David, who became the great exemplar of Jewish piety. Historical super-scriptions assigned events hinted at in the poetry of a psalm to a specific event in the life of David. Psalms 51, 54, 56, 57, 59, 60 form a cluster of psalms all of which have these superscriptions, even though many of them were composed long after David and even after the demise of the monarchy. But the superscription then makes them each a 'Psalm of David'. They are then read with reference first and fore-most to David, and lessons about piety and obedience can be learnt by those reading it with this focus in mind some centuries later. Furthermore, the *Midraš T'hillîm*, the greatest Rabbinic commentary on the psalms, compiled between the third and thirteenth centuries CE, confirms this interpretation 'David-wards' in its own exegesis. The interpretation emphasizes the origins of a psalm in the lifetime of David. One of the best examples is the commentary on Psalm 51, verses 3 to 5, which uses the superscription and comments as if the setting assumes David's adultery with Bathsheba; this interpretation then seeks to apply lessons learnt by David for life in the present community.

The emphasis on the halakhic approach in using the law would have contributed to this Davidic mode of interpretation, whereby the psalms encouraged 'torah-piety', and 'torah-piety' encouraged the reading of the psalms. And throughout this time, the synagogue schools would have played an important part in furthering the use of the psalms in this way. Indeed, the didactic element is so much a part of the later use of psalmody that U. Simon, in *Four Approaches to the Book of Psalms*, sees the instructional approach as primary in Jewish tradition, calling the book of Psalms 'a second Pentateuch' because of its tendencies towards commandment and admonition.

The prophetic use of psalms is particularly evident in the period between the second and third centuries CE. The best example, which we have already noted, is in Qumran, in the *pēšer* approach, which used a psalmic text in order to show how the promises made by the psalmist were being fulfilled in the life of the Qumran community. The text which most clearly shows this is Psalm 37, and the Qumran text is 4 Q 171 (see p. 120 earlier). Another example is found in a scroll from Cave 11. There reference is made to David as the composer of 3,600 hymns and songs (noting again the emphasis on David as the composer and model of psalmic piety) and the reference ends: 'All these he uttered *through prophecy* which was given him from before the Most High.' By terming the psalms 'prophecies', inspired by the great figure-head David, the *pēsher* method of interpretation is thus justified even further; these are prophetic texts, and the times of Qumran signal the time of fulfilment of the promises once made to David.

This is very close to the use of the prophecy/fulfilment method taken up by Jewish writers in the New Testament, such as Matthew, Paul and the writer of Hebrews, all referred to earlier. Certainly each of these writers draws from the psalms, and does so by assuming the citations had a prophetic worth. Examples from just two psalms by each of these writers should illustrate this point. For instance, all three use Psalm 8 in this way. Psalm 8.3 is used in Matthew 21.16 (at the time of the entry into Jerusalem); Psalm 8.5–7 is used in Hebrews 2.6–7 (to show it was Jesus foretold in the psalm, as one a little lower than the angels), and Psalm 8.8 is used in 1 Corinthians 15.27, to show that the one under whom everything was to be subject in the psalm is in fact Christ. Psalm 110 is another much-used example. Psalm 110.1 is used in Matthew 22.24 and 26.64, to speak of Christ fulfilling the promises made in part to David, and also by Paul in Romans 8.34 and Colossians 3.1, to show the further fulfilment of the psalm in the time of Christ by way of his ascension into heaven. Psalm 110.4 is used in Hebrews 5.6 and 7.17 to show that Christ is the fulfilment of the priestly promises made to David. In each case, and in different ways, the text of a psalm is used to illustrate that what was a promise to David *then* is fulfilment in Christ *now*.

The same prophetic use of the psalms is also found in the *Midraš T'hillîm*. Psalm 2 was originally a psalm probably composed for use in the royal court, and hence is focused on the Davidic king and so acclaims him as one anointed by God and adopted by him as a son:

> I will tell of the decree of the Lord:
> He said to me, 'You are my son,
>   today I have begotten you.
> Ask of me, and I will make the nations your heritage,
>   and the ends of the earth your possession.'
>
> (Psalm 2.7–8)

In *Midraš T'hillîm* the 'you' addressed in Psalm 2.7–8 is no longer the Davidic king, but instead is the coming Messiah. After a period of suffering, God will bring the Messiah, his anointed one, into the world to redeem the world from sin. This psalm is thus a promise made not only to David, but also to the future Messiah. In this sense it is still a prophetic text but, according to the *Midraš T'hillîm*, the time of fulfilment has not been yet fulfilled by any other; it has simply not yet come about.

The prophetic interpretation of psalmody in Jewish tradition is also referred to by U. Simon. The second chapter of *Four Approaches to the Psalms* deals with the Karaite approach to psalmody, which was a way of reading the texts in a literalist way, whereby the psalms were understood literally as prophetic prayers for their own time. Simon's fourth chapter looks at Abraham Ibn Ezra, referred to earlier, and again shows that the interpretation of the psalms as inspired and prophetic poetry, by means of the application of the allegorical approach, was also evident in the Jewish tradition even as late as the twelfth century CE. The psalms thus become an important means of looking ahead to the fulfilment of prophecy in the future, as well as the fulfilment in the present (as in the Qumran community and in the New Testament writers).

The spiritual use of psalmody in the Jewish tradition is in some way related to the more personal didactic use, although it is broader than it. Its emphasis is more on religious experience acquired through praying the psalms. This interest is expressed by the psalmists themselves. Psalm 69.30, for example, speaks of the importance of prayer even when sacrifice accompanying prayer is not possible (thus perhaps reflecting the concerns of those in exile, deprived of the sacrificial system). Psalm 141.2 speaks similarly of prayer being more important than, for example, the offering of incense in the Temple. Given the emphasis on ritual and sacrifice in the priestly tradition, expressed particularly in the books of Leviticus and Numbers, the emphasis in the psalms on the words being as important as the rites was important in Judaism for preparing for the final destruction of the Temple, when ritual and sacrifice were no longer possible, and prayer and praise was the most vital form of access to God.

This emphasis on reflective prayer and experience of God through meditation is very much part of the Jewish mystical tradition. Although other biblical texts were more important (Ezekiel 1, the vision of the chariot throne, being one of the best examples), the emphasis on the kingship of God in so many hymns and royal psalms meant that the psalms were another important resource in this tradition.

Whether the psalms were used in public liturgy, or as teaching aids in the life of the community, or as inspired texts which spoke of the fulfilment of an inspired prophetic hope, or as words inspiring religious experience through prayer, their theological message in the Jewish tradition is undoubtedly diverse.

THEOLOGICAL APPROACHES TO THE PSALMS IN THE CHRISTIAN
TRADITION

The Psalter was one of the key texts in Christian liturgy from the
second century CE onwards. The Psalms enabled the early Church to
remember their Jewish roots, and they also allowed the Church a fixed
text which could be adapted for specifically Christian use. By the end of
the second century, according to Tertullian, the psalms were used
along with prayers, preaching and blessings in the Sunday vigil service.
By the fourth century, the Psalter played such a central part in the vigils
of the church that John Chrysostom could speak of the psalms as
follows:

> If we keep vigil in the Church, David comes first, last and midst. If early in
> the morning we seek for the melody of hymns, first last and midst is David
> again. If we are occupied with the funeral solemnities of the departed, if
> virgins sit at home and spin, David is first, last and midst ... O marvellous
> wonder! Many who have made but little progress in literature, many who
> have scarcely mastered its first principles, have the Psalter by heart.

By the sixth century, the Canonical Hours of Prayer, taken by the
Western Church from the East, refers to eight daily offices; the psalms
play a central part in each. The 'Primer' of the Middle Ages, which was
essentially a prayer book for the laity, keeps the psalms at the centre of
its offices. In eucharistic theology, in the divine offices, the importance
of the Psalter in Protestant and Catholic tradition is evident from
Reformation times onwards. The metrical use of the psalms, and the
place of the psalms in the Book of Common Prayer, as well as the use of
psalms in the Catholic tradition through the music of Gelineau and
Taizé, all illustrate this point. Whether speaking of formal offices or
liturgies, homilies and devotions, or the hymnic tradition inspired by
Herbert, Wesley, Watts, Wyatt, Vaughan, Milton, Lyte, Keble and Tate
and Brady, the psalms have played a central part in Christian worship
through the ages.

The Psalter has also been used a good deal by Christians for didactic
purposes. The monastic tradition and the emphasis on private reading
as well as the public lectionaries furthered this. This coincides with the
importance of individual exemplary piety in Jewish tradition, which
focused on David; the contrast in the Christian tradition is that this
example is found not as much in David, as in Christ; these are thus not
so much the psalms of David as the psalms prayed by Christ. The
beginning of this mode of interpretation is found in the Gospels. The
passion narratives have a number of references to the way in which
Christ prayed the psalms in the last week of his life, whether at the last

supper (Psalm 41.9; see Matthew 26.24 and Luke 24.25), or in the Garden of Gethsemane (Psalm 42.3, 11 and 43.5; see Mark 14.34 and Matthew 26.38). The final words on the cross suggest several verses from the psalms: 'I thirst' (John 19.28) echoes Psalms 22.15 and 69.21; 'My God – why has thou forsaken me?' (Mark 15.34; Matthew 27.46) echoes Psalm 22.1; and 'Into thy hands I commit my spirit' (Luke 23.46) is from Psalm 31.5. Consequently the pattern is 'from obedience to faith' – Christ's example, resourced from the Psalms, becomes the example for every Christian disciple to follow.

This same type of instructional use of the psalms is carried on in Origen's commentaries on the psalms, in Jerome's small commentary on the Psalter, in Theodore of Mopesuestia's commentary on over half of the Psalter, and in the use of the psalms in the divine office of the Western and Eastern Churches, especially in the monastic traditions. One perceives throughout this strain that the Psalms were as a 'second law' – in this sense, a law which was written on hearts, and not on tablets of stone. The psalms were, in brief, an incitement to morality through the medium of prayer. This is continued further in the commentary on the Psalms by Calvin (*c.* 1557) which is essentially preaching in its style, as also in Luther's several commentaries and works on the Psalms (1513–16, 1519–21 and 1532–3 [the latter, on the Gradual Psalms]). It is important to see that most commentaries on the Psalms, at least until the rise of historical-critical studies in the early nineteenth century, are in fact as much homily as exegesis and, as Christian homily, they develop their interpretation Christ-wards rather than David-wards. Hence the psalms were used as a form of instruction, not least for the purpose of motivating personal faith and trust in God, and this is as much a feature of the Christian tradition as it is of the Jewish tradition.

The prophetic use of the psalms in the Christian tradition begins within the New Testament itself, as we have already seen in part in relation to the Jewish writers such as in Matthew, Paul and Hebrews. But the prophetic use of the Psalms is broader than the use of the *pēsher* method evidenced in examples from these particular texts. As in Qumran, 'David the prophet' is a phrase occurring frequently in New Testament texts. For example, in Acts 2.25–36, in a speech by Peter intended to show how the resurrection of Christ was foretold in the Hebrew Scriptures, the passage includes a quotation from Psalm 16.8–11:

For David says concerning him,
'I saw the Lord always before me,
    for he is at my right hand that I may not be shaken …

For thou wilt not abandon my soul to Hades,
   nor let thy Holy One see corruption.'

(Acts 2.25, 27)

The passage continues, speaking of David (verses 30ff.):

Being therefore a prophet ... he foresaw and spoke of the resurrection of
the Christ, that he was not abandoned to Hades, nor did his flesh see
corruption. This Jesus God raised up, and of that we all are witnesses.

This passage is an important illustration of the way in which David was
understood as a prophet. The psalms were thus seen as prophecies,
and the present age is the time of the fulfilment of the psalms-as-
prophecies; again, there are echoes here of Qumran. This happens
elsewhere in the book of the Acts of the Apostles (see 4.23–31;
13.26–43).

The break with the Jewish roots became more marked after the
destruction of the Temple in 70 CE, and after the dispersion of the Jews
in the middle of the second century, and hence the need to use the
Jewish Scriptures in this immediate prophetic way receded. This was
also in part due to the increasing number of Gentile converts to the
Christian faith. However, one of the most recent traces of the same
approach is found in the millenarian Christian groups seeking the
reconversion of the Jews during the middle of the nineteenth century.
Such an approach requires a specific belief in the inspiration and application of Scripture, and a particular view of the Jewish faith.

The spiritual interpretation of the psalms in the Christian tradition
is, as in the Jewish tradition, closely associated with both the didactic
and the liturgical ways of reading. Its essential difference is in the way
the psalms are now read, not as prophecies *about* Christ, nor as prayers
of Christ, but rather as prayers addressed to Christ. Christ becomes the
one addressed as 'Lord', so that the metaphorical language once
describing God in the psalms is now understood as speaking more
particularly of Christ. Thus Christ is the one whose presence is *hidden*
in the psalms, as the king, judge, deliverer, protector, shepherd, way,
rock, life. In part this provides ideal material for an allegorical adaptation of psalmody, but because it focuses more on prayer than on the
use of the psalms in Christian apologetics, it is more bound up with the
reflective, contemplative tradition.

In Christian theology, this way of reading the psalms has been particularly influenced by the monastic tradition – for example, in the *lectio
divina* way of reading and praying, set out in the Benedictine Rule,
which gives instructions for the entire Psalter to be recited once a week,
using twelve psalms at the night office (as well as Psalms 4, 95 and 51)

and three psalms at each of the lesser hours. This way of reading has also been popularized by various contemporary Christian writers such as, for example, T. Merton, D. Bonhoeffer, C. S. Lewis and M. Israel. Its emphasis is on the value of the psalms as prayers. Its focus on Christ is a feature brought to the psalms, rather than arising out of them. One has to recognize, therefore, that this is as much a reading into the psalms as it is a reading out of them. That it is one which has been widely practised in Christian tradition – Protestant, Catholic and Orthodox alike – testifies to its usefulness; hymns and prayer-like imitations of psalms down the ages give ample testimony to it. A book written at the beginning of this century by R. E. Prothero, entitled *The Psalms in Human Life*, is a useful historical survey in this respect, giving an extensive list of Christian figures throughout church history who have lived and died with the words of psalms on their lips, addressing their prayers to Christ as the revealer of God to us.

Thus whether in liturgy, in instruction, in Christian interpretation or as a spiritual resource, the theological reading of the Psalms is as diverse in the Christian tradition as it has been seen to be in Jewish use. And yet the theological approach, however extensive, is by no means the only way of reading the Psalms; there is an equally wide range of historical and literary approaches, as the following two sections will seek to illustrate.

The Psalter and Historical Approaches

The major concern in a historical reading of the psalms is to ascertain their setting within the religion of ancient Israel. Questions of contemporary relevance, of utmost importance in the theological and literary approaches, are of less significance. The interest in the psalms as ancient literature and ancient liturgy is evident in all six approaches listed below. (For a summary of these approaches, see the diagrams on p. 170 in Chapter 6).

HIGHER CRITICISM

The interest in personality and hence in authorship is the main hallmark of this approach. The laws are of Moses; the proverbs, of Solomon; and the psalms, of David. The fact that so many of the psalms (seventy-three in all) have the title 'A Psalm of David' encouraged this approach.

However, during the last century, when in historical criticism the interest in date and place and authorship was still paramount, the

211

attention moved from assuming Davidic authorship to acknowledging that the psalms were written by a number of individuals. This was in part on account of reading 'A Psalm of David' in a different way. The preposition *lᵉ*, translated 'of' can also mean 'for' or 'to' or 'belonging to', indicating a psalm dedicated to the memory of David, or associated with a Davidic tradition, or even a psalm to be assigned for personal use. The practice of tracing many traditions back to the house of David was a common one in post-exilic times (for example, the Chronicler does it too) and this was certainly how the historical headings were understood to have developed over time. Hence higher criticism established a now commonly held view, that David may have been the 'patron' of psalmody, and although many of the psalms may have been products of the royal cult, David was not the 'author', or original composer, of many of the psalms, in the strict sense. (One notable and very recent exception to this view is M. Goulder's *The Prayers of David* [1990]. Goulder holds that psalms with headings setting the work in the life of David [in Psalms 51—72] are actual records of David's sufferings during the last years of his life. The narrative in 1–2 Samuel, Goulder believes, forms the background to this tradition.)

The caution about Davidic authorship in higher criticism during the middle of the last century meant that other theories had to be proposed about the identities of the psalmists. The following views were the most acceptable with regard to the authorship of the psalms.

First, because of the aesthetic interest in religious poetry (in part a legacy of the Romantic movement), there was an interest in the psalmists as individual poets, writing 'from the heart to the heart'. Because this presumed some individual creativity, the dating proposed was usually late – many scholars accepted a time as late as the second century BCE – when individualism within Judiasm was believed to be more prevalent. A second view, which was contemporaneous with the first (that is, throughout the middle and latter part of the nineteenth century), and which was influenced more by the resurgence of national consciousness on account of current events, was a belief in the national, corporate element in psalmody. The psalmists were seen as representatives of the nation – poet laureates – composing psalms for all the community to use. This could be at times of national celebration (victory in war, good harvest, and events in the life of the king or community leader) or national crisis (military defeat, plague and famine, and conflicts in religious and political leadership). Again the dating proposed for such psalms was quite late; the post-exilic period was seen to be the key influence.

A third proposal, held by commentators in the very early part of this century, was to see the psalms as products of the liturgical community, written by gifted cultic officials, for use at the main annual festivals. One sees again the influence of the history of religions school, and with this, the realization that many of the psalms had incorporated a good deal of mythical material which they had borrowed from their neighbours and which, as in foreign cults, they acted out in the rituals of the cult. The psalms were in fact the 'rubrics' which accompanied those rituals. The dating was now monarchic, because a good deal of the mythical material was believed to be played out in the royal cult, celebrating the sacral role of the Davidic king in the Jerusalem Temple. The psalms which spoke of the king and his close relationship with God (for example, Psalms 2, 45, 89, 110, 132) were especially relevant in this respect. Also important were psalms which spoke of the kingship of God and his presence in Zion, and these psalms (for example, Psalms 46, 47, 48, 93, 95—9) were believed to have been used at an annual autumnal festival, at the beginning of a new (agricultural) year.

Whereas in earlier studies the chief proponents were from Germany and England, a large number of Scandinavians (of whom the name of S. Mowinckel is perhaps the best known) contributed to this part of the debate in its earliest stages. One of the most recent additions to this argument is M. Goulder's *The Psalms of Asaph and the Pentateuch* (1996). Goulder has proposed that the superscriptions 'A Psalm of Asaph', at the beginning of Psalms 50, 73—83, indicate the origins of these psalms, not their later use. He argues that their interest in the Exodus tradition, and in the traditions of the north at a time of military catastrophe, suggest that they were composed for an autumn festival not in Jerusalem, but in Bethel, in the 720s, before the fall of the north. This view, which has some similarities with Goulder's view about the early liturgical origins of the Psalms of Korah, and his thesis concerning the Davidic authorship of Psalms 51 to 72, is a contrast to the predominant theories about psalms being composed for the Jerusalem Temple in the south. According to Goulder, the Psalms of Asaph represent an early, northern liturgical collection.

Two other modifications have been evident during the post-war years. On the one hand, a number of German scholars have developed the idea that the cult in ancient Israel was equally important for ordinary individuals, and that many of the psalms were composed as prayers (perhaps as incantations) for individuals to read before the priest at the Temple or local sanctuary at times of sickness, sorcery, persecution, trials of justice and community conflict. Following from this – and perhaps in some ways preparing the way for the more literary approach – the 'life-centredness' of the psalms has been another concern in interpretation, whereby any specific setting, whether communal or individual, public or private, is deemed to be unclear; the ambiguity of the poetry of the psalms makes any such proposals hazardous. Hence all we can know is that the psalms were composed, using basic praise and lament forms to cater for the heights and depths of all life-experiences at all stages in Israel's history. (The names C. Westermann and W. Brueggemann are the best known with regard to this approach). Such 'life-centredness' makes them accessible beyond any one particular historical setting and reusable in many others.

What should be clear from all the above five views is that not one of them is able to contain the entire number of psalms within its basic thesis. What is proposed is a basic emphasis (communal or individual), a general date (mainly pre-exilic, or mainly post-exilic) and a common location (the Temple, and local sanctuary groups). The 'Quest for the Historical David', seen by the majority of scholars to be a doubtful exercise, thus diversified into a number of permutations, and yet none of them has been capable of explaining the provenance and authorship of more than one third of the extant psalms, and even here the results were by no means proven. On this account, higher criticism within the Psalter has not really produced any clear answers to its own questions.

SOURCE CRITICISM

Within the five books of the Psalter, at least ten collections, of varying sizes, are visible. These are discernible by way of the title over the psalm, assigning their use (although not necessarily their origin) to a particular concern, whether by way of cultic figurehead (David, Asaph, Korah) or by way of a particular theme (kingship of God, *Hallel*) or by cultic use (the Songs of Ascents). These collections, and their associated concerns, can be seen in Figure 21.

It may seem a far cry from the source-critical theory in the Pentateuch to label each of these separate collections as 'sources', but they are indeed the smaller parts which make up the larger whole; and just as in Genesis and Exodus, a comparison of the differences between P and J is part of the source-critical method, so in the Psalter, the comparison of the different 'sources' or collections reflects a similar method. Indeed, this is what was applied earlier, with respect to the discussion of the differences between almost identical psalms such as Psalms 14 and 53, 40 and 70, and 108, 57 and 60; all three examples occurred in different Davidic collections.

As well as identifying sources through the collections in the larger blocks of material, another way of using source-criticism is in individual psalms. This would involve, for example, ascertaining possible 'northern' and 'southern' sources. Several of the so-called Asaph and

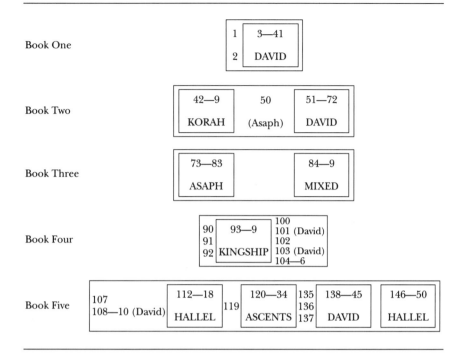

Figure 21   The Five Books of the Psalter

Korah psalms provide interesting material in this respect. Or it could involve ascertaining a 'Temple' source, for example, in some of the Zion hymns; or a 'royal source', for example in some of the royal psalms; or a 'scribal source', within the wisdom psalms. The concern is first with a particular interest within a psalm, and second with assigning the psalm into a particular category, where it is compared with other psalms which suggest similar interests. One might argue that here is a certain circularity. The source-critical method has produced no more assured results than has higher criticism.

FORM CRITICISM

Form criticism is a natural ally of source criticism, insofar as it deals with the even smaller components of the text in question. Form-critical studies were really initiated by H. Gunkel, in his introduction, unfinished commentary and several articles on the Psalms. Because of the wide variety of literary and liturgical interests, form-critical studies have made an important contribution to our understanding of the origins and growth of the psalms.

At the very beginning of this chapter we assessed the two most prominent psalmic forms, namely lament and praise, and noted their distribution throughout the Psalter (see p. 190). We also noted that liturgies, historical psalms, and prophetic exhortations were also very much in evidence, not least in the communal psalms, and that psalms of thanksgiving and instructional psalms ('wisdom psalms') were also important ways of determining more personal compositions. (Another psalm category, the royal psalms, is not really a form-critical category, because its classification is more dependent upon the contents than on the outer form; indeed, royal psalms encompass a wide variety of forms.) Taking three main categories – namely the hymns, the laments, and miscellaneous forms – their listing and distribution throughout the Psalter would look similar to what is shown in Table 15.

Table 15   The Basic Forms Used in the Psalter

Hymns

General Hymns: 8, 29, 33, 100, 103, 104, 111, 113, 114, 117, 135, 136, 145, 146, 147, 148, 149, 150.
Also: 78, 105.
Zion Hymns: 46, 48, 76, 87, 122.
Kingship Hymns: 47, 93, 96, 97, 98, 99.

Laments

Individual Laments: 3, 5, 6, 7, 12, 13, 17, 22, 25, 26, 28, 31, 35, 36, 38, 39, 42—3, 51, 54, 55, 56, 57, 59, 61, 63, 64, 69, 70, 71, 86, 88, 102, 109, 120, 130, 140, 141, 142, 143.
Communal Laments: 44, 60, 74, 77, 79, 80, 82, 83, 85, 90, 94, 106, 108, 123, 126, 137.

Miscellaneous Forms

Royal Psalms: 2, 18, 20, 21, 45, 72, 89, 101, 110, 132, 144.
Individual Thanksgivings: 9—10, 30, 32, 34, 40, 41, 92, 107, 116, 138.
Communal Thanksgivings: 65, 66, 67, 68, 118, 124.
Individual Psalms of Confidence: 4, 11, 16, 23, 27, 62, 84, 91, 121, 131.
Communal Psalms of Confidence: 115, 125, 129, 133.
Liturgies: 15, 24, 134.
Prophetic Exhortations: 14, 50, 52, 53, 58, 75, 81, 95.
Didactic Psalms: 1, 19, 37, 49, 73, 112, 119, 127, 128, 139.

We noted in Chapter 6 (p. 164) that the problems with form criticism arise when it is viewed too rigidly, and when it is assumed that the 'determining of form' then also leads to the 'determining of cultic-setting'. The outer form which a psalmist may choose does not necessitate a specific use in one pre-determined cultic setting; the psalmists adapt in a creative way several of the traditional forms, and the mistake of form-critical studies has been to apply its own rules too inflexibly especially where a poetic medium such as psalmody is concerned. More often than not, the poetic content determines the form, not vice versa. The large category entitled 'miscellaneous forms' in the list in Table 15 shows just how difficult it is to set every psalm into one fixed category, and if this is the case, how much more difficult it is to presume one cultic setting out of such a mixed category.

But the usefulness of form criticism is that it offers some insights into poetic conventions (and from this, poetic originality) from earliest times. It is quite clear that the forms of praise and lament are paramount; it is similarly clear that these forms were freely adapted, and they were not always used with a cultic occasion in view. Nevertheless, while realizing its limitations, form criticism is one of the more useful historical approaches to psalmody.

TRADITION CRITICISM

If one interprets tradition criticism in terms of the theological influences through socio-religious groups, then the psalmists reflect some interesting associations. For example, the traditions of the prophets, with their concern about social justice and about true worship due to God alone is found in a number of psalms (40, 50, 52, 60, 75, 81, 82, 85, 125); and the traditions of the wise, with their plea for the separation of the pious and righteous, and for the obedience to the law, is also prevalent (1, 9—10, 19, 25, 32, 34, 36, 37, 49, 62, 90, 102, 111, 112, 119, 127, 128, 141). The traditions of the Levites, of court officials, of the family, and even of the Deuteronomists are also to be found in several other psalms. Hence, by way of using tradition criticism, the many different socio-religious interests of the psalmists soon become apparent, and the theological diversity within the Psalter as a whole becomes clearly visible.

If one interprets 'tradition' in terms of a particular theological theme, such as 'Exodus', or 'Zion', or 'Creation', then other interesting observations arise concerning the interplay of theologies (and ideologies) within liturgy. For example, it is noteworthy that several psalms use the Exodus tradition – a tradition about a wandering people, without land or statehood, being promised protection by a

217

deity who also had no fixed abode (Psalms 77, 78, 80, 81, 105, 106, 114, 135, 136 are the best examples). This makes an interesting complement to the collection of material which is essentially from the southern, royal, Jerusalem Temple, where God was believed to dwell. Or again, it is significant that creation traditions have been used in some psalms (for example, Psalms 8, 29, 33, 104, 136, 139). These serve to enlarge the vision beyond national and communal concerns alone. (The Zion tradition is of course far more widely used; its interaction with the other less likely traditions creates the most interest in the way it interacts with the different theology in the greater whole.)

If form criticism and source criticism each tell us about *how* a psalm was composed, then tradition criticism seeks to answer in part the question *why* it was written. In this way it offers an important complementary understanding – albeit still in general terms – of the nature of psalmody.

REDACTION CRITICISM

In its concern with the 'final form', redaction criticism applies both to each psalm and to the Psalter as a whole. As far as the entire Psalter is concerned, one obvious point of concern is the doxologies, for these suggest ways in which the redactors subdivided the collections into five different books. The interest in these doxologies then raises questions about the close relationship between the first three doxologies marking out Books One to Three (at 41.14; 72.18–20 and 89.52). This may well illustrate how these first books were united at an earlier stage. This then leads on to the question of the doxology in 106.45, and how this enabled the creation of Books Four and Five at a much later stage.

When reading individual psalms, one of the useful contributions of redaction criticism is ascertaining how redactors readapted earlier psalms (for instance, those designed for individual use) into psalms which could be used by the entire community. Examples include the endings to Psalm 22 (verses 23–31) and, more briefly, 51 (verses 18–19), 69 (verses 34–6), 77 (verses 16–20), and perhaps especially 130 (verses 7–8) and 131 (verse 3), where the main body of the psalm suggests more personal concerns, and the communal concern is presented suddenly and interupts the mood of trust in the earlier part of the psalm.

Again in individual psalms, redactional activity might be seen in the joining of two entirely different psalms to make up one whole. Psalm 19 is the best example. The first half is a creation psalm, and the second half is on the importance of keeping the law. The purpose of redaction criticism is to ask where the joining is to be found, and why it was done. Psalm 108, joining together Psalms 57.1–11 and 60.5–12, is another relevant psalm for redaction criticism. So too are Psalms 18 and 144, and 115 and 135; these are both 'pairs' which have a number of internal correspondences, and each pair suggests the work of a redactor in conforming the later psalm (144 and 135) to the earlier (18 and 115).

The most extensive redactional activity must be seen in the super-scriptions, which are almost certainly later additions from post-exilic times; the superscriptions served to join psalms together according to usage and theme, hence assigning them into particular collections. (It is noteworthy, in the light of our earlier comments about Books One to Three being earlier than Books Four to Five, that almost all of these psalms take superscriptions, and there are far fewer superscriptions in the latter two books, almost twenty having none at all.) Giving a psalm a particular title was clearly a complex activity, and many psalms possess a number of different superscriptions all in the same heading – some personal, some liturgical, some both. For example, Psalm 22 has three: 'to the choirmaster' (indicating musical use); 'to the Hind of Dawn' (possibly denoting a hymn tune); and 'a Psalm of David' (possibly indicating a more personal psalm). Psalm 45 has four or possibly five headings: (the choirmaster; the hymn tune; the guilds of singers; a 'maskil' – instructional psalm; and a love song – its contents). So too Psalms 46, 54, 56, 57, 58, 59 and 60 have multiple superscriptions, each indicating accumulative uses. But redaction criticism is important in each of these cases because it seeks to discover (as far as is possible) the purpose of the text in its final stages.

CANON CRITICISM

Canon criticism reads the Psalter only as a book. Whether this is as a book which is primarily liturgical, primarily poetic, or whether it is primarily a prayer book begs many questions about the greatest emphasis of the final whole. Psalm 1, as a fitting prologue, might indi-cate the book is for reflective private prayer; Psalm 150, as a psalm of praise by way of conclusion, might indicate that the book is more for liturgical use. The problem with canon criticism is that it has to decide on the *one* final form, and the truth lies somewhere between two – or three – such forms.

As we noted earlier, canon criticism raises as many questions about theology as it does about final form. For it is possible to find one theo-logical theme which aptly brings together the sum of the smaller parts. Either it is too narrow (take, for example, 'God's dealings with his people throughout their history, expressed in praise and prayer') and so excludes a very large number of the psalms in question; or it is too broad (for example, 'the kingship of God') and so includes a large number of psalms which do not really use this theme at all. It is possible to ascertain one theological theme in a particular psalmic collection, or even one such theme in one of the five books; but it is extremely difficult to do this within the Psalter as a whole.

The survey of the canonical history of the Psalter, through Jewish and through Christian tradition (see pp. 195–6) served to confirm this view. The Psalter is too diverse to be classified with one theological emphasis appropriate for all its uses.

We noted with regard to our first example of the historical method – the search for the date, place and author of each psalm under the subheading 'Higher Criticism' – that this method cannot answer all these questions with any great precision. It is impossible to work back into the historical background, and, through the medium of the poetry (often highly ambiguous poetry) to gain any clear answers about the provenance of any one psalm. Only general observations can suffice. So too, with regard to the final example of the historical method, canon criticism also cannot answer its own questions. In each case, one is left with partial insights – important, but by no means complete. The question remaining is whether the literary-critical approaches perform any better.

The Psalter and Literary Approaches

Using the literary approach, one works at the opposite end of the spectrum to the historical approach. Questions of contemporary relevance are very much to the fore; the emphasis is thus much more on 'why' than on 'how'. For a summary of how much this is so, review Figures 19 and 20 on p. 172 in Chapter 7.

SEMANTIC AND LINGUISTIC READINGS

This approach is basically concerned with the questions about *why* various biblical terms have been used rather than any others, and what the relationship between the different terms within the poem as a whole might be.

It could be argued that this approach to psalmody has been used for at least two centuries. One of the key ways of understanding the semantics of Hebrew poetry is by way of its parallelism, and one of the first English scholars to lecture on this was one Robert Lowth, Praelector of Poetry at Oxford in the 1740s, who argued that one of the distinctive features of Hebrew poetry, in comparison with its Greek and Latin counterparts, was its 'economy and uniformity of expression' mediated through its *parallelism,* a quality which (unlike other classical poetry) made it translatable into languages without destroying its essence. This feature, according to those later influenced by Lowth, appears to have influenced the binary ideas in the poetic diction of English poets such as Wordsworth, Coleridge and Keats.

Few would doubt that parallelism marks the essence of Hebrew poetry, and that this element is very much part of the way of communicating in Semitic languages. It is also in evidence in the New Testament tradition. So much of Christ's purported teachings (in the spoken Semitic language of Aramaic, not Hebrew) were couched in parallel terms. Take, for example, the maxim, 'My yoke is easy/and my burden light' (Matthew 11.30) or – by way of using opposite ideas – the teaching that 'Every one who exalts himself will be humbled, and he who humbles himself will be exalted' (Luke 18.14). The psalms, set some five hundred years earlier, work in the same way. Three examples will illustrate this. First, a hymn:

A   When Israel went forth from Egypt,
A   the house of Jacob from a people of strange language,
B   Judah became his sanctuary,
B   Israel his dominion.

(Psalm 114.1–2)

Here the two parallel ideas are found in two contrasting lines (AA and BB). Similar ideas are expressed in parallel ways in the lament in Psalm 31.10:

A   For my life is spent with sorrow
A   and my years with sighing;
B   my strength fails because of my misery,
B   and my bones waste away.

Here the parallel ideas are found in the first two and second two lines. Another shorter form of this is found in Psalm 19.1, where the parallelism is set over two contrasting lines rather than four:

A   The heavens are telling the glory of God;
B   and the firmament proclaims his handiwork.

There are many different ways in which binary ideas are expressed in the psalms – sometimes echoing each other within the same verse (or within two verses), and sometimes set out in contrast within two juxtaposed verses. Sometimes the echoing ideas extend over several

221

lines, and form some sort of pattern within the psalm as a whole, be it in terms of chiasmus or by way of refrains. Psalms 8 (verses 1, 9) and 118 (verses 1, 29) as well as Psalms 49, 57, 99 (all with two refrains) and Psalms 42 to 3 and 46 (with three refrains) and Psalms 59 and 80 (with four refrains) serve to show just how complex this patterning can be.

As well as determining the meaning of a psalm by way of its echoing or opposing words and phrases, other ways of reading the psalms lay stress not so much on the sense expressed in the parallelism as on the sound of the words in Hebrew. The acrostics, referred to earlier, might be included here; but equally important are psalms where the alliteration of the words or syllables is important (that is, in the use of consonants). In addition, assonance (that is, in the use of vowel sounds) is similarly an observable technique. One example of alliteration is Psalm 122.6–7, where the longing for Jerusalem is intensified through the sounds of the -sh and -l in the words:

sha'ālû shĕlôm Yĕrûshalayim	Pray for the peace of Jerusalem!
yishlayû 'ohăbhayîkh	'May they prosper who love you!
yĕhî shalôm bĕhêlekh	Peace be within your walls,
shālwah bĕ'armĕnôthayîkh.	and security within your towers!'

An example of assonance (in the *-enu* and *-ehu* sounds) is from Psalm 90.17, in a prayer for God to give the people his favour:

wîhî no'am 'ădhonay 'ĕlohênû 'ālênû	Let the favour of the Lord be upon us
uma'ăseh yādhênû kônĕnāh 'alênû	and establish thou the work of our hands upon us
uma'ăseh yādhênû kônĕnēhû	yea, the work of our hands establish thou it.

Whereas the historical method would be concerned with the grammatical and etymological understanding of these terms, the literary approach is more interested in an aesthetic understanding in attempting to interpret the parts played by each of these words – both in terms of their sense and their sound – within the psalm as a whole.

POETIC CRITICISM

Perhaps two of the most influential writers in the area of poetic criticism, especially with regard to the psalms, are R. Alter and L. Alonso Schökel. Both recognize that a knowledge of Hebrew is required before a full understanding can be achieved of the way in which each psalm works, although their studies are intelligible to those with no knowledge of Hebrew at all. Even so, the arguments of both writers are

supplemented by those of two writers on poetry who had no ﹍
of the Hebrew, yet still understood how well the Hebrew co﹍
with all its precision, balance, and symmetry, even in translati﹍
Eliot associates poetry with 'a raid on the inarticulate' – all ɹoetry,
Hebrew psalmody included, has within it an element of mystery, and
thus cannot be defined or over-classified. And C. S. Lewis speaks of
poetry as an 'artistic imitation of reality' – like a little incarnation,
it reveals enough for us to understand it in new ways, but a good deal is
still hidden.

These insights are important regarding Hebrew poetry, particularly
psalmody, with its strong liturgical affiliations, for they help to explain
how and why this poetry is not exhausted by its first liturgical context,
and how and why it is eminently reusable in other settings, not necessarily liturgical ones. Frances Young, writing in *The Art of Performance*, is
most helpful here. Comparing the biblical text to a score of music, she
notes how it is possible to move from the lexical level of the score to the
performance level of the poem where it is adapted – like a musical
performance – in settings other than those of the composer of the
score. Although Young does not make a particular point of this analogy
with respect to the psalms, it is clear that psalmody, having so many
liturgical connotations and thus being so clearly available for performance week after week, year after year, is very much a performative art
– beginning more often than not in liturgy, but continuing by way of its
survival not only within it but also beyond it.

In this way, Alter's comments on the steady progression of images
and themes which intensify, like images thrown on a cinema screen, as
a poem progresses, may well best be understood by those with a
working knowledge of Hebrew, but such an observation can also be
understood by anyone who looks for the 'performative art' in psalmody
in general. Word pairs, for example, may make a good deal more sense
when one understands and hears them in Hebrew; but they can be
translated so that their binary appeal – whether of repetition or of
contrast – is not lost, and so their performance value outlasts the
culture which gave rise to it. Similarly Schökel's appeal to *appreciate* the
word-pairing in psalmody rather than constantly attempting to take it
apart and *classify* it also has a relevance beyond the appeal of a psalm
through the Hebrew medium alone; for if this were all there were to a
poem, the search for the many different layers of meaning would be an
irrelevant exercise.

In this way, poetic criticism is not only an analytical process, but an
intuitive one as well; it looks for the performative value of a psalm in
the here and now – in our language and in our culture – instead of
trying to understand its performative value back in ancient times.

STRUCTURALIST CRITICISM

In some ways poetry is not a good medium for structuralism, if one is to accept Schökel's maxim about appreciating the psalm before trying to classify it. For, as we have noted earlier, structuralism is very much about classification – hence the way in which it was compared earlier to the similar interest in classification in form criticism.

One of the key areas which has interested structuralists has been that of mythical representations and, although this has usually been studied in narrative forms, the psalms offer a rich resource for this approach (see p. 146 listing the different myths used in various psalms). Two particular myths might be singled out for such study. The first is the myth of the heavenly council (Psalm 82.1: 'God has taken his place *in the divine council, in the midst of the gods* he holds judgement' and Psalm 89.6–7: 'Who among the heavenly beings is like the Lord, a God feared *in the council of the holy ones?*') The second myth is that of God's ordering of creation, first by calming the sea, and then by slaying a fearful monster of the deep (for example, Psalm 74.13: 'Thou didst divide the sea by thy might; *thou didst break the heads of the dragons on the waters*' and Psalm 89.9–10: 'Thou dost rule the raging of the sea; when its waves rise, thou stillest them. *Thou didst crush Rahab like a carcass*'). Such myths are prevalent elsewhere in biblical literature, and elsewhere in the literature of the ancient Near East, as also in different forms in Greek and Roman mythology. A structuralist approach would use the psalm(s) in order to perceive the structures of reality which lie behind the presentation of the material in a poetic and liturgical form.

But structuralism can also take one psalmic unit without begging questions about associations with other psalms or indeed with other literature. An early example of this is a study of the structure of Psalm 2 by P. Auffret (1977). A more recent example is a study of Psalm 18 by D. K. Berry (1993). Although more engaged with reader-response issues than with structuralism *per se*, Berry, like Auffret, takes the idea of the psalm being a 'speech act' with contemporary performative value, and examines the psalm by way of assessing its structures through the form and language used.

Other recent studies, like Berry's, make use of the structuralist approach, but by no means exclusively so. However, unlike those of Berry and Auffret, this idea is applied to more than one psalm. One example is a study of the theme of 'Yahweh as refuge' throughout the Psalter by J. F. D. Creach (1996). This deals with the metaphor as well as with the social world of the psalmists, in terms of their threatened securities, and so makes use of the structuralist concerns. Another study, by M. R. Hauge (1995) examines the use of 'Sheol, Temple and Way' in those psalms where the 'I' form predominates, and depicts similarly the uncertain world of the psalmists, who try to dispel their insecurities and especially their fear of the threat of death by way of patterned and stereotypical language. So too H. J. Levine's selected studies in *Sing unto God a New Song* (1995) consider the motifs of time and eternity, and of the absence and presence of God in the Psalms. Both Hauge and Levine, to some degree, apply structuralist concerns. But it has to be said that in each of these recent studies, the structuralist concerns are more coincidental; they are part of the discourse about the binary ideas in the psalms (God as refuge/people as under threat, Sheol/Temple, eternity/time, the absence and the presence of God). Other than a few other isolated articles in books on literary criticism (for example, D. M. Howard's contextual study of Psalms 90–4 in *The Shape and Shaping of the Psalter*, ed. J. C. McCann, 1993), structuralist studies in the Psalter have hardly been prolific.

RHETORICAL CRITICISM

We have already noted how rhetorical criticism looks at the text as a vehicle of persuasion, looking for the silences and gaps in the text in order to make it 'mean' something from the viewpoint of the reader. Both this approach and the reader-response approach are, in different degrees, ways in which the gender-orientated and the politically motivated readings (of feminist criticism and liberation theology respectively) take the text and turn the meaning round to suit their own purpose.

Very little has been written by way of using rhetorical-critical studies to achieve a feminist reading of the Psalms. Given that in narrative texts outside the Psalter, women are described as using psalms in praise or prayer on several occasions (Miriam in Exodus 15; Deborah in Judges 5; Hannah in 1 Samuel 3; Judith in Judith 16; and Mary in Luke 1) one might expect more to have been written on this subject within the psalms themselves. One obvious place is the superscription to Psalm 46. This reads, literally, 'according to the Alamoth', and it is probably a reference to women singers (the plural form *-oth*, in Hebrew, is the feminine). This, in the light of above references to Miriam and Deborah, with their own role in leading liturgy, need not be surprising. A rhetorical-critical study would then look at the rest of Psalm 46 through women's eyes as well as through women's voices; the references to God as the refuge in times of trouble (46.1–3) and the silence before God (46.10) would play a part in this. Furthermore, other psalms might receive this treatment, too. Psalms 68.25 and

148.12–13 both suggest the presence of women in the liturgy, so the rest of the psalms could be filled out accordingly to reflect a woman's experience in worship despite the male voice of the composer.

Some would see this as a rather tame type of rhetorical criticism, playing around with details rather than attending to the heart of the issue. If women are assumed to be present in the liturgy at all, and hence are part of the 'you' being addressed and the 'we' who respond in so many of the communal psalms, then feminist readings are intended to enter more fully into all of these psalms and so offer them a different voice. And if the 'I' form could be seen to be representative, and hence also inclusive of women, the same appropriation applies here as well. In brief, almost all the entire Psalter is by implication inclusive of women, who have been excluded only on account of the maleness of the composer and the later interpreters. This sort of recognition and correction is what M. V. Reinstra, for example, has done in her reflective readings in a book entitled *Swallow's Nest: A Feminine Reading of the Psalms* (1992).

One could take this a rhetorical study further still. Also worthy of a feminist reading are the psalms of protest and the cries for help expressed in the laments. So too are the psalms of creation, about the re-establishing of the proper order of things, expressed in the hymns; and the psalms of indictment on the lack of justice in the community, expressed in the prophetic exhortations and in some of the wisdom psalms, could be part of this approach as well. In this sense there are many categories of psalms open to a feminist 'reversal'.

Another kind of rhetorical criticism is called 'liberation theology'. As with feminist readings, it is again surprising how little the psalms have been used in this way. Liberation studies, even those using the Bible, have very few references to the psalms in their indices. But there are at least two ways forward for this sort of rhetorical reading. On the one hand, the Exodus tradition in psalmody (for example, in Psalms 77.19–20; 78.12–14; 80.8; 81.2, 10; 105.37–8; 106.7–12; 114.1, 3, 5; 135.9 and 136.11–15) offers an interesting example of the critique of the status quo from within, and hence of the way even liturgy mediates some form of political ideology and social critique. For the Exodus tradition is a reminder about God being on the side of the oppressed and the marginalized; although it seems to have been used in the psalms as a means of legitimizing the community's right to think of themselves as the elect people of God, chosen out of Egypt, this was not what the essence of the tradition itself was about. Hence the task of rhetorical criticism in each these psalms would be to offer a critique of the way in which the tradition has been used – and abused – in each of these psalms.

Another way in which rhetorical criticism might work in psalmody through a liberation theology lens is by using those psalms which speak of God's protection of the 'poor and needy'. Although this may well beg questions of a more historical nature, concerning the date of such psalms and hence a definition of just who exactly the poor and needy were, there is plenty of scope for a semantic and structuralist reading of the Hebrew terms for poor. For instance, the word *dal*, implying the economically poor, occurs for example in Psalms 41, 72, 82 and 113; the word *'ebyōn*, used sometimes with *dal* and hence also implying the materially poor, is found in fifteen other places where the meaning could be either spiritual or material; the word *'ānî*, which also has associations with physical poverty, is to be found in Psalms 9—10, 18, 68 and 74; the word *'ānāw*, which seems to describe mainly spiritual needs, occurs in at least nine psalms; and the term *'ānî w*e* *'ebyōn*, used in twelve psalms, represents overall an inner poverty of spirit. One might deduce from this that there is scope for a critical evaluation of the 'poor' in the psalms, whoever they may be. A rhetorical-critical analysis could be just the way to do it.

We are again brought back to the same point: literary studies has not yet really attended to the poetry of the Old Testament in detail, least of all to the Psalter. But there is certainly scope for such approaches.

READER-RESPONSE CRITICISM

The reader-response way of reading the psalms has been mainly engaged with the performative value of psalmody within a believing tradition, stressing the performance (and the reader's response) in terms of prayer or of acts of worship. One example might be the *lectio divina* used in the contemplative tradition, as well as the responses of writers such as Bonhoeffer, Merton, and Israel, referred to earlier, and so illustrating how close this particular way of reading can be to the spiritual reading listed under theological approaches. Certainly, in terms of the response of the reader by way of prayer, this approach is as old as the psalms themselves.

A less explicitly confessional response is evident in studies by W. Brueggemann and J. Magonet. We have referred earlier to Brueggemann, on account of his interest in the life-centredness of the psalms, so it should be no surprise to find that, by taking some of his interpretative categories from P. Ricoeur, Brueggemann is able to offer a reader-response theory in terms of orientation (in the psalms of praise), disorientation (in the psalms of lament) and reorientation (in the psalms of thanksgiving).

J. Magonet, in *A Rabbi Reads the Psalms*, is perhaps one of the few writers in this area who can show that reader-response theory can be for the simple pleasure of reading – in his terms, 'for the fun of exploring their inner dynamic and meaning'. Showing the wrong uses of a literalist reader-response reading (for example in the Middle Ages – when Psalm 8 was used for crying children, Psalm 23 for interpreting dreams, Psalm 35 against mischievous busybodies, Psalm 58 against vicious dogs, and Psalm 146 for sword wounds), Magonet then seeks to demonstrate an alternative reading which makes sense of the whole psalm, and so avoids the quasi-magical focus illustrated above. The psalms have to be read as whole units, and the search for concentric patterns in their use of language and forms can lead to new ways of understanding this. Praise and prayer take on a very different focus as, in eight different psalms, Magonet outlines the interrelationship of words within the same psalm-unit (first from the Hebrew, then into English) and observes how the occurrences of the same words in different verses thus create a particular pattern within the psalm as a whole. Magonet reverses a good number of more traditional readings by way of this approach. Psalm 22, for example, is not only about vicarious suffering, but also about the outrage of one deprived of power and control; and Psalm 23 is not so much about security with God, as about the dangers of living by faith.

The approach is still about living with God, and the cost of faith; but it is very much about the active role of the reader. It contrasts with the more receptive role often used with the prayerful approach and, as such, shows how a reader-response approach can be a creative and literary activity and not only a passive response.

HOLISTIC CRITICISM

The approach of holistic criticism brings us back to the need to read *between* the psalms; this means that instead of viewing separate psalms, the focus is on the whole text of the whole Psalter.

This is perhaps the one area in literary studies in the Psalter where more discourse has taken place. Two important contributors are G. H. Wilson (1985), whose studies began with the uses of the Psalter at Qumran, and K. Seybold (1990), whose introduction to the psalms started with the final form and worked backwards, positing some wisdom influence on the whole. Hence from influences such as these, it is clear that the roots of holistic criticism in psalmody are historical-critical, even though its present interests are undoubtedly literary. This will be seen in the following discussion.

Three books have been particularly important in this respect: *The Shape and Shaping of the Psalter* (ed. J. C. McCann); the April 1992 edition of the journal *Interpretation*; and N. Whybray's *Reading the Psalms as a Book*. Overall, at least three different ways emerge with respect to a viewing of the Psalter holistically.

The first is a possible royal theme, proposed initially by Wilson. This notes how Psalms 2, 72 and 89, all royal psalms, occur at the 'seams' of Books One, Two and Three, and hence lay stress on the importance of the house of David and God's promises to the king. But Psalm 89.49, at the end of Book Three, ends with a cry of despair about the end of the Davidic line ('Lord, where is thy steadfast love of old, which by the faithfulness thou didst swear to David?') thus suggesting the period of exile when the monarchy was in disarray and the promises seemed to be broken. Book Four (Psalms 90 onwards) resolves this tension by taking attention away from the human Davidic king, and focusing instead on God as king; and Book Five takes this further, appealing to reliance on God alone. Furthermore, in Books Four and Five, more didactic elements are paramount; hence these two books are more likely to be the work of the wise, while the previous three books are probably more the work of those from the royal court. Thus, speaking holistically, the Psalter in its final form is a combination of the interests of the royal house of David before the Exile, and the scribes exercising some wisdom influence on the Psalter after the Exile. The holistic way of reading the psalms is thus to view them as memories of the past, concerning the rise and fall of the house of David, readapted into the life of the present community.

The second holistic emphasis, which is part of Seybold's thesis, and is developed by D. M. Howard, is to focus on the wisdom traditions and to see that right the way throughout the Psalter, the didactic influence is paramount. Psalms 1 and 119 bear witness to these traditions in their stress on the importance of the law. These psalms once formed the beginning and end of the first edition of the Psalter, to which other didactic psalms were later added. Hence the Psalter overall has a didactic emphasis by way of the psalms which have been brought into its seams, and which form the beginning and ending. The problem here (and one which is posed particularly by W. Brueggemann) is the fact that the Psalter now ends with the paean of praise in Psalm 150. This surely shows that liturgical and theological interests were as important at the *end* as were the didactic and wisdom interests at the *beginning*. Furthermore, particular placing of the hymnic material, especially in Books Four and Five, shows that liturgical concerns were certainly at work; hymns have been added not only at the end of the Psalter itself (Psalms 146—50) but also at the end of other collections. For example, Psalm 100 closes the collection 95—9; Psalm 118 closes the group known as the Great Hallel; Psalm 134 closes the Song of

Ascents collection; and Psalm 145 closes the David collection. Hence, again speaking in terms of the literary sense of the final whole, the effect of the whole is not so much about the wisdom material alone; it is about the way this is integrated with hymnody, and about how the present needs of the community are thus served by both instruction and praise of God.

A variation on this theme has been developed in part by J. C. McCann. By looking at the placing of the royal psalms in Books One to Three, it is possible to see this as a way of reaching beyond the disappointed hopes of the fallen monarchy to inspire a new vision of an entirely new theocratic age beyond the covenant made with David. Hence the voice of the Psalter as a whole is not so much about the house of David as about the breaking in of a new rule of God. Books Four and Five develop this in new ways, and their emphasis on the kingship of God at the beginning (Psalms 93, 95—9) and at the end (Psalms 145—50) shows the eschatological, future-orientated shape of the Psalter in its final form. Already, on this account, speaking holistically, the Psalter is basically about the future. It is to be seen as prophecy, and as such it offers promises about the future kingdom of God. This may well explain why the community at Qumran and the New Testament writers chose to speak about the psalms as 'prophecies'.

Whybray's book, *Reading the Psalms as a Book*, is, however, a timely warning about using a holistic approach in any one exclusive way. Whybray observes that there are attractions in all the above theories, yet there are limitations as well. The Psalter is not only a politico-religious book, looking back to the memory of the House of David, in the hope of some restoration to this 'golden age' once again; nor is it only a teaching and liturgical handbook from the religious leaders to the laity, offering insights as to how to keep the faith in the present time, when all is party-strife and international turmoil; nor is it essentially only a prophetic book, inspiring the people with new hope concerning the future with promises about the coming of God soon to be fulfilled. The sheer variety of these holistic approaches shows that no one systematic view of the Psalter as a whole can really work. Thus, following our own proposals, pluralism is indeed the key – in relation to each of the six approaches, as well as within each method itself.

Summary

Before attempting to study Psalm 8 by using a combination of all the above approaches, Table 16 gives a summary of the ways in which we have looked at the psalms over these last three sections. It looks in turn at the theological, historical, and literary approaches, and is intended to be a guide for the reading of *any* biblical text. Clearly not every single one of the questions asked in this chart can usually be answered in one biblical passage. Good reading cannot be categorized quite as simply as this, for it has to be undertaken in a more integrative and intuitive way. Nevertheless, to know what questions to ask is an important start for knowing what answers to give.

The final chapter has selected Psalm 8 as a very good example of a psalm which is in fact open to offering answers to most of the questions asked in Table 16. Table 16 is therefore intended as a particular guideline in this respect.

Table 16 Questions to Ask when Reading the Psalms

Theological Approaches	*Historical Approaches*	*Literary Approaches*
What is the **liturgical** meaning?	What are its **origins**? • *Who* was the psalmist? • *When* did he write? • *Where* did he write from?	How does the **text** work? • its order in the sense? (in its parallelism) • its order in the sound? (in its assonance, alliteration)
What is the **didactic** meaning?	What **sources** were used? • e.g. northern or southern? • e.g. priestly or prophetic? • e.g. ancient Near Eastern?	How does the **poetry** work? • as performative art? • as ambiguity?
What is the **prophetic** meaning?	What **forms** were used? • praise? • lament? • mixed?	How do **structures** work? • the mythical patterning? • the binary ideas? • in individual psalms? • in the Psalter overall?
What is the **spiritual** meaning?	What **traditions** were used? • e.g. Exodus? • e.g. Zion? • e.g. creation?	How does **rhetoric** work? • feminist readings? • liberationist readings?
	What **redaction** was used? • in each of the five books? • in each psalm? • endings? • joinings? • superscriptions?	How does a reader **respond**? • by way of prayer • discovering concentric patterns
	What of the whole **Canon**? • what is its overall form? • what is its overall theology?	How does the '**whole**' work? • a shaping through the past? • a shaping for present help? • a shaping for future hope?

9

From Theory to Practice: Readings of Psalm 8

RSV Translation of Psalm 8

To the choirmaster: according to The Gittith. A Psalm of David

1 a   O LORD, our Lord,
   b   how majestic is thy name in all the earth!

   c   Thou whose glory above the heavens is chanted
2 a   by the mouth of babes and infants,
   b   thou hast founded a bulwark because of thy foes,
   c   to still the enemy and the avenger.

3 a   When I look at thy heavens, the work of thy fingers,
   b   the moon and the stars which thou hast established;
4 a   what is man that thou art mindful of him,
   b   and the son of man that thou dost care for him?

5 a   Yet thou hast made him little less than God,
   b   and dost crown him with glory and honour.
6 a   Thou hast given him dominion over the works of thy hands;
   b   thou hast put all the things under his feet,
7 a   all sheep and oxen,
   b   and also the beasts of the field,
8 a   the birds of the air, and the fish of the sea,
   b   whatever passes along the paths of the sea.

9 a   O LORD, our Lord,
   b   how majestic is thy name in all the earth!

Historical Approaches

Lower Criticism

Lower criticism begins by noting that Psalm 8 is a hymn of praise to God as Creator. In the Hebrew, it has evidence of a regular rhythm of two groups of three beats to each line (3:3), especially noticeable in verses 4, 5, 6 and 7, a rhythm which is typical of several hymns. Three points may be noted with regard to the Hebrew text.

232

(i) Verse 1c is corrupt, and it is difficult to know whether to read it as an independent unit (translating it literally 'You have *set* your glory above the heavens') or to link it to verse 2a, and reading the verb as 'chant' rather than 'set, place', as does the RSV translation above.

(ii) The phrase 'because of your foes' in verse 2b is omitted in some manuscripts, and is left out of some versions. It is not essential.

(iii) The word translated as 'God' in verse 5 ('little less than God') is correct from the Hebrew text, but the Greek uses the word 'angels'; the reading 'you have made him a little less than the angels' is what is used in the quotation of this verse in Hebrew 2.7 – for it is using the Greek text, not the Hebrew.

Higher Criticism

Higher criticism would start with questions about the date, place and author of the psalm. As far as the date for this psalm is concerned, it is almost certainly *post-exilic*, for it seems to be a development of Genesis 1 in its description of the ordering of creation and the belief that mankind is at the pinnacle of the created order. The mythological influences (concerning a heavenly council with other deities, and the great deep waters of chaos, about which, see below) are evident, but they have been suppressed. This shows the more cautious view of mythology and the greater consciousness of monotheism in later times – its theological and demythologizing tendencies are like Genesis 1, but developed even further.

As far as the place is concerned, the psalm could be used *anywhere*. The Temple does not feature at all; God's presence is to be found throughout the whole created order (again a later idea). Thus it could be used for private reflection, but equally it could be part of public liturgy. It could well have been composed away from the Temple.

As far as the author is concerned, the post-exilic date makes it impossible that the psalmist is the king. The 'Psalm of David' in the superscription should be read in terms of a psalm belonging to the Davidic collection, preserved as part of the tradition belonging to the patron psalmist, David. The subject of the psalm is therefore any archetypal figure – *'everyman'* – no single individual, whether priest, prophet, or king, could be proposed as composer of the psalm. This is a case of a psalm being written by a representative of the people for anyone to use.

233

Source Criticism

Two key *sources* for this psalm have already been referred to – Genesis 1, and the mythological accounts of creation taken from other cultures. As far as *Genesis 1* is concerned, the ordering of creation expressed in this psalm – the heavens, the moon, the stars (verse 3) is the same as in Genesis 1.14–19. Humankind as the climax of creation (verse 5) also echoes Genesis 1.26–7. The hierarchy in creation, whereby man has authority over the entire created order – the beasts and the birds and the fish of the sea (verses 7 and 8) also echoes Genesis 1.29–30, in style as well as in theology. Genesis 1 is quite different from the creation account in Genesis 2 in all these respects; and the most important theme – that of God being transcendent over all the created order, rather than being immanent within it (as is presented in Genesis 2, where God walks and talks in the garden of Eden) – is very much the same theme in Psalm 8. If Psalm 8 did borrow from Genesis 1, then it is also possible that Genesis 1 in turn borrowed from an earlier creation psalm, Psalm 104, which itself has correspondences with an Egyptian hymn to the sun-god, Amon-Re, found on a tomb in Tell el-Amarna, dating from the fourteenth century BCE. Hence Psalm 8 may be derived from several sources, in several ways.

Another source which the psalmist may have drawn from, less explicitly, is the accounts of creation in *the myths of other cultures*. At least two features come to light in this psalm, although (because the psalm is later) these have been suppressed. The first is the belief in a *heavenly council*, with a pantheon of gods, where the chief deity (often called 'El') would send out decrees to those other deities who were to execute his command. (Psalm 82.1–2: 'God has taken his place in the divine council; in the midst of the gods he holds judgement' has a more explicit hint of this idea; it is earlier.) The idea of a heavenly council could be seen in the word 'God' in verse 5. Although a common name for Israel's deity, it is a plural form, and so could also read 'gods' (this is the word translated as 'angels' in the Greek). The idea of a heavenly council is also apparent in verses 1b and 2, where God's glory is described as chanted by heavenly beings (as in Isaiah 6.3, where the prophet sees a vision of God in heaven and hears the seraphim chanting God's glory).

The second mythological motif, also suppressed, is that of a deity's battle with *a monster of the deep*, the god's victory over which brings about the ordering of chaos and so enables the creation of the world. The psalms which use this theme of God fighting a dragon of the deep include

Psalms 74.12–17 and 89.5–11. The latter psalm, 89, also has the heavenly council motif. The expression in verse 8b, 'whatever passes along the paths of the sea' could allude to this; but more especially, a further allusion is evident in the unusual use of the term '*behemoth*' which has been translated as 'beasts of the field' in verse 7b. '*Behemoth*' here is a plural noun, but may be translated as a singular noun and is also a depiction of a primeval monster, rather like a hippopotamus. But here the psalmist has deliberately adapted the primordial allusion – the monster, tamed by God, is just like an ordinary beast of the field.

Form Criticism

In terms of the *form* of this psalm, we have already noted that the rhythm of the psalm gives it associations with several of the hymns which also use a 3:3 metre. Thus the psalm could be classified as a *hymn*, for use in liturgy. However, there is no reference to any rituals, processions, festivals, or life in the Temple; and the creation theme is one widely used in didactic literature (for example, in Proverbs 8 and Job 38—42), so that the psalm could be as much a reflective wisdom poem as it is a liturgical hymn. Other psalms with creation themes similarly suit a more private and reflective *wisdom* orientation – for example, Psalms 19, 90 and 139. The only features pointing to a liturgical setting are the smaller forms within the psalm itself – the movement between communal praise in verses 1 and 2, to individual praise (using the archetypal 'I' form) in verses 3 to 8, and then back to communal praise in verse 9, which altogether might suggest some antiphonal usage, where the liturgical leader speaks and the congregation responds. The fact that verses 1 and 9 are the same, being usable as a *refrain*, may add weight to the possible liturgical orientation of the psalm.

Tradition Criticism

As far as the use of *traditions* is concerned, Psalm 8 is firmly linked to the *creation tradition* as expressed particularly in Genesis 1. As was noted briefly earlier, this is in contrast to another creation tradition – the one mostly associated with Genesis 2. Genesis 2 speaks of man as the dust of the earth, more vulnerable and contingent upon creation, unlike the more exalted view of man in Genesis 1 and Psalm 8. This psalm is also more like Genesis 1, and hence less like Genesis 2, in its emphasis on the beauty and order in the cosmos (in Genesis 1 this is expressed in the refrain 'and God saw that it was good'; Genesis 2, by contrast, ends with a view of creation where the land is cursed, and humankind's survival in the world involves toil and conflict). A further link between Psalm 8 and Genesis 1, and hence the contrast of both with Genesis 2, is the emphasis on the distance of God from his created order. God looks down on his world, and is in harmony with all that he has made, but does not engage with the humans in any relational way. (By contrast, in Genesis 2—3, God walks in the garden, talks to the created couple, and is angry at their unwillingness to obey him, shown when they take the fruit from the tree.) In summary, Psalm 8, like Genesis 1, sees the grandeur of creation, the glory of humankind, and the transcendence of God: this then is certainly a tradition of creation, but it is a very particular adaption of that tradition.

Redaction Criticism

The link with Genesis 1, known as the *priestly* account of creation because of its repetitive style and refrain-like quality, may suggest that Psalm 8 too has passed through priestly hands. If *redactional activity* is to be seen through the headings of the psalms, then this may well indicate a priestly influence in the later stages. For, whatever we may postulate about its earlier origins on account of its form (that is, whether composed as a reflective poem or as a liturgical hymn being unclear), the later usage as seen through the role of the redactors certainly suggests a place in liturgy. The first term in the superscription, 'to the choirmaster', is used in fifty-five other psalms and indicates some use in the guilds of singers in the second Temple.

The second term, 'according to the Gittith' (also found in Psalms 81 and 84) could have several connotations, all liturgical. 'Gittith' could mean some sort of instrument, like a lyre, thus emphasizing again the musical use of the psalm. Or 'Gittith' could mean a winepress, and so indicate that this was a creation psalm to be used at the end of the vintage season, in autumn, at the turn of the year. If so, it was probably used at one of the three great annual festivals, Tabernacles, which took place at the turn of the year in autumn-time. Or it could simply mean a hymn tune, as seems to be the case with other archaic headings such as in Psalms 22 and 45.

The final part of the superscription, 'Psalm of David', is thus best read as ascriptive. This is a psalm belonging to the post-exilic royal collection, to be sung in memory of

236

the Davidic house, in a similar way to the other seventy-two psalms which bear this same Davidic heading.

Canon Criticism

In terms of its place in the *canonical collection*, it could be argued that Psalm 8 stands in a close relationship to *Psalms 7 and 9*, and this indicates its inclusion here at quite a late stage. Psalm 7.17 ends: 'I will give to the Lord the thanks due to his righteousness, and I will sing praise to the name of the Lord, the Most High.' Psalm 9.1 begins: 'I will give thanks to the Lord with my whole heart; I will tell of thy wonderful deeds. I will be glad and exult in thee, I will sing praise to thy name, O Most High.' It is quite possible that Psalm 8 was placed between these two psalms as an example of the song of praise which is referred to at the end of the one psalm and alluded to at the beginning of the other. Certainly, when one looks at all the other creation psalms in Book One (Psalms 19, 29 and 33) it could be argued in each case that they have been inserted at a later stage, and that each of them has been included to add light to the predominant theme of lament and complaint in the psalms which enclose them. The fact that Psalm 8 was included between two predominantly lament and complaint psalms (7, 9—10) illustrates this well.

Literary Approaches

Moving now from the history of the psalm to the meaning of the text, the focus has changed from asking questions about *how the psalm was composed*, to asking questions about *what the psalm now means*.

Semantic and Linguistic Readings

In terms of the *semantics of the language*, Psalm 8 is an interesting psalm on account of its frequent *word-pairing*. Even the first verse does this by using the two contrasting names for God: 'Yahweh', the name of God which is not to be spoken, and 'Lord', or more accurately, '*ādônênû* ('our Lord', or, in some translations, 'our Governor'), the more familiar name for God. Verse 4 offers a contrast of the two names of man – the more general term '*enōš*, and the more personal term *ben-adām* – the son of man (though not of course used here in the sense of being a title, as it was in New Testament times). Two other interesting pairs of contrasts are the 'babes and sucklings' and the 'foe and the avenger' in verse 2, which bring out the meaning of the weak and vulnerable confounding the mighty and the strong. The two verbs in the parallelism of verse 4 ('to remember' and 'to care for') again offer a contrasting device for depicting two aspects of the protection of God. Further pairings – of the moon and stars (verse 3), the glory and honour (verse 5) the hands and feet (verse 6), sheep and oxen, birds and fish (verses 7 to 8) – all create comparisons in the descriptions of God's creative care for things both great and small. And within the psalm overall, its setting between the heavens (verses 1 and 9) and the earth (verses 2 to 8) further adds dimension to the dual comparison between the majesty of God and the dignity of humankind.

Poetic Criticism

The *performative nature of the poetry* could be illustrated in many ways. Two examples, the first taken from *The Liturgical Psalter* and the second from a new translation/meditation by J. Cotter are shown in Figures 22 and 23, musical and poetic versions of Psalm 8. Again, we may note the correspondences with theological readings, not least those with a more spiritual interest. To these two illustrations we might also have added more visual ones, depicting the psalm by way of paintings or photographs. The 'performative' reading is the most difficult to represent in a book, for 'performance' may not use words at all, but may be embodied in painting, sculpture, music or dance.

Structuralist Criticism

A *structuralist reading* is closely related to the semantic reading outlined above. Its concern is thus also with the *word-pairing and parallelism* in separate verses, but in addition it is concerned with the structure of the greater whole – for example, with the balance between the heavens and the earth in verses 1 and 9 and 3 to 8 respectively. It is also concerned with the structure of the smaller parts within the whole – for example, in verses 3 to 8 (concerning the earth), the balance between the cosmos and humankind (verses 3 and 4) and between humankind and the created order (verses 5 to 8). Within these concentric 'balances', a further study could include the balancing found within the mythical allusions of first, the deity and heavens, in the allusion to the motif of the heavenly council and second, the deity and the earth, in the allusion to the motif of the chaos monster now tamed. The concern for order, and the displacement of chaos by the use of the patterns and of ideas, is a vital means

238

Words: Psalm 8 from *The Liturgical Psalter*
David Frost and others
Music: G. M. Garrett (1834–97)
Descant: John Barnard

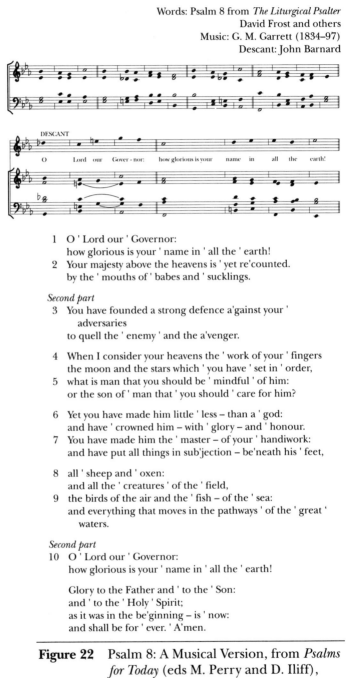

1   O ' Lord our ' Governor:
    how glorious is your ' name in ' all the ' earth!
2   Your majesty above the heavens is ' yet re'counted.
    by the ' mouths of ' babes and ' sucklings.

Second part
3   You have founded a strong defence a'gainst your '
        adversaries
    to quell the ' enemy ' and the a'venger.

4   When I consider your heavens the ' work of your ' fingers
    the moon and the stars which ' you have ' set in ' order,
5   what is man that you should be ' mindful ' of him:
    or the son of ' man that ' you should ' care for him?

6   Yet you have made him little ' less – than a ' god:
    and have ' crowned him – with ' glory – and ' honour.
7   You have made him the ' master – of your ' handiwork:
    and have put all things in sub'jection – be'neath his ' feet,

8   all ' sheep and ' oxen:
    and all the ' creatures ' of the ' field,
9   the birds of the air and the ' fish – of the ' sea:
    and everything that moves in the pathways ' of the ' great '
        waters.

Second part
10 O ' Lord our ' Governor:
    how glorious is your ' name in ' all the ' earth!

    Glory to the Father and ' to the ' Son:
    and ' to the ' Holy ' Spirit;
    as it was in the be'ginning – is ' now:
    and shall be for ' ever. ' A'men.

Figure 22   Psalm 8: A Musical Version, from *Psalms for Today* (eds M. Perry and D. Iliff), Hodder & Stoughton, 1990.

Stewards of
Creation

Refrain: Creator God, Source of all life,
how gloriously does your name resound,
echoing to the bounds of the universe!

The morning stars sing for joy, and the youngest child cries your
    name.
The weak in the world shame the strong, and silence the proud
    and the rebellious.

When I look at the heavens, even the work of your fingers,
the moon and the stars majestic in their courses –
the eagle riding the air, the dolphin ploughing the sea,
the gazelle leaping the wind, the sheep grazing the fells –
who are we human beings that you keep us in mind,
children, women, and men that you care so much for us?

Yet still you bring us to life, creating us after your image,
stewards of the planet you give as our home.
How awesome a task you entrust to our hands.
How fragile and beautiful is the good earth.

Creator God, amid the immensities of the universe you seek us out
and call us to be partners in your work of creating. May we not
fail you.

Figure 23   Psalm 8: A Poetic Version, from J. Cotter,
                   Through Desert Places, Cairns
                   Publications, 1989, p. 13.

through which the poem itself brings about a well-
ordered world for a community who may well have felt the
threat of chaos close at hand. Hence the means (the well-
ordered poem) becomes a sign of the end (a well-ordered
world). Figure 24 explains this in more graphic detail.

Rhetorical
Criticism

A *rhetorical-critical reading* of this psalm takes us into the
interpretation of it from several other angles. On the one
hand, following the pattern of Genesis 1, this is a psalm
which is *gender-inclusive*, for it depicts the creation of
both man and woman (through the use of the general
Hebrew term for 'humankind' in verse 4), although
the predominant male interpretation of this psalm
throughout its history has usually inferred the archetype
to be 'man' alone. Hence a feminist reading would be to
take what is actually implied in the Hebrew noun by
'humankind' and so redress the balance of the place of
woman as well as man in the created order, following the
pattern of 'male and female created in the image of God'
in Genesis 1.

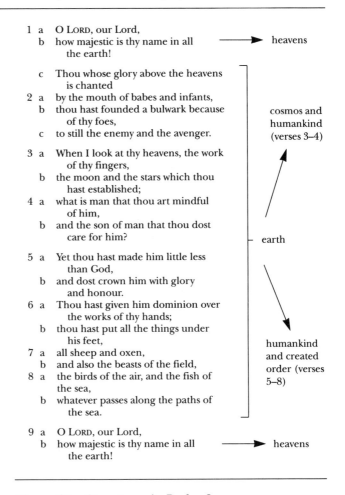

1 a O Lord, our Lord,
  b how majestic is thy name in all   ⟶ heavens
     the earth!

  c Thou whose glory above the heavens
     is chanted
2 a by the mouth of babes and infants,
  b thou hast founded a bulwark because   cosmos and
     of thy foes,   humankind
  c to still the enemy and the avenger.   (verses 3–4)

3 a When I look at thy heavens, the work
     of thy fingers,
  b the moon and the stars which thou
     hast established;
4 a what is man that thou art mindful
     of him,
  b and the son of man that thou dost   earth
     care for him?

5 a Yet thou hast made him little less
     than God,
  b and dost crown him with glory
     and honour.
6 a Thou hast given him dominion over
     the works of thy hands;
  b thou hast put all the things under
     his feet,   humankind
7 a all sheep and oxen,   and created
  b and also the beasts of the field,   order (verses
8 a the birds of the air, and the fish of   5–8)
     the sea,
  b whatever passes along the paths of
     the sea.

9 a O Lord, our Lord,
  b how majestic is thy name in all   ⟶ heavens
     the earth!

Figure 24   Structures in Psalm 8

Furthermore, another rhetorical response could be by way of questioning the hierarchical placing of humankind *over* creation, which could be inferred by a reading of verses 6 to 8. The sense of the *codependency* of humans with the created order, and the *stewardship* of creation, closer to the account in the creation story of Genesis 2, would be deemed a more sensible reading of the psalm, particularly in the light of ecological issues today. Such an 'ecological' reading necessitates a critique of the values implied by the psalmist, and this can be done by referring to other texts (such as Genesis 2) which redress the balance. This 'ecological' rhetorical way of reading, by use of 'corrective' texts, stands in contrast with the first (more feminist) rhetorical way of reading, which simply uses what is already implied within the text itself. But each approach is rhetorical-critical, insofar as each looks at the text from outside 'in', as it were, and seeks to change its art of persuasion to suite a more contemporary setting.

Reader-Response Criticism

A *reader-response approach* can do many things with this psalm. One way could be to take the emphasis on the *children's praise* in verse 2, and to observe that this illustrates how those with simple trust are more able to perceive the beauty of the created order in ways in which a sceptical adult might never be able to do. This 'reader-response' could then link this with the use of the same verse in Matthew 21.16. On entering Jerusalem on the donkey, accompanied by the praises of the crowds (singing 'Hosanna to the Son of David ... blessed is he who comes in the name of the Lord'), Jesus confronts the cynicism of the scribes and chief priests who seek to mock the simple praise of the children: 'Have you never read, "Out of the mouths of babes and sucklings thou hast brought perfect praise"?' The praise of the simple may well be a perception of simple truths; but simple truths can also be profound, and the praise of the simple is not to be despised. 'Whoever receives one such child in my name receives me; but whoever causes one of these little ones who believe in me to sin, it would be better for him to have a great millstone fastened round his neck and to be drowned in the depth of the sea' (Matthew 18.5–6). This sort of verse-association shows how a reader-response approach can take a theme in the text, and allow it to create correspondences with the theme in other texts, and so to the theme in other texts beyond. Using reader-response theory, one text can produce infinite readings.

Holistic Criticism

A *holistic reading*, by starting with the psalm as a whole, might be by way of *comparing* the meaning of Psalm 8 in its entirety *with other creation psalms* – Psalms 19, 29, 33, 104 and 139 in particular – and so establishing some overall themes of the theology of creation throughout the entire Psalter. Another way would be to take Psalm 8, as an example of a later, more reflective psalm on creation, and contrast it in terms of structure and meaning with a very different psalm – for example, with *Psalm 29*, which is as much concerned with the *sounds* in creation (for it is a psalm with a sevenfold structure which is about the seven-fold voice of God heard through a thunderstorm) as Psalm 8 is with the *imagery* within the created order. And as Psalm 8 is about the visionary aspect of creation, it is also about the beauty and order within it. Its emphasis on the beauty of the natural order again makes it a good contrast with Psalm 29, for here, through the sounds of the storm, the psalmist is more concerned with the destructive aspects of creation. The 'awe and fear' before God as Creator thus mean quite different things when one compares these two different creation psalms. In this sense, holistic readings might be used by way of comparing the whole text with other similar texts; and in the case of the psalms, the concern is as much with the theological ideas as it is with the literary presentation of them.

Theological Approaches

Many of the points one would make in a *theological appreci-ation* of Psalm 8 have already appeared in other approaches. This underlines the multifaceted way in which different types of reading impinge upon each other. Some *liturgical* interpretation has already been noted in our discussion of form criticism; some *spiritual* interpretation, under poetic criticism; and some *didactic* interpretation under rhetorical criticism and under the reader-response readings. The distinctively theological observation to be made here is how this psalm was used in the *Christian tradition* in particular. For example, the 'Lord' addressed at the beginning of the psalm is inter-preted by Christians as Christ himself, and from this he is understood as the Lord who, having brought about creation, can accept the children's praises (Matthew 21.16 again).

Furthermore, as seen in the middle of the psalm, the figure is human as well as divine, and so the term 'son of man' is now his by right. (In this sense, 'son of man' as used earlier to refer to everyman is now invested with a good deal of extraneous tradition to refer explicitly to *the* 'Son of Man' of the Gospels: it is now a *title* for Christ himself.) This then means that Christ, born into the world and so 'a little lower than the angels' has, by returning to the heavens after his death and resurrection, created a new way of humankind knowing God through him (noting here the two New Testament references alluded to earlier: Hebrews 2.6–7, referring to Psalm 8.4–5; and 1

Corinthians 15.27, referring to Psalm 8.6). With this sort of 'prophetic' interpretation, achieved by way of finding 'hidden meanings' in the text, Psalm 8, once composed and used to reflect upon *creation* now is recomposed and reused to reflect upon *redemption.*

From this only a very small adjustment is required in making this same psalm one of the most important psalms used in liturgy at Ascensiontide. In so doing, Christ is thus the Lord whose name is majestic in all the earth; he is the one robed in majesty, who receives the praise of his people because by becoming man, and by dying, rising and ascending into heaven, he has put all things (in a spiritual sense) in subjection under him. As the writer to the Ephesians puts it, alluding to this psalm, and speaking of Christ's rule in heavenly places (1.17ff.) 'he has put all things under his feet and has made him the head over all things for the church' (Ephesians 1.22).

Conclusion

Towards the end of his six-hundred-page work on biblical hermeneutics, Anthony Thiselton's last few pages focus entirely on the issue of what he calls 'hermeneutical pluralism'. By this, Thiselton means the tension between the need for openness to each and every mode of interpreting the biblical text, and at the same time the need to exercise some discretion over this openness, lest pluralism itself becomes another ideology. The irony in a pluralistic approach is that it too can become a dogma. By its very claim to 'open-endedness' in its reading, pluralism can be as assertive and as abrasive in its approach as all the other approaches which it seeks to denounce. Thiselton puts it like this: 'To seek to *impose* some universal model, or even to impose a model onto other readers as "primary" would be to operate in the same authoritarian terms that social pragmatists use but disguise as liberal pluralism.' (*New Horizons in Hermeneutics: The Theory and Practice of Transforming Bible Study*, HarperCollins, 1992, p. 612).

An appeal to read the Bible in a pluralistic way is thus in need of some sort of self-critique. Thiselton, as a Christian theologian, proposes that this could be achieved by the new horizons which are found in the cross and resurrection: the *cross*, because it reverses all our expectations of what is effective, and challenges our very concept of power and understanding, and even alienates us from all we may believe about 'wisdom, religion and power politics of ... society'; and the *resurrection*, because it offers us a world-view which cannot be evaluated by any systematic predetermined way of thinking. Thiselton's argument is in some ways quite compelling. The cross and resurrection, in their different ways, challenge the core of *both* a closed, systematic way of thinking about the Bible as Scripture *and* an open-ended, liberal, pluralistic way of thinking about biblical texts. The ultra-orthodox and ultra-liberal approaches to the Bible are equally extreme, and the truth may well lie somewhere between the two.

But where? We have in this book made such an appeal to the diversity in the making of the Bible, and hence the necessity of diverse approaches in the reading of it, that it may seem strange at the end to undermine the very plea for pluralism with which this book began. But this would be to misunderstand the message of the beginning.

For the real concern in this book is that the Bible is text which is more vulnerable than most to the abuse of '-isms'. By this, we mean that, in a **theological** understanding of the text, *fundamentalism* can so easily emerge as a subtle form of control – a control which implies that it alone offers the true (spiritual) meaning of the text, and that one particular meaning, now properly understood and interpreted, should control the lives of those who come into contact with others who believe this way. But there are other '-isms' as well. The **historical** approach is equally prone to falling prey to a *historicism*, whereby the 'accidental truths of history' become the means of determining whether a religion is true or false, or whether the interpretation of that religion through a religious text is true or false. Similarly, the **literary** approach is in danger of taking the form of a bookish *literarism*. In presuming that the text must be understood primarily as good literature, aesthetic concerns can become a similar limitation, whereby the exploration of different sorts of concerns is deemed less relevant. And so when set alongside these extremes of fundamentalism, historicism and literarism, *pluralism* too can take on a different meaning; it can be just as insidious, and just as much an ideology as the other three.

For what lies behind all these '-isms' is the ideology of control. It is what David Clines, in his *Interested Parties: The Ideology of Writers and Readers of the Hebrew Bible*, calls 'the will to power' – 'whether it is, for instance, the royal ideology of ancient Israel or the religious ideology of the guild of modern biblical scholars' (p. 11). It is what Walter Brueggeman in his *Israel's Praise: Doxology against Idolatry and Ideology* calls 'a vested interest which is passed off as truth, partial truth which counterfeits as whole truth, theological claim functioning as a mode of social control' (p. 111). And it is the same issue which Rex Mason seeks to address with his book, *Propaganda and Subversion in the Old Testament*. Whether we look at this issue from within the biblical texts themselves, or whether we focus instead on the readers and users of the texts, the problem is the same. To return to Clines again:

> Writers do not, on the whole, write their texts for the fun of it; they have a case to put, an argument to advance, or an opponent to overcome. And since the name for their case, their argument, their position, is their 'ideology', I say that their text is a realization of their ideology, a performance of their investment in their ideology; one could say that ideology if 'inscribed' in their texts, meaning that the texts themselves are ways of thinking and speaking ideologically ... On their surface, their texts lay claim

to coherence and rationality, and they give the appearance of sincerity and either moral fervour or objectivity. But beneath the surface there are issues of power, of self-identity and security, of group solidarity, of fear and desire, of need and greed, that have played a role in the production of the text, sometimes a leading role.

(*Interested Parties*, Sheffield Academic Press, 1995, pp. 23, 24)

Every 'criticism' falls under this reproach: higher criticism, lower criticism, source criticism, form criticism, tradition criticism, redaction criticism, canon criticism – all the various approaches of historical criticism can have within them a tendency to presume a right of ownership of the text and so to control it. So too semantic criticism, poetic criticism, structuralist criticism, rhetorical criticism, reader-response criticism, holistic criticism – all these easily become different ways of 'reader-centredness' whereby the reader assumes the same right to a proper interpretation of a text, and so ends up trying to control it. And, finally, theological readings, tied so closely to religious beliefs and to an accepted confessional approach to the text, are equally guilty in this respect.

So where does this leave us? It leaves us still with an appeal to pluralism, and so to accepting a diversity of approaches to the biblical text, for it is in the safety of a number of approaches that the tendency to power and control can best be dissipated. But it also leads us with a sense that we should be as critical of pluralism *per se* as we should be critical of any exclusivist approach which assumes that it alone has the key control. An appeal to pluralism does not then mean accepting everything about postmodernism; ironically this would be making another ideological claim.

Our approach to good reading of the Bible should begin with a recognition that there is something both 'fixed' (the text itself) and yet at the same time 'open' (the many voices which are found in the text). It is clear that the Bible cannot be constrained by any one system of reading; it has constantly eluded the many attempts to simplify and control its meaning. Thus the basic premise for any biblical student is an acceptance of the fact that the texts will always be something of a mystery; and herein lies the challenge of biblical studies as an academic discipline.

Bibliography

[* indicates most significant and relevant books quoted]

General Reading

* P. R. Ackroyd and C. F. Evans (eds), *The Cambridge History of the Bible*, Vols. I–III, CUP, 1963–70.

J. Barton, *Reading the Old Testament*, London, DLT, revd. edn 1996.

G. L. Bray, *Biblical Interpretation Past and Present*, Leicester, Apollos, 1996.

R. P. Carroll and A. G. Hunter, *Words at Work: Using the Bible in the Academy, the Community and the Churches: Essays in Honour of Robert Davidson*, Glasgow, Trinity St Mungo Press, 1994.

B. Chilton (ed.), *Beginning New Testament Study*, London, SPCK, 1986.

* R. J. Coggins and J. L. Houlden (eds), *A Dictionary of Biblical Interpretation*, Philadelphia, Trinity and, London, SCM, 1990.

D. N. Freedman (ed.), *The Anchor Bible Dictionary*, Vols. 1–6, New York and London, Doubleday, 1992.

R. M. Grant and D. Tracy, *A Short History of the Interpretation of the Bible*, London, SCM, revd edn 1984.

J. C. de Moor (ed.), *Synchronic or Diachronic? A Debate on Method in Old Testament Exegesis*, Leiden, Brill, 1995.

* R. Morgan with J. Barton, *Biblical Interpretation*, OUP, 1989.

S. Prickett and R. Barnes (eds.), *The Bible: Landmarks of World Literature*, CUP, 1991.

C. S. Rodd, *Thinking Things Through: I. The Bible*, London, Epworth, 1996.

J. Rogerson (ed.), *Beginning Old Testament Study*, London, SPCK, 1983.

J. Rogerson, C. Rowland and B. Lindars (eds), *The Study and Use of the Bible*, Grand Rapids, Eerdmans and, Basingstoke, Marshall Pickering, 1988.

H. G. M. Williamson and R. E. Friedman (eds.), *The Future of Biblical Studies: The Hebrew Scriptures*, Atlanta, Scholars Press, 1987.

Introduction

* J. Barr, *The Bible in the Modern World*, London, SCM, 1973.

Z. Bauman, *Intimations of Postmodernity*, London, Routledge, 1992.

* W. Brueggemann, *The Bible and Postmodern Imagination: Texts under Negotiation*, London, SCM, 1993.

F. B. Burnham (ed.), *Postmodern Theology: Christian Faith in a Pluralist World*, San Francisco, Harper, 1989.

* R. P. Carroll, *Wolf in the Sheepfold: The Bible as a Problem for Christianity*, London, SPCK, 1991.

R. P. Carroll, *Under Erasure: The Bible as a Premodern Book in a Postmodern Time* (as yet unpublished paper read at SOTS, 4 January 1996).

E. A. Castelli, S. D. Moore, G. A. Phillips and R. M. Schwartz, *The Postmodern Bible: The Bible and Culture Collective*, New Haven and London, Yale University Press, 1995.

D. Christopher-Smith (ed.), *Text and Experience: Towards a Cultural Exegesis of the Bible*, Sheffield, JSOT Press, 1995.

A. D. Clarke and B. W. Winter (eds), *One God, One Lord in a World of Religious Pluralism*, Cambridge, Tyndale House Press, 1991.

S. Connor, *Postmodernist Culture: An Introduction to Theories of the Contemporary*, Oxford, Blackwell, 1989.

T. Docherty, *Postmodernism: A Reader*, New York and London, Harvester Wheatsheaf, 1993.

T. Eagleton, *The Illusions of Postmodernism*, Oxford, Blackwell, 1996.

S. E. Fowl (ed.), *The Theological Interpretation of Scripture: Classic and Contemporary Readers*, Oxford, Blackwell, 1997.

C. Grenholm, *The Old Testament, Christianity and Pluralism*, Tübingen, J. C. B. Mohr (Paul Siebeck), 1996.

D. Harvey, *The Condition of Postmodernity*, Oxford, Blackwell, 1989.

J. Hick, *Problems of Religious Pluralism*, London, Macmillan, 1985.

B. D. Ingraffia, *Postmodern Theory and Biblical Theology: Vanquishing God's Shadow*, CUP, 1995.

D. L. Jeffrey, *People of the Book*, Philadelphia, Fortress, 1996.

J.-F. Lyotard, *The Post-modern Condition: A Report on Knowledge*, Minneapolis, Augsburg, 1984.

E. V. McKnight, *Post-Modern Use of the Bible: The Emergence of Reader-Oriented Criticism*, Nashville, Abingdon, 1988.

* R. Middleton and B. J. Walsh, *Truth is Stranger than It Used To Be: Biblical Faith in a Postmodern Age*, London, SPCK, 1995.

* M. Saebø (ed.), *Hebrew Bible/Old Testament: The History of its Interpretation, Volume 1. From the Beginnings to the Middle Ages. Part I. Antiquity*, Göttingen, Vandenhoeck and Ruprecht, 1996.

A. C. Thistelton, *Interpreting God and the Post-modern Self: On Meaning, Manipulation and Promise*, Edinburgh, T. & T. Clark, 1995.

* F. C. Tiffany and S. H. Ringe, *Biblical Interpretation: A Roadmap*, Nashville, Abingdon, 1996.

* D. Tracy, *The Analogical Imagination: Christian Theology and the Culture of Pluralism*, London, SCM, 1981.

* D. Tracy, *Plurality and Ambiguity: Hermeneutics, Religion, Hope*, London, SCM, 1988.

* F. Young, *Biblical Exegesis and the Formation of Christian Culture*, CUP, 1997.

N. Zurbrogg, *The Parameters of Postmodernism*, London, Routledge, 1993.

* The journal, *Semeia*, 51 (1990) also has several useful articles on the Bible and Postmodernism.

Chapter 1 – A Biblical Library? The Smaller Parts of the Greater Whole

B. W. Anderson, *The Living World of the Old Testament*, London, DLT Longman, revd edn 1988.

D. E. Aune, *The New Testament in Its Literary Environment*, Philadelphia, James Clark, 1987.

* J. Barton, *What is the Bible?* London, Triangle, 1991.

* L. Boadt, *Reading the Old Testament*, New York, Paulist Press, 1984.

S. Brown, *The Origins of Christianity*, OUP, revd edn 1994.

R. E. Clements (ed.), *The World of Ancient Israel*, CUP, 1989.

* J. and K. Court, *The New Testament World*, CUP, 1990.

H. C. Kee, *Knowing the Truth: A Sociological Approach to New Testament Interpretation*, Philadelphia, Fortress, 1975.

H. C. Kee, *Christian Origins in Sociological Perspective*, Atlanta, Scholars Press and, London, SCM, 1980.

* H. C. Kee and J. Jacob, *The Social World of Formative Christianity and Judaism*, Philadelphia, Fortress, 1988.

A. Malherbe, *Social Aspects of Early Christianity*, Philadelphia, Fortress, 1983.

J. Neusner (ed.), *Christianity, Judaism and Other Graeco-Roman Cultures*, Leiden, Brill, 1975.

J. K. Riches, *Jesus and the Transformation of Judaism*, London, DLT, 1980.

* J. Rogerson and P. Davies, *The Old Testament World*, CUP, 1989.

* C. Rowland, *Christian Origins*, London, SPCK, 1985.

M. Smith, *Palestinian Parties and Politics that Shaped the Old Testament*, London, SCM, revd edn 1987.

J. Stambaugh and D. Balch, *The Social World of the First Christians*, Philadelphia, Fortress and, London, SCM, 1986.

G. Theissen, *The Open Door*, Philadelphia, Fortress, 1991.

D. Tidball, *An Introduction to the Sociology of the New Testament*, Exeter, Paternoster, 1983.

Chapter 2 – A Biblical Theology?
Two Testaments, One Book?

General Works

J. Barr, *The Semantics of Biblical Language*, OUP, 1961.

* J. Barr, *Old and New in Interpretation*, London, SCM, 1966.

* J. Barr, *The Scope and Authority of the Bible: Explorations in Theology 7*, London, SCM, 1980.

J. Barr, *Biblical Faith and Natural Theology*, Oxford, Clarendon, 1993.

* B. S. Childs, *Biblical Theology in Crisis*, Philadelphia, Fortress, 1970.

* P. D. Hanson, *The Diversity of Scripture: A Theological Interpretation*, Philadelphia, Fortress, 1982.

J. D. Smart, *The Past, Present and Future of Biblical Theology*, Philadelphia Fortress, 1979.

S. Terrien, *The Elusive Presence: Towards a New Biblical Theology*, San Francisco, Harper, 1978.

Old Testament Theology

S. Ackermann, *Under Every Green Tree: Popular Religion in Sixth-Century Judah*, Atlanta, Scholars Press, 1992.

* R. Albertz, *A History of Israelite Religion in the Old Testament Period*, 2 Vols, E. tr. from German, London, SCM, 1993 and 1995.

B. W. Anderson (ed.), *The Old Testament and the Christian Faith*, London, SCM, 1963.

F. F. Bruce, *This is That*, Carlisle, Paternoster, 1968.

* W. Brueggemann, *Old Testament Theology*, Philadelphia, Fortress, 1992.

* B. S. Childs, *Biblical Theology of the Old and New Testaments*, London, SCM, 1992.

R. E. Clements, *Old Testament Theology: A Fresh Approach*, London, Marshall, Morgan & Scott, 1978.

W. Eichrodt, *A Theology of the Old Testament*, 2 Vols, E. tr. from German, London, SCM, 1961 and 1967.

* J. Goldingay, *Theological Diversity and the Authority of the Old Testament*, Carlisle, Paternoster, 1995.

A. T. Hanson, *The Living Utterances of God: The New Testament Exegesis of the Old*, London, DLT, 1983.

J. Høgenhaven, *Problems and Prospects of Old Testament Theology*, Sheffield, JSOT Press, 1987.

E. Jacob, *A Theology of the Old Testament*, E. tr. from French, London, Hodder & Stoughton, 1958.

R. Knierim, *The Task of Old Testament Theology: Substance, Method and Cases*, Grand Rapids, Eerdmans, 1995.

G. A. F. Knight, *A Christian Theology of the Old Testament*, London, SCM, 1964.

H. D. Preuss, *Old Testament Theology*, 2 Vols, E. tr. from German, Edinburgh, T. & T. Clark, 1995, 1996.

* G. von Rad, *Old Testament Theology*, 2 Vols, E. tr. from German, Edinburgh, T. & T. Clark, 1962, 1965.

* R. Rendtorff, *Canon and Theology*, E. tr. from German, Edinburgh, T. & T. Clark, 1993.

* H. G. Reventlow, *Problems of Old Testament Theology in the Twentieth Century*, London, SCM, 1985.

H. H. Rowley, *The Faith of Israel*, London, SCM, 1961.

* W. H. Schmidt, *The Faith of the Old Testament*, E. tr. from German, Oxford, Blackwell, 1983.

N. H. Snaith, *The Distinctive Ideas of the Old Testament*, London, Epworth, 1944.

W. Vischer, *The Witness of the Old Testament to Jesus Christ*, E. tr. from German, London, Lutterworth, 1949.

Th. C. Vriezen, *An Outline of Old Testament Theology*, E. tr. from Dutch, Oxford, Blackwell, 1960.

* C. Westermann, *The Old Testament and Jesus Christ*, E. tr. from German, Minneapolis, Augsburg, 1970.

* G. E. Wright, *The Book of the Acts of God*, London, Duckworth, 1960.

W. Zimmerli, *Old Testament Theology in Outline*, E. tr. from German, Edinburgh, T. & T. Clark, 1978.

New Testament Theology

* R. Bultmann, *Theology of the New Testament*, 2 Vols, E. tr. from German, London, SCM, 1952, 1955.

* H. Conzelmann, *An Outline of the Theology of the New Testament*, E. tr. from German, London, SCM, 1969.

J. and K. Court, *The New Testament World*, CUP, 1990.

*O. Cullmann, *Salvation as History*, E. tr. from German, London, SCM, 1967.

C. H. Dodd, *The Apostolic Preaching and its Development*, London, Hodder & Stoughton, 1936.

* J. D. G. Dunn, *Unity and Diversity in the New Testament*, London, SCM, 1977.

J. D. G. Dunn with J. P. Mackey, *New Testament Theology in Dialogue*, London, SPCK, 1987.

* R. Grant, *Gods and the One God: Christian Theology in the Graeco-Roman World*, London, SPCK, 1986.

* M. Hengel, *Judaism and Hellenism*, E. tr. from German, London, SCM, 1974.

A. M. Hunter, *Introducing New Testament Theology*, London, SCM, 1957.

J. Jeremias, *New Testament Theology: The Proclamation of Jesus*, E. tr. from German, London, SCM, 1965.

E. Käsemann, *Essays in New Testament Themes*, Philadelphia, Fortress, 1964.

W. G. Kümmel, *The New Testament: The History of the Investigation of its Problems*, E. tr. from German, London, SCM, 1973.

* R. Morgan, *The Nature of New Testament Theology*, London, SCM, 1973.

* S. Neill and T. Wright, *The Interpretation of the New Testament 1861–1986*, OUP, revd edn 1988.

* J. Reumann, *Variety and Unity in New Testament Thought*, OUP, 1991.

A. Richardson, *An Introduction to the Theology of the New Testament*, London, SCM, 1958.

A. Schweitzer, *The Quest of the Historical Jesus*, E. tr. from German, London, A. & C. Clark, 1910.

* E. Stauffer, *New Testament Theology*, E. tr. from German, London, SCM, 1963.

G. Theissen, *The First Followers of Jesus*, London, SCM, 1978.

J. Weiss, *Jesus' Proclamation of the Kingdom of God*, E. tr. from German, London, SCM, 1971.

Chapter 3 – A Biblical Corpus? The Canon and the Boundaries of Faith

P. R. Ackroyd, *Studies in the Religious Tradition of the Old Testament*, London, SCM, 1987.

J. Barr, *The Bible in the Modern World*, London, SCM, 1973.

* J. Barr, *Holy Scripture: Canon, Authority, Criticism*, Oxford, Clarendon, 1983.

J. Barton, *Oracles of God: Perceptions of Ancient Prophecy in Israel after the Exile*, London, DLT, 1986.

* J. Barton, *People of the Book? The Authority of the Bible in Christianity*, London, SPCK, 1988.

J. Barton, *The Spirit and the Letter: Studies in the Biblical Canon*, London, SPCK, 1997.

R. Beckwith, *The Old Testament Canon of the New Testament Church and its Background in Early Judaism*, London, Fontana Press, 1986.

W. Beuken and S. Freyne, *The Bible as Cultural Heritage* [*Concilium*], London, SCM, 1995.

J. Blenkinsopp, *Prophecy and Canon*, Notre Dame Indiana, Notre Dame University Press, 1977.

* M. G. Brett, *Biblical Criticism in Crisis? The Impact of the Canonical Approach on Old Testament Studies*, CUP, 1991.

R. Cameron (ed.), *The Other Gospels: Non-Canonical Gospel Texts*, Guildford, Lutterworth, 1983.

J. H. Charlesworth (ed.), *The Old Testament Pseudepigrapha*, Vols I and II, London, DLT, 1983, 1985.

B. S. Childs, *Introduction to the Old Testament as Scripture*, London, SCM, 1979.

D. Clines, S. Fowl and S. Porter (eds), *The Bible in Three Dimensions*, Sheffield, JSOT Press, 1990.

E. E. Ellis, *The Old Testament in Early Christianity: Canon and Interpretation in the Light of Modern Research*, Tübingen, J. C. B. Mohr (Paul Siebeck), 1991.

H. Y. Gamble, *The New Testament Canon: Its Making and Meaning*, Philadelphia, Fortress, 1985.

* S. Z. Leiman (ed.), *The Canonisation of Hebrew Scripture: The Talmudic and Midrashic Evidence*, Hamden, Conn., Academy of Archon Books, 1974.

* J. W. Miller, *The Origins of the Bible: Rethinking Canon History*, New York, Paulist Press, 1994.

G. W. E. Nickelsburg, *Jewish Literature between the Bible and the Mishnah*, London, SCM, 1981.

E. Pagels, *The Gnostic Gospels*, New York, Weidenfeld & Nicolson, 1989.

* R. Rendtorff, *Canon and Theology*, E. tr. from German, Edinburgh, T. & T. Clark, 1993.

J. M. Robinson (ed.), *The Nag Hammadi Library*, Leiden, Brill, 1977.

J. A. Sanders, *Torah and Canon*, Philadelphia, Fortress, 1972.

J. A. Sanders, *Canon and Community: A Guide to Canonical Criticism*, Philadelphia, Fortress, 1984.

J. A. Sanders, *From Sacred Story to Sacred Text: Canon as Paradigm*, Philadelphia, Fortress, 1987.

W. Schneemelcher and E. Hennecke (eds), *New Testament Apocrypha Vols I and II*, E. tr. from German, Guildford, Lutterworth, 1965.

H. F. D. Sparks, *The Apocryphal Old Testament*, OUP, 1984.

M. E. Stone (ed.), *Jewish Writings of the Second Temple Period*, Philadelphia, Fortress, 1984.

P. Stuhlmacher, *Historical Criticism and Theological Interpretation of Scripture*, London, SPCK, 1979.

A. C. Sundberg, *The Old Testament of the Early Church*, Cambridge, Mass., Harvard University Press, 1964.

* G. M. Tucker, D. L. Petersen and R. R. Wilson (eds), *Canon, Theology, and Old Testament Interpretation*, Philadelphia, Fortress, 1988.

C. Tuckett, *Nag Hammadi and the Gospel Tradition*, Edinburgh, T. & T. Clark, 1986.

C. Tuckett, *Reading the New Testament: Methods of Interpretation*, Philadelphia, Fortress, 1987.

Chapter 4 – A Biblical Text? The Variety of Versions

Η ΚΑΙΝΗ ΔΙΑΘΗΚΗ, London, British and Foreign Bible Society, 1988.

Biblia Hebraica Stuttgartensia, Stuttgart, Deutsche Bibelgesellschaft, 1984.

The Pentateuch in Hebrew, London, William Clowes and Sons, 1951.

Septuagint, Stuttgart, Deutsche Bibelgesellschaft, 1979.

K. Aland and R. Aland, *The Text of the New Testament*, E. tr. from German, Grand Rapids, Eerdmans, 1987.

J. Backhouse, *The Lindisfarne Gospels*, London, Phaidon Press with British Library, 1981.

* J. Barr, *Comparative Philology and the Text of the Old Testament*, OUP, 1968.

S. A. J. Bradley, *Anglo-Saxon Poetry*, London, Everyman, 1995.

M. Broshi, *Psalms Scroll from Qumran*, Jerusalem, The Israel Museum (no publication date).

F. F. Bruce, *The New Testament Documents*, Grand Rapids, Eerdmans, 1981.

* F. M. Cross and S. Talmon (eds), *Qumran and the History of the Biblical Text*, Cambridge, Mass., Harvard University Press, 1976.

D. S. Daniell and G. W. H. Lampe, *Discovering the Bible*, University of London Press, 1970.

J. D. Douglas and N. Hillyer (eds), *New Bible Dictionary*, Leicester, Inter-Varsity Press, 1982.

J. K. Elliott, *A Survey of Manuscripts Used in the Editions of the Greek New Testament*, Leiden, Brill, 1987.

E. Earle Ellis, *The Old Testament in Early Christianity: Canon and Interpretation in the Light of Modern Research*, Grand Rapids, Eerdmans, 1991.

M. Godden and M. Lapidge (eds), *The Cambridge Companion to Old English Literature*, CUP, 1991.

* R. Gordis, *The Biblical Text in the Making*, Philadelphia, Fortress, revd edn 1971.

* J. H. Greenlee, *Introduction to New Testament Textual Criticism*, Grand Rapids, Eerdmans and, Carlisle, Paternoster, 1996.

* S. Jellicoe (ed.), *Studies in the Septuagint: Origins, Recensions and Interpretation*, New York, Ktav Publishing House, 1974.

R. W. Klein, *Textual Criticism of the Old Testament*, Philadelphia, Fortress, 1974.

P. Kyle McCarter Jr., *Textual Criticism: Reclaiming the Text of the Hebrew Bible*, Philadelphia, Fortress, 1986.

R. M. Liuzza (ed.), *The Old English Version of the Gospels*, OUP, 1994.

P. K. McCarter, *Textual Criticism*, Philadelphia, Fortress, 1986.

* B. Metzger, *The Early Versions of the New Testament: Their Origins, Transmission and Limitations*, Oxford, Clarendon, 1977.

* B. Metzger, *The Text of the New Testament: Its Transmission, Corruption and Restoration*, Oxford, Clarendon, revd edn 1992.

M. C. Morrell, *A Manual of Old English Biblical Materials*, Knoxville, Tennessee, University of Tennessee Press, 1965.

J. D. Purvis, *The Samaritan Pentateuch and the Origin of the Samaritan Sect*, Cambridge, Mass., Harvard University Press, 1968.

* B. J. Roberts, *The Old Testament Text and Versions*, Cardiff, University of Wales Press, 1951.

J. R. Rosenbloom, *The Dead Sea Isaiah Scroll*, Grand Rapids, Eerdmans, 1970.

* J. A. Sanders, *The Psalms Scroll of Qumran Cave 11*, Clarendon Press, 1965.

B. Smalley, *The Study of the Bible in the Middle Ages*, Oxford, Blackwell, 1983.

A. H. Smith (ed.), *Three Northumbrian Poems*, London, Methuen, 1933.

* G. Vermes, *The Dead Sea Scrolls: Qumran in Perspective*, London, SCM, 1982.

* J. Weingreen, *Introduction to the Critical Study of the Text of the Hebrew Bible*, Oxford, Clarendon, 1982.

E. Würthwein, *The Text of the Old Testament: An Introduction to Biblia Hebraica*, Oxford, Blackwell, revd edn 1979.

Chapter 5 – Theological Approaches to the Bible

General Works

* J. Barr, *The Scope and Authority of the Bible: Explorations in Theology 7*, London, SCM, 1980.

G. B. Caird, *The Language and Imagery of the Bible*, London, Duckworth, 1980.

D. A. Carson and H. G. M. Williamson (eds), *It is Written: Scripture Citing Scripture*, CUP, 1988.

R. E. Clements, *A Century of Old Testament Study*, London and Guildford, Lutterworth, 1976.

B. Drewery and R. J. Bauckham (eds), *Scripture Tradition and Reason*, Edinburgh, T. & T. Clark, 1988.

* M. Fishbane, *Biblical Interpretation in Ancient Israel*, Oxford, Clarendon, 1985.

* M. Fishbane, *The Garments of Torah: Essays in Biblical Hermeneutics*, Bloomington, Indiana, Indiana University Press, 1989.

* H. W. Frei, *The Eclipse of Biblical Narrative: A Study in Eighteenth- and Nineteenth-Century Hermeneutics*, New Haven, Yale University Press, 1974.

R. W. Funk, *Language, Hermeneutics and the Word of God*, New York, Harper & Row, 1966.

H. G. Gadamer, *Philosophical Hermeneutics*, Berkeley, University of California Press, 1976.

H. G. Gadamer, *Truth and Method*, London and New York, Sheed & Ward, 1979.

J. Habermas, *Knowledge and Human Interests*, Boston, Heinemann, 1971.

R. C. Hobb, *Reception Theory*, London and New York, Methuen, 1984.

S. McFague, *Metaphorical Theology: Models of God in Religious Language*, London, SCM, 1983.

* D. E. Nineham, *The Uses and Abuses of the Bible: A Study of the Bible in an Age of Rapid Cultural Change*, London, SPCK, 1978.

H. G. Reventlow, *The Authority of the Bible and the Rise of the Modern World*, E. tr. from German, London, SCM, 1984.

P. Ricoeur, *The Conflict of Interpreters*, Evanston, Northwestern University Press, 1974.

P. Ricoeur, *Interpretation Theory*, Fort Worth, Texas Christian, 1976.

* P. Ricoeur, *Hermeneutics and the Social Sciences*, CUP, 1981.

J. Rogerson, *Old Testament Criticism in the Nineteenth Century in Germany*, London, SPCK, 1984.

G. Theissen, *Biblical Faith: An Evolutionary Approach*, London, SCM, 1984.

J. B. Thompson, *Critical Hermeneutics: A Study of the Thought of Paul Ricoeur and Jurgen Habermas*, CUP, 1981.

G. Vermes, *The Complete Dead Sea Scrolls in English*, Harmondsworth, Middlesex, Penguin, 1997.

* F. Young, *The Art of Performance*, DLT, 1990.

Theological Approaches

K. Barth, *The Word of God and the Word of Man*, E. tr. from German, New York, Harper & Row, 1987.

J. Bowker, *The Targums and Rabbinic Literature*, CUP, 1969.

C. R. Braaten and R. W. Jenson, *Reclaiming the Bible for the Church*, Edinburgh, T. & T. Clark, 1995.

F. F. Bruce, *Biblical Exegesis in the Qumran Texts*, London, Tyndale, 1960.

R. Bultmann, *Faith and Understanding*, E. tr. from German, London, SCM, 1969.

R. P. Carroll and A. G. Hunter, *Words at Work: Using the Bible in the Academy, the Community and the Churches: Essays in Honour of Robert Davidson*, Glasgow, Trinity St Mungo Press, 1994.

P. R. Davies, *Whose Bible Is It Anyway?* Sheffield, SOT Press, 1995.

C. F. Evans, *Is 'Holy Scripture' Christian?* London, SCM, 1971.

J. Goldingay, *Models for Scripture*, Carlisle, Paternoster, 1994.

J. Goldingay, *Models for the Interpretation of Scripture*, Carlisle, Paternoster, 1995.

J. Goldingay, *Theological Diversity and the Authority of the Old Testament*, Carlisle, Paternoster, 1995.

* J. L. Houlden, *Bible and Belief*, London, SPCK, 1991.

* J. L. Houlden, *The Interpretation of the Bible in the Church*, London, SCM, 1995.

D. H. Kelsey, *The Uses of Scripture in Recent Theology*, London, SCM, 1975.

M. J. Mulder (ed.), *Miqra: Reading, Translation and Interpretation of the Hebrew Bible in Ancient Judaism and in Early Christianity*, Philadelphia, Fortress, 1984.

* J. Neusner, *What is Midrash?* Philadelphia, Fortress, 1987.

J. Neusner, *Christian Faith and the Bible of Tradition: The Use of Scripture*, Atlanta, Scholars Press, 1990.

M. Reu, *Luther and the Scriptures*, Colombus, Ohio, Columbia University Press, 1944.

S. Safarai (ed.), *The Literature of the Sages: Midrash, Mishnah, Talmud*, Philadelphia, Fortress, 1984.

S. M. Schneiders, *The Revelatory Text*, San Francisco, Harper, 1991.

D. C. Smith (ed.), *Text and Experience: Towards a Cultural Exegesis of the Bible*, Sheffield, JSOT Press, 1995.

J. Spong, *Rescuing the Bible from Fundamentalism*, San Francisco, Harper, 1991.

R. B. Tollinton, *Selections from the Commentaries and Homilies of Origen*, London, SPCK, 1929.

G. Vermes, *Scripture and Tradition in Judaism*, Leiden, Brill, revd edn 1973.

F. Watson (ed.), *The Open Text*, London, SCM, 1993.

* F. Watson, *Text, Church and Word: Biblical Interpretation in Theological Perspective*, Edinburgh, T. & T. Clark, 1994.

* F. Watson, *Text and Truth: Redefining Biblical Theology*, Edinburgh, T. & T. Clark, 1997.

Liberation Theology and Theological Approaches to the Bible

N. S. Ateek, *Justice and Only Justice: A Palestinian Theology of Liberation*, Maryknoll, New York, Orbis, 1989.

F. Belo, *A Materialist Reading of the Gospel of Mark*, Maryknoll, New York, Orbis, 1981.

P. Berryman, *Liberation Theology: Essential Facts about the Revolutionary Movements in Latin America and Beyond*, Philadelphia, Temple University Press, 1987.

C. Boff, *Theology and Praxis: Epistemological Foundations*, Maryknoll, New York, Orbis, 1987.

C. and L. Boff, *Introducing Liberation Theology*, Maryknoll, New York, Orbis, 1988.

M. Clevenot, *Materialist Approaches to the Bible*, Maryknoll, New York, Orbis, 1985.

M. Ellis, *Towards a Jewish Theology of Liberation*, Maryknoll, New York, Orbis, 1987.

T. Gorringe, *Discerning Spirit*, London, SCM, 1989.

* N. Gottwald (ed.), *The Bible and Liberation: Political and Social Hermeneutics*, Maryknoll, New York, Orbis, 1983.

* G. Gutierrez, *A Theology of Liberation*, Maryknoll, New York, Orbis, 1974.

G. Gutierrez, *The Power of the Poor in History*, London, SCM, 1983.

G. Gutierrez, *We Drink from Our Own Wells*, Maryknoll, New York, Orbis, 1988.

* N. H. Lohfink, *Option for the Poor: The Basic Principle of Liberation Theology in the Light of the Bible*, Berkeley, BIBAL Press, 1987.

J. P. Miranda, *Marx and the Bible: A Critique of the Philosophy of Oppression*, London, SCM, 1977.

C. Myers, *Binding the Strong Man: A Political Reading of Mark's Story of Jesus*, Maryknoll, New York, Orbis, 1988.

G. Pixley, *God's Kingdom: A Guide for Biblical Study*, London, SCM, 1987.

* C. Rowland, *Radical Christianity*, Oxford and Cambridge, Polity Press, 1988.

* C. Rowland and M. Corner, *Liberating Exegesis: The Challenge of Liberation Theology to Biblical Studies*, London, SPCK, 1990.

C. Rowland and J. Vincent (eds), *Liberation Theology UK, Vol. I*, Sheffield, Urban Theology Unit, 1995.

J. L. Segundo, *The Liberation of Theology*, Maryknoll, New York, Orbis, 1976.

J. Sobrino, *Spirituality of Liberation*, Maryknoll, New York, Orbis, 1988.

T. Wievliet, *A Place in the Sun; An Introduction to Liberation Theology in the Third World*, Maryknoll, New York, Orbis, 1978.

Feminist Theology and Theological Approaches to the Bible

* M. Bal, *Lethal Love: Feminist Literary Readings of Biblical Love Stories*, Bloomington, Indiana, Indiana University Press, 1987.

* M. Bal, *Anti-Covenant: Counter-Reading Women's Lives in the Bible*, Sheffield, Almond Press, 1989.

* P. Bird, *Feminism and the Bible: A Critical and Constructive Encounter*, Winnipeg, Manitoba, CMBC, 1994.

L. Boff, *The Maternal Face of God: The Feminine and its Religious Expressions*, Collins Religious, 1989.

* A. Brenner, *The Israelite Woman: Social Role and Literary Type in Biblical Narrative*, Sheffield, Almond Press, 1985.

A. Brenner and F. Van Dijk-Hemnes, *On Gendering Texts: Female and Male Voices in the Hebrew Bible*, Leiden, Brill, 1993.

* A. Y. Collins, *Feminist Perspectives in Biblical Scholarship*, Chico, California, Scholars Press, 1985.

M. Daly, *The Church and the Second Sex*, London, Dublin, G. Chapman, 1968.

M. Daly, *Beyond God the Father*, Boston, Beacom Press, 1973.

* J. C. Exum, *Fragmented Women: Feminist (Sub)versions of Biblical Narrative*, Sheffield, Almond Press, 1993.

D. N. Fewell and D. M. Gunn, *Gender, Power and Promise: The Subject of the Bible's First Story*, Nashville, Abingdon, 1993.

T. Frymer-Kemsky, *In the Wake of the Goddess: Women, Culture and the Biblical Transformation of Pagan Myth*, London and New York, Maxwell MacMillan International, 1992.

* D. Hampson, *Theology and Feminism*, Oxford, Blackwell, 1990.

D. Hampson (ed.), *Swallowing a Fishbone? Feminist Theologians Debate Christianity*, London, SPCK, 1996.

M. Hayter, *The New Eve in Christ: The Use and Abuse of the Bible in the Debate about Women in the Church*, London, SPCK, 1987.

A. Laffey, *Wives, Harlots and Concubines*, London, SPCK, 1990.

A. Loades (ed.), *Feminist Theology: A Reader*, London, SPCK, 1993.

C. Meyers, *Discovering Eve: Ancient Israelite Women in Context*, Oxford, OUP, 1998.

E. Moltmann-Wendel, *The Women around Jesus*, London and New York, Crossroad, 1988.

E. Moltmann-Wendel, *A Land Flowing with Milk and Honey: Perspectives in Feminist Theology*, London, SCM, 1986.

S. Niditch, *Chaos to Cosmos: Studies in Biblical Patterns of Creation*, Atlanta, Scholars Press, 1985.

I. Pardes, *Countertraditions in the Bible: A Feminist Approach*, Cambridge, Mass., Harvard University Press, 1992.

* J. Plaskow, *Standing again at Sinai: Judaism from a Feminist Perspective*, New York, HarperCollins, 1990.

R. Radford Ruether, *Sexism and God-Talk: Towards a Feminist Theology*, London, SCM, 1982.

I. N. Rashkow, *The Phallacy of Genesis: A Feminist-Psychoanalytic Approach*, Louisville, Westminster, John Knox Press, 1993.

* L. M. Russell, *Feminist Interpretation of the Bible*, Oxford, Blackwell, 1985.

E. Schüssler Fiorenza, *In Memory of Her: A Feminist Theological Reconstruction of Christian Origins*, London and New York, Crossroad, 1984.

* E. Schüssler Fiorenza, *Bread not Stone: The Challenge of Feminist Biblical Interpretation*, Boston, Beacon Press, 1984.

* E. Schüssler Fiorenza (ed.), *Searching the Scriptures: A Feminist Introduction, Vol. 1*, London, SCM, 1994.

M. A. Tolbert (ed.), *The Bible and Feminist Hermeneutics* (*Semeia* 28), Atlanta, Scholars Press, 1983.

* P. Trible, *God and the Rhetoric of Sexuality*, Philadelphia, Fortress, 1978.

* P. Trible, *Texts of Terror*, Philadelphia, Fortress, 1984.

R. J. Weems, *Battered Love: Marriage, Sex and Violence in the Hebrew Prophets*, Minneapolis, Augsburg, 1995.

E. van Wolde, *Words become Worlds: Semantic Studies of Genesis 1–11*, Leiden, Brill, 1994.

Chapter 6 – Historical Approaches to the Bible

B. Albrektson, *History and the Gods: An Essay on the Idea of Historical Events as Divine Manifestation in the Ancient Near East and in Israel*, Lund, C. K. Gleerup, 1967.

R. Alter, *The World of Biblical Literature*, London, SPCK, 1982.

* J. Bartlett, *The Bible: Faith and Evidence: A Critical Enquiry into the Nature of Biblical History*, British Museum Publications, 1990.

G. Bornkamm, *Jesus of Nazareth*, E. tr. from German, London, Hodder & Stoughton, 1962.

G. Bornkamm, *Tradition and Interpretation in Matthew*, E. tr. from German, London, SCM, 1963.

W. Brueggemann and H. W. Wolff, *The Vitality of Old Testament Traditions*, Atlanta, John Knox Press, 1975.

B. S. Childs, *Memory and Tradition in Israel*, London, SCM, 1962.

H. Conzelmann, *Acts of the Apostles: A Commentary*, E. tr. from German, Philadelphia, Fortress, 1987.

J. D. Crossan, *The Historical Jesus: The Life of a Mediterranean Jewish Peasant*, Edinburgh, T. & T. Clark, 1991.

J. D. Crossan, *The Essential Jesus: Original Sayings and Earliest Images*, San Francisco, Harper, 1994.

J. D. Crossan, *The Essential Jesus: What Jesus Really Taught*, San Francisco, Harper, 1996.

R. C. Culley, *Themes and Variations: A Study of Action in Biblical Narrative*, Atlanta, Scholars Press, 1992.

G. Ebeling, *The Nature of Faith*, E. tr. from German, London, Collins, 1961.

E. Fuchs, *Studies of the Historical Jesus*, E. tr. from German, London, SCM, 1964.

H. Gunkel, *What Remains of the Old Testament and Other Essays*, London, G. Allen & Unwin, 1928.

* H. Gunkel, *The Folklore of the Old Testament*, E. tr. from German, Sheffield, JSOT Press, 1987.

* A. van Harvey, *The Historian and the Believer: The Morality of Historical Knowledge and Christian Belief*, London, SCM, 1966.

J. Jeremias, *The Parables of Jesus*, London, SCM, 1954.

E. Käsemann, *Commentary on Romans*, E. tr. from German, London, SCM, 1980.

D. A. Knight (ed.), *Tradition and Theology in the Old Testament*, London, SPCK, 1977.

K. Koch, *The Growth of Biblical Tradition*, London, Black, 1969.

E. Krentz, *The Historical Critical Method*, Philadelphia, Fortress, 1975.

W. K. Kümmel, *The New Testament: The History of the Interpretation of its Problems*, E. tr. from German, London, SCM, 1970.

R. Lane Fox, *The Unauthorized Version: Truth and Fiction*, London, Viking, 1991.

J. D. Levenson, *The Hebrew Bible, the Old Testament and Historical Criticism*, Louisville, Kentucky, Westminster John Knox Press, 1993.

W. Marxsen, *Mark the Evangelist: Studies in the Redaction History of the Gospel*, E. tr. from German, Nashville, Abingdon, 1969.

P. D. Miscall, *The Workings of Old Testament Narrative*, Philadelphia, Fortress, 1983.

M. Noth, *The Laws in the Pentateuch*, E. tr. from German, London, Oliver & Boyd, 1966.

N. Perrin, *Jesus and the Language of the Kingdom: Symbol and Metaphor in New Testament Interpretation*, Philadelphia, Fortress and, London, SCM, 1976.

N. Perrin, *Rediscovering the Teaching of Jesus*, London, SCM, 1976.

G. von Rad, *The Problem of the Hexateuch and Other Essays*, E. tr. from German, London, SCM, 1966.

W. Rast, *Tradition, History and the Old Testament*, Philadelphia, Fortress, 1975.

J. M. Robinson, *A New Quest of the Historical Jesus*, London, 1959.

J. A. T. Robinson, *The Priority of John*, London, Xpress Reprints, 1995.

E. P. Sanders, *Paul and Palestinian Judaism*, London, SCM, 1977.

* E. P. Sanders, *Jesus and Judaism*, London, SCM, 1985.

* J. A. Sanders, *Canon and Community: A Guide to Canonical Criticism*, Philadelphia, Fortress, 1984.

D. F. Strauss, *The Life of Jesus Critically Examined*, E. tr. from German (1837), London, SCM, 1973.

* D. F. Strauss, *The Christ of Faith and the Jesus of History*, E. tr. from German (1865), London, SCM, 1977.

C. H. Talbert (ed.), *Reimarus: Fragments*, London, SCM, 1970.

* J. Wellhausen, *Prolegomena to the History of Israel*, E. tr. from German, London, A. & C. Black, 1885.

J. Weiss, *Jesus' Proclamation of the Kingdom of God*, E. tr. from German, London, SCM, 1971.

M. J. Wilkins and J. P. Moreland (eds), *Jesus under Fire: Modern Scholarship Reinvents the Historical Jesus*, Carlisle, Paternoster, 1996.

N. T. Wright, *Jesus and the Victory of God*, London, SPCK, 1996.

Chapter 7 – Literary Approaches to the Bible

R. Alter, *The Art of Biblical Narrative*, London, Allen & Unwin, 1981.

* R. Alter and F. Kermode (eds), *The Literary Guide to the Bible*, London, Fontana, 1987.

R. Alter, *The Pleasures of Reading in an Ideological Age*, New York and London, Simon & Schuster, 1989.

D. Barratt, R. Polley and L. Ryken (eds), *The Discerning Reader: Christian Perspectives on Literature and Theory*, Leicester, Apollos, 1995.

R. Barthes, *Structural Analysis and Biblical Exegesis: Interpretational Essays*, E. tr. from French, Pittsburgh, Pickwick Press, 1974.

R. Barthes, *Image, Music, Text: Essays Selected and Translated by Stephen Heaton*, London, Fontana, revd edn 1993.

W. A. Beardslee, *Literary Criticism of the New Testament*, Philadelphia, Fortress, 1970.

* A. Berlin, *Poetics and the Interpretation of Biblical Narrative*, Sheffield, Almond Press, 1983.

* W. Beuken, S. Freyne and A. Weiler (eds), *The Bible and Its Readers*, Philadelphia, Fortress and, London, SCM, 1991.

D. J. A. Clines, *et al, Art and Meaning*, Sheffield, JSOT Press, 1982.

D. J. A. Clines (ed.), *The Dictionary of Classical Hebrew* (to appear in 8 volumes) Sheffield, JSOT Press, 1993–.

R. A. Culpepper, *Anatomy of the Fourth Gospel: A Study in Literary Design*, Philadelphia, Fortress, 1983.

T. Eagleton, *Literary Theory: An Introduction*, Oxford, Blackwell, 1983.

T. S. Eliot, *Selected Essays*, London, Faber & Faber, 3rd edn 1951.

* T. S. Eliot, *The Frontiers of Criticism*, Minneapolis, University of Minnesota Press, 1956.

* J. C. Exum and D. J. A. Clines (eds), *The New Literary Criticism and the Hebrew Bible*, Sheffield, Almond Press, 1993.

* H. Frei, *The Eclipse of Biblical Narrative: A Study in Eighteenth- and Nineteenth-Century Hermeneutics*, New Haven, Yale University Press, 1974.

* N. Frye, *The Great Code: The Bible and Literature*, New York, Routledge & Kegan Paul, 1982.

* N. Frye, *The Anatomy of Criticism: Four Essays*, Harmondsworth, Middlesex, Penguin, 1957, revd edn 1990.

J. A. Gabel, C. B. Wheeler and A. D. York (eds), *The Bible as Literature: An Introduction*, OUP, 3rd edn 1995.

E. M. Good, *Irony in the Old Testament*, Sheffield, Almond Press, 2nd edn 1981.

A.-J. Greimas, *Sign, Language, Culture*, E. tr. from Dutch, The Hague, Mouton, 1970.

* D. M. Gunn and D. N. Fewell, *Narrative in the Hebrew Bible*, OUP, 1993.

T. R. Henn, *The Bible as Literature*, London, Lutterworth, 1970.

W. Iser, *The Act of Reading*, E. tr. from German, Baltimore, Johns Hopkins, 1991.

* G. Josipovici, *The Book of God*, New Haven, Yale University Press, 1988.

G. A. Kennedy, *New Testament Interpretation through Rhetorical Criticism*, Chapel Hill, North Carolina Press, 1984.

F. Kermode, *The Genesis of Secrecy: On the Interpretation of Narrative*, Cambridge, Mass., Harvard University Press, 1979.

L. Koehler, W. Baumgartner and M. E. J. Richardson (tr. ed.), *The Hebrew and Aramaic Lexicon of the Old Testament* (projected 4 vols.), E. tr. from German, Leiden, Brill, 1994–.

C. Lévi-Strauss, *Anthropology and Myth*, E. tr. from French, Oxford, Blackwell, 1987.

* A. Loades and M. McLain (eds), *Hermeneutics, the Bible and Literary Criticism*, New York, Macmillan, 1992.

E. McKnight, *The Bible and the Reader: An Introduction to Literary Criticism*, Philadelphia, Fortress, 1985.

P. D. Miscall, *The Workings of Old Testament Narrative*, Philadelphia, Fortress, 1983.

R. Morgan and J. Barton, *Biblical Interpretation*, OUP, 1989.

R. G. Moulton, *The Literary Study of the Bible*, London, A. & C. Black, 1899.

C. Myers, *Binding the Strong Man: A Political Reading of Mark's Story of Jesus*, Maryknoll, New York, Orbis, 1988.

N. R. Petersen, *Literary Criticism for New Testament Critics*, Philadelphia, Fortress, 1978.

R. M. Polzin, *Biblical Structuralism: Method and Subjectivity in the Study of Ancient Texts*, Philadelphia, Fortress, 1977.

M. A. Powell (ed.), *The Bible and Modern Literary Criticism: A Critical Text and Annotated Bibliography*, New York and London, Greenwood Press, 1992.

* S. Prickett, *Words and the Word: Language, Poetics and Biblical Interpretation*, CUP, 1986.

S. Prickett, *Reading the Text: Biblical Criticism and Literary Theory*, OUP, 1991.

V. Propp, *Theory and History of Folklore*, E. tr. from Russian, Minneapolis, University of Minnesota Press, 1984.

I. A. Richards, *Principles of Literary Criticism*, London, Routledge, 1989.

A. Robertson, *The Old Testament and the Literary Critic*, Philadelphia, Fortress, 1977.

F. de Saussure, *Course in General Linguistics with added authors*, E. tr. from French, London, Duckworth, 1983.

* M. Sternberg, *Poetics of Biblical Narrative: Ideological Literature and the Drama of Reading*, Bloomington Indiania, Indiania University Press, 1985.

F. Temple, B. Jarrett *et al* (eds), *Essays and Reviews*, Longman, Green, Longman and Roberts, 1861.

* A. C. Thiselton, *New Horizons in Hermeneutics: The Theory and Practice of Transforming Bible Study*, London, HarperCollins, 1992.

J. P. Tompkins, *Reader-Response Criticism: From Formalism to Post-Structuralism*, Baltimore, John Hopkins Press, 1980.

M. Weiss, *The Bible from Within: The Method of Total Interpretation*, Jerusalem, Magnes Press, Hebrew University of Jerusalem, 1984.

A. N. Wilder, *Early Christian Rhetoric: The Language of the Gospel*, London, SCM, 1964.

* A. N. Wilder, *The Bible and the Literary Critic*, Philadelphia, Fortress, 1991.

The journal, *Semeia*, has several articles on the Bible and literary criticism.

Chapter 8 – The Many Voices in the Psalms

Commentaries

* A. A. Anderson, *Psalms 1–72, Volume I* (New Century Bible Commentary) Grand Rapids, Eerdmans and, London, Marshall, Morgan & Scott, 1972.

A. A. Anderson, *Psalms 73–150, Volume II* (New Century Bible Commentary) Grand Rapids, Eerdmans and, London, Marshall, Morgan & Scott, 1972.

C. A. Briggs, *The Book of Psalms, Volume I I–L* (International Critical Commentary) Edinburgh, T. & T. Clark, 1906.

C. A. Briggs, *The Book of Psalms, Volume II LI–CL* (International Critical Commentary) Edinburgh, T. & T. Clark, 1907.

* P. C. Craigie, *Psalms 1–50* (World Biblical Commentary 19), Waco, Texas, Word Books, 1983.

M. E. Tate, *Psalms 51–100* (Word Biblical Commentary 20), Dallas, Texas, Word Books, 1990.

L. C. Allen, *Psalms 101–150* (Word Biblical Commentary 21), Waco, Texas, Word Books, 1983.

M. Dahood, *Psalms I: 1–50* (Anchor Bible Commentary 16), Garden City, New York, Doubleday, 1966.

M. Dahood, *Psalms II: 51–100* (Anchor Bible Commentary 17), Garden City, New York, Doubleday, 1968.

M. Dahood, *Psalms III: 101–150* (Anchor Bible Commentary 17A), Garden City, New York, Doubleday, 1970.

* H.-J. Kraus, *Psalms 1–59 Volume I* (Augsburg), E. tr. from German, Minneapolis, Augsburg, 1988.

H.-J. Kraus, *Psalms 60–150 Volume II* (Augsburg), E. tr. from German, Minneapolis, Augsburg, 1989.

C. S. Rodd, *Psalms 1–72*, London, Epworth, 1963.

C. S. Rodd, *Psalms 73–150*, London, Epworth, 1964.

A. Weiser, *The Psalms: A Commentary* (Old Testament Library), E. tr. from German, London, SCM, 1962.

General Works

P. R. Ackroyd, *Doors of Perception: A Guide to Reading the Psalms*, London, SCM, 1978.

A. Aejmelaeus, *The Traditional Prayer in the Psalms*, Berlin, De Gruyter, 1986.

* R. Alter, *The Art of Biblical Poetry*, New York, Basic Books, 1985.

* L. Alonso Schökel, *A Manual of Hebrew Poets*, E. tr. from Spanish, Rome, Editrice Pontificio Istituto Biblio, 1988.

P. Auffret, *The Literary Structure of Psalm 2*, Sheffield, JSOT Press, 1977.

D. K. Berry, *The Psalms and their Readers: Interpretive Strategies from Psalm 18*, Sheffield, JSOT Press, 1993.

D. Bonhoeffer, *The Psalms: Prayer Book of the Bible*, E. tr. from German, Oxford, SLG Press, 1982.

R. G. Bratcher and W. D. Reyburn, *A Translator's Handbook on the Book of Psalms*, New York, United Bible Societies, 1991.

C. C. Broyles, *The Conflict of Faith and Experience in the Psalms*, Sheffield, JSOT Press, 1989.

* W. Brueggemann, *Israel's Praise: Doxology against Idolatry and Ideology*, Philadelphia, Fortress, 1988.

W. Brueggemann, *The Psalms and the Life of Faith*, Minneapolis, Fortress, 1995.

T. Carmi (ed.), *The Penguin Book of Hebrew Verse*, Harmondsworth, Middlesex, Penguin, 1981.

B. S. Childs, *Biblical Theology of the Old and New Testaments: Theological Reflection on the Christian Bible*, London, SCM, 1982.

B. S. Childs, *Old Testament Theology in a Canonical Context*, London, SCM, 1985.

D. Cohn-Sherbok, *Atlas of Jewish History*, London and New York, Routledge, 1994.

J. Cotter, *Through Desert Places*, Sheffield, Cairns Publications, 1989.

J. F. D. Creach, *The Choice of Yahweh as Refuge and the Editing of the Psalter*, Sheffield, JSOT Press, 1996.

S. J. L. Croft, *The Identity of the Individual in the Psalms*, Sheffield, JSOT Press, 1987.

R. C. Culley, *Oral Formulaic Language in the Biblical Psalms*, Toronto, University of Toronto Press, 1967.

* J. Day, *Psalms* (Old Testament Guides), Sheffield, JSOT Press, 1990.

J. Eaton, *The Psalms* (Torch Bible Commentary), London, SCM, 1967.

D. Frost, *et al* (eds), *The Liturgical Psalter*, Collins Liturgical Publications, 1977.

E. S. Gerstenberger, *Psalms: Part I, with an Introduction to Cultic Poetry*, Grand Rapids, Eerdmans, 1988.

S. E. Gillingham, *The Poems and Psalms of the Hebrew Bible*, OUP, 1994.

M. Goulder, *The Psalms of the Sons of Korah: A Study in the Psalter*, Sheffield, JSOT Press, 1982.

M. Goulder, *The Prayers of David (Psalms 51–72): Studies in the Psalter II*, Sheffield, JSOT Press, 1990.

M. Goulder, *The Psalms of Asaph and the Pentateuch: Studies in the Psalter III*, Sheffield, JSOT Press, 1996.

G. Guiver, *Company of Voices: Daily Prayer and the People of God*, London, SPCK, 1988.

* H. Gunkel, *The Psalms*, E. tr. from German, Philadelphia, Fortress, 1967.

M. R. Hauge, *Between Sheol and Temple: Motif, Structure and Function in the 'I' Psalms*, Sheffield, JSOT Press, 1995.

K. G. Hoglund, *et al* (eds), *The Listening Heart: Essays in Wisdom and the Psalms in Honour of Roland E. Murphy, O Carm*, Sheffield, JSOT Press, 1987.

* W. L. Holladay, *The Psalms through Three Thousand Years: Prayerbook of a Cloud of Witnesses*, Minneapolis, Fortress, 1993.

M. Israel, *A Light on the Path: An Exploration of Integrity Through the Psalms*, London, DLT, 1990.

A. R. Johnson, *The Cultic Prophet and Israel's Psalmody*, Cardiff, University of Wales Press, 1979.

C. Jones, G. Wainwright and E. Yarnold (eds), *The Study of Liturgy*, London, SPCK, 1978.

J. Keble, *The Psalter in English Verse*, London, Gresham Publishing Company, 1839.

* H.-J. Kraus, *Theology of the Psalms* (Augsburg), E. tr. from German, Minneapolis, Augsburg, 1986.

H. Küng, *Judaism: The Religious Situation of Our Time*, E. tr. from German, London, Crossroad, 1992.

* H. J. Levine, *Sing unto God a New Song: A Contemporary Reading of the Psalms*, Bloomington, Indiana, Indiana University Press, 1995.

C. S. Lewis, *Reflections on the Psalms*, Glasgow, G. Bles, 1961.

* J. C. McCann (ed.), *The Shape and Shaping of the Psalter*, Sheffield, JSOT Press, 1993.

* J. Magonet, *A Rabbi reads the Psalms*, London, SCM, 1994.

T. Merton, *On the Psalms*, London, Sheldon Press, 1957.

P. D. Miller, *Interpreting the Psalms*, Philadelphia, Fortress, 1986.

* S. Mowinckel, *The Psalms in Israel's Worship*, Vols. I and II, E. tr. from Norwegian, Oxford, Blackwell, 1962.

C. A. Newsom and S. H. Ringe (eds), *The Women's Bible Commentary*, London, SPCK, 1992.

W. O. Oesterley, *The Psalms*, London, SPCK, 1939.

M. Perry and D. Iliff (eds), *Psalms for Today: Full Music Edition*, London, Hodder & Stoughton, 1990.

R. E. Prothero, *The Psalms in Human Life*, London, John Murray, 1909.

* S. C. Reif, *Judaism and Hebrew Prayer: New Perspectives on Jewish Liturgical History*, CUP, 1993.

M. V. Reinstra, *Swallow's Nest: A Feminist Reading of the Psalms*, Leominster, Gracewing, 1992.

* L. Sabourin, *The Psalms: Their Origin and Meaning*, New York, Alba House, 1974.

* J. A. Sanders, *The Psalms Scroll of Qumran Cave 11*, OUP, 1962.

* K. Seybold, *Introducing the Psalms*, E. tr. from German, Edinburgh, T. & T. Clark, 1990.

* U. Simon, *Four Approaches to the Book of Psalms*, E. tr. from Hebrew, New York, State University of New York Press, 1991.

P. W. Skehan, E. C. Ulrich and J. E. Sanderson (eds), *The Dead Sea Scrolls: Qumran Cave 4, Paleo-Hebrew and Greek Biblical Manuscripts*, Oxford, Clarendon Press, 1992.

E. Werner, *The Sacred Bridge: The Interdependence of Liturgy and Music in Synagogue and Church during the First Millennium*, New York, Columbia University Press, London, Dennis Dobson, 1959.

C. Westermann, *The Psalms: Structure, Content and Message*, E. tr. from German, Minneapolis, Augsburg, 1980.

* C. Westermann, *Praise and Lament in the Psalms*, E. tr. from German, Edinburgh, T. & T. Clark, 1981.

* N. Whybray, *Reading the Psalms as a Book*, Sheffield, JSOT Press, 1996.

* G. H. Wilson, *The Editing of the Hebrew Psalter*, Chico, California, Scholars Press, 1985.

F. Young, *The Art of Performance*, London, DLT, 1990.

See also *The Book of Psalms* (*Interpretation* [April 1992]); and articles in: *Journal of Biblical Literature* (JBL); * *Journal for the Study of the Old Testament* (JSOT); and *Vetus Testamentum* (VT).

Conclusion

* W. Brueggemann, *Israel's Praise: Doxology against Idolatry and Ideology*, Philadelphia, Fortress, 1989.

* D. J. A. Clines, *Interested Parties: The Ideology of Writers and Readers of the Hebrew Bible*, Sheffield, JSOT Press, 1995.

R. B. and M. P. Coote, *Power, Politics and the Making of the Bible*, Minneapolis, Fortress, 1990.

* P. R. Davies, *Whose Bible Is It Anyway?* Sheffield, JSOT Press, 1995.

T. Eagleton, *Criticism and Ideology: A Study in Marxist Literary Theory*, London, Verso, 1978.

T. Eagleton, *Against the Grain; Selected Essays*, London, Verso, 1986.

G. Garbini, *History and Ideology in Ancient Israel*, E. tr. from Italian, New York and London, Crossroad, 1988.

N. Gottwald, *The Bible and Liberation: Political and Social Hermeneutics*, Maryknoll, New York, Orbis, 1983.

* D. Jobling (ed.), *Ideological Criticism of Biblical Texts* (*Semeia* 59), Atlanta, Scholars Press, 1992.

G. Lüdemann, *The Unholy in the Holy Scripture: The Dark Side of the Bible*, London, SCM, 1996.

J. Magonet, *The Subversive Bible*, London, SCM, 1997.

R. Mason, *Propaganda and Subversion in the Old Testament*, London, SPCK, 1997.

D. Penchansky, *The Politics of Biblical Theology: A Postmodern Reading*, Macon, Georgia, University of Mercer Press, 1995.

J. F. A. Sawyer, *The Fifth Gospel: Isaiah in the History of Christianity*, CUP, 1995.

A. C. Thiselton, *New Horizons in Hermeneutics: The Theory and Practice of Transforming Bible Study*, London, HarperCollins, 1992.

Subject Index

271

Author Index

275

Bible Reference Index